Land of
A THOUSAND EYES

PETER OLSZEWSKI has had a long career in the Australian print media as a journalist, columnist and editor. He has also worked as a radio broadcaster for English and US networks. In recent years he has worked as a freelancer, writing for many major newspapers and magazines, has been a university lecturer in journalism and communications, and most recently a journalism trainer in Myanmar. He currently lives in Queensland and doesn't have a cat.

Peter is also the author of *A Dozen Dopey Yarns: Tales from the Pot Prohibition* (JJ McRoach) and *A Salute to the Humble Yabby*.

Land of

A THOUSAND EYES

*The subtle pleasures of everyday life
in Myanmar*

PETER OLSZEWSKI

A SUE HINES BOOK
ALLEN & UNWIN

First published in 2005

A Sue Hines Book
Allen & Unwin
83 Alexander Street
Crows Nest NSW 2065
Australia
Phone: (61 2) 8425 0100
Fax: (61 2) 9906 2218
Email: info@allenandunwin.com
Web: www.allenandunwin.com

National Library of Australia
Cataloguing-in-Publication entry:

Olszewski, Peter, 1948- .
Land of a thousand eyes.

ISBN 1 74114 507 4.

1. Olszewski, Peter, 1948- - Journeys - Burma. 2.
Journalists - Burma - Biography. 3. Burma - Description
and travel. I. Title.

070.92

Edited by Catherine Hammond
Text design by Phil Campbell
Typeset by Midland Typesetters
Printed in Australia by McPherson's Printing Group

10 9 8 7 6 5 4 3 2 1

For Ma Pan Cherry and her love

Author's Note

Almost all modern books written about Myanmar by Westerners document the writers' dedicated pursuits of evidence of human rights abuses and atrocities. Some writers undertake great risk to do this, often illegally crossing borders and joining the ranks of armed insurrectionists.

I've done none of this.

I'd read widely about Myanmar before I arrived to live in Yangon and realised I still had no idea what ordinary life in the capital was like and how ordinary people survived, coped and lived.

What I subsequently saw and experienced is what I've written about, including what I like to refer as the 'Chestertonian' trivialities of life, and at times the perceptions are subtle, as is the nature of the Myanmar.

The most pleasing critique of this book came from a Myanmar journalist who, after reading the manuscript, said, 'You are the first foreign writer to get under the skin of my people.'

So this book isn't about revealing or documenting atrocities or abuse; others such as Bertil Lintner, Shelby Tucker and Andrew Marshall have already done this.

This book is about understanding; understanding a people who have been hidden from our gaze for more than half a century, and it is intensely personal because life is, after all, rather personal.

Most of the names of 'ordinary' people and some of their occupations have been changed, as have some of the places, times or contexts in which conversations and meetings appearing in this book have taken place, in the interests of politeness, privacy and protection. In some cases, particularly in regards to 'Western foreigners,' changes have been made to protect the guilty. But the names and details of all major players remain unchanged, as have details of events that may have historical significance or may be considered matters of record.

Thanks to the many, many people who helped, who are, unfortunately, far too numerous to mention here.

Flying astounds me. I have never lost the sci-fi sense of wonder associated with it because flying is so odd. One day you are here in this culture. You step into an aluminium canister with massive engines, you blast into the sky, and the next day you are there, in that culture.

Last night I had dinner in Brisbane, Australia, and soon, in several hours, I will be having lunch in Yangon.

I'm on the midnight flight to Singapore en route to Yangon, Myanmar, my home-to-be for the immediate future. The jet slices through the night sky as I watch the in-flight news service. It is January 2003 and war is in the air, thrumming through the space-age criss-cross of electric communication circuitry encircling our planet and increasingly binding us to the one common fate.

America is preparing to bomb Baghdad, and Washington spin doctors are at work, prepping the world for what is to come by broadcasting demonic images of Saddam Hussein's inherent evilness, broadcasting satellite images of buildings said to house terrible weapons of mass destruction, broadcasting images of dead Kurds littering the streets.

I'm restless so I read a little of the history of the country I'll soon be calling home, a country of river plains historically cut off from world view by a curtain of misty, mysterious mountains.

I read how the late nineteenth-century British press prepped the public for the coming final invasion of Burma. The British occupied Rangoon and lower Burma in 1824 and, fearing an alliance between the new Burmese king, Thibaw, and the French, they invaded upper Burma in 1885.

The British press had a ready-made horror story guaranteed

to appal British readers, making them bay for Burmese blood. When new Burmese kings were installed, an obligatory purging of the realm occurred. Members of the royal families were massacred by whichever family member ascended to the throne. When King Mindon died in 1878, royal intrigue pushed an insignificant son, Thibaw, who had lived most of his life in a monastery, into the limelight. Thibaw's first task was to carry out the requisite purging, and over a two-day period his Royal Guard engaged in the ritual slaughter of 83 royal family members. As the shedding of royal blood was taboo, the princesses were strangled, according to custom. The princes were sewn into red velvet sacks and beaten to death with paddles. The account I'm reading claims the princes were 'gently beaten to death', although I'm not sure how a gentle but fatal beating is effectively administered.

The bodies were interred in a mass grave in the Mandalay palace courtyard, but afterwards the ground erupted with the pressure of escaping gases. Elephants were brought in to tamp down the mess, and news of both the killing and the sordid detail of behemoths stamping on distended guts incensed the British public when it was reported in their press. But there was more to come.

When Thibaw ascended to the throne he also buried jars of oil in the palace foundations. The oil turned sour, a bad omen, and soothsayers said the situation could only be put right if a few hundred people, including some Europeans, were put to death. Thousands fled Mandalay, including the entire population of Europeans, and the British had the pretext they needed to invade.

A blitzkrieg armada sailed up the Irrawaddy River from Rangoon, and Thibaw was captured before he fully realised he had been invaded. He was exiled to India, his great palace became a British officers' club, and the Burmese monarchy was finished.

After the Singapore changeover, I drift off to sleep until the breakfast clatter and cabin announcements waken me. Landing preparations are underway and once again I observe how flying is a series of sexy cinematic clichés. Cut to the interior of the plane as it yaws to the left to begin its descent into Yangon. Cut to the passenger looking out the window. Cut to the view from the window. Huge rivers snaking hither and thither through the lush green rice-growing delta lands of southern Myanmar, the famed Delta of Sorrows.

Ka-thump, ka-thump. Our wheels go down in preparation for landing. The view from my window is now of an expanse of green tree tops interspersed with glimpses of buildings. There it is, the green city, the mysterious, isolated Yangon, formerly known as Rangoon. And then the glint of gold of the city's most dominant feature, the magnificent Shwedagon pagoda, the holiest of Buddhist holies, the Mecca of the Theravada Buddhist world—to mangle a religious metaphor.

An estimated US$600 million worth of gold and gems adorn the world's largest and richest pagoda in one of the world's poorest countries, but light-fingered Westerners should never be tempted to filch the gold from this or from the many other thousands of pagodas dotting the Myanmar landscape. The last Westerner to attempt to do so, Philip De Brito, was impaled at Syriam in 1613. He did not cooperate with his executioner—he was reluctant to present his posterior to the stake, hence it failed to cleanly skewer vital organs on its passage through his anus and into his body. Therefore death was not quick. He lay in a courtyard in the sun, impaled, for two days before succumbing.

Violent death is no stranger to the pariah country I am about to live in. Myanmar, a country about a third of the size of Queensland, with a population of about 52 million, has mostly been under repressive rule since 1962, run for the greater part of that time by a military junta known by the creepy name of SLORC, or State Law and Order Restoration Council, and practising what has been dubbed 'voodoo socialism'.

In September 1988, while the Olympic Games took place in nearby Seoul, hundreds—maybe thousands—of students and protesters were methodically slaughtered in a chilling precursor to the Tiananmen Square massacre in China less than a year later. After the Myanmar bloodbath a new junta was formed, the State Peace and Development Council (SPDC), which still runs the country. Headed by the ageing Senior General Than Shwe, its reign is flawed by the presence of a beautiful princess-like woman, the democracy leader Aung San Suu Kyi, an heroic and articulate international symbol and a perpetual thorn in the side of the Myanmar military.

The passengers on our plane are restless and anxious as we prepare to land. They're paranoid. That's the feeling most foreigners have as they enter Yangon, myself included. Well, actually I have good reason to be.

In January 1978—several passports and a quarter of a century ago—I entered the Revolutionary Socialist Republic of the Union of Burma, as it was then called, and after six days I was detained and questioned. Ultimately, to put a dramatically official spin on those strangely distant events, I was deported and warned never to return.

Back in 1978, Burma had only recently opened up for tourism and I grabbed the chance to visit this mysterious country, which I'd always viewed romantically. I applied for the only visa

PETER OLSZEWSKI

available at that time, a seven-day visa, at the Burmese embassy in Bangkok, where I was given a verbal mauling by a stocky woman who, had it not been for her Asian face, could have been an inspirational model for the heroic tractor-driving peasant women glorified in Russian propaganda posters. Eventually she relented, giving me a visa that in turn gave me passage to Rangoon on a dangerously decrepit, juddering Burma Airlines plane.

When I arrived in Rangoon, I endured a four-hour customs going-over that included grappling with complex and almost illegible forms, printed on pulpy Third-World paper with not enough room to print my answers. I had to empty my pockets and list every small coin of the various currencies I'd collected during my assorted Asian peregrinations. An officer noted that my planned itinerary form stated I would stay in Rangoon for the entire seven days of my allotted week. I was told I could not stay in Rangoon and I was instructed to take the road to Mandalay or Bagan.

I argued that it had been a lifelong dream of mine to visit Rangoon. I was told to check into the Strand Hotel for the interim, and from there a hotel manager took me to a small Rangoon shop-front possessing Rangoon's only neon light, which identified the establishment as the Ministry of Tourism office. A miniscule man, who reminded me of the Jiminy Cricket cartoon character, informed me he was the actual Minister of Tourism. His English was quaintly colonial, with numerous quotes from Kipling, and he too advised me to take the famous road to Mandalay. 'No tourist would want to stay in Rangoon, sir. Much better that you join the other tourists in Mandalay or Bagan or both.'

I reiterated details of my boyhood ambitions and eventually he acceded, telling me that if I intended to remain in Rangoon, I could do so providing I stayed for the week at the Strand Hotel.

The Strand was an archetypal British colonial hotel and a

monument to British imperialism, albeit frayed and dusty. Like other famous archetypal British colonial Asian hotels including the Eastern and Oriental in Penang and Raffles in Singapore, it had been built by the Armenian Sarkie brothers.

The Strand, like Rangoon itself, was a sad testament to the decline brought about by the dysfunctional dictatorial regime of the mad General Ne Win, who ruled this socialist republic for so many years and who, while reputedly bathing in dolphin's blood, turned the once prosperous nation into the economic basket-case of South-East Asia.

I crossed the dusty marble floor of the Strand and, after a long drawn-out checking-in process, stepped into an ornate wrought-iron lift and learnt my first Burmese lesson—Never Use Lifts. The power supply in Burma is erratic, and on this occasion the power cranked down, the lift stopped mid-floor and I was trapped for more than an hour.

Many years later I chanced upon a dusty Burmese magazine—the August 1996 issue of *Panorama*, the front cover of which announced the opening of the Unity Hotel in Mandalay, noting that it offered 'Day and Night elevator service'. An inset photo on the front cover showed a gleaming chrome lift and, inside, an article extolled the virtues of this significant development, stating: 'Everybody likes upper floors that command beautiful panoramic views. But you need an elevator that works around the clock to take you up and down. There, Unity Hotel has it for you!'

The lost-property cabinet in the foyer of the Strand was famous for its contents. The cabinet was a time capsule cataloguing the upmarket detritus of the grand old days, the days when the British ruled in stuffy Victorian splendour and partied at the Strand, leaving behind jewellery, gloves, cufflinks and binoculars to sit, unclaimed, in this dusty display cabinet for a hundred years or so.

Over the years I've read dozens of accounts of the contents

of this display case and the claim that the sanctity of this lost property is inviolate—nothing can be bought, nothing can be purloined. Except that, after two days of my offering bribes, the cabinet was unlocked and I bought a magnificently ornate Victorian English necklace for my then wife. It had thick, finely worked filigree silver, studded with large twinkling blue stones that could well have been sapphires. Unfortunately the necklace was stolen in Calcutta and I never determined whether I had made the purchase of a lifetime.

On this 1978 trip, I explored Rangoon. The city was grey, depressing and moribund. Nothing seemed to work, there was nothing to buy, no life, no joy. The Minister of Tourism was right. No tourist would want to stay in Rangoon. Ironically, the locals pronounced their country as 'Bummer', popular hippy slang for a bad time. 'Excuse me, sir, how are you liking Bummer?' 'Oh man, I'm having a bummer.' 'Very good, sir.'

But at the same time there was a beauty and graciousness about Burma that was almost elusive. At times the country revealed tantalising inklings of itself that took my breath away and made me want so much to understand this strange yet dignified city with its strange yet dignified way of life and its strange yet dignified people. In the evenings I'd sit by the banks of the Rangoon River as the big orange-red orb of the tropical sun—shrouded at times with a shimmering mist of wood-fire smoke and petrol fumes, other times partly hidden by grey-black inky smudges of cloud—rapidly and dramatically slid through the sky and sank into an incongruous horizon, a farrago of black-silhouetted snaggle-toothed British colonial tenement buildings and the elegant tapering spires of Rangoon's many Buddhist pagodas.

The thin, mangy pariah dogs slunk from their daytime hidey-holes to forage and howl in unison. Crows flapped and settled on roofs, scratching the guttering with their grasping, ugly claws. Bats darted and exploded through the thick air, and sensuously slinky-hipped women carrying baskets of produce on their heads glided by, chatting and presumably reviewing the day's events.

During the day the streets became automobile museums, with the cars all exhibiting a commonality: they were battered, clapped-out and ancient. Pre-WWII cars shared the road with rattling Indian-manufactured cars, including the ubiquitous Ambassadors. The only modern cars were gleaming military Mercedes, which swooshed silently through the streets with flags fluttering or were parked in a guarded semi-circle outside the Socialist Revolutionary Republic headquarters.

I engaged Solomon to become my driver in his old Chevrolet for the duration of my stay. But on the first morning, when I went out into the street to hail him, I watched his entire family unpack their bedrolls and belongings from the car, in which they obviously lived. I was relegated to the back seat of Solomon's car because an unexplained and unintroduced gentleman sat in the passenger seat, accompanying us wherever we went. He wore a grey Chairman Mao jacket and hat, and of course I christened him Chairman Mao.

My questions about his identity and presence went unanswered. When Solomon discussed his economic plight and apologised for the bumpy ride, explaining that he had to stuff his tyres with rags because tubes could not be purchased, Chairman Mao pulled out a notebook and scribbled ominously, causing Solomon obvious distress. During our bumpy perambulations we passed many sports fields, which were mostly parking lots for tanks and armoured vehicles covered with camouflage netting.

The bar at the Strand could possibly have been the inspiration for the famous *Star Wars* bar scene. Strange quasi-military types huddled and whispered together—espionage and intrigue were as thick in the air as the mingled roiling smoke of countless cheap Asian cigarettes and Burmese cheroots. Asians with strange top-knot hairdos conspired with bulldog-faced Americans wearing military attire from the waist up, civilian clothing from the waist down. No-one would acknowledge me, no-one would speak to me. Everyone was guarded and, well, paranoid. And I loved it. This was Adventure with a capital A.

I learnt how the black market worked, selling cigarettes, jeans and any other Western flotsam and jetsam I possessed. But the huge wad of the local currency—kyats—that I carted to my hotel room and covered my bed and floor with was useless. The kyats couldn't be spent outside Burma, and they couldn't really be spent inside Burma because there wasn't much to buy. There was a sort of duty-free store, the Diplomat Store, but this hardly contained any stock—just a few cheap, thin wooden versions of the Burmese chinthe, a mythical lion-like creature that guards pagodas, plus a few dusty packets of crappy Indian cigarettes and some bolts of boring cloth.

I unloaded a kilo of my useless kyats at Rangoon's only expensive restaurant, a floating extravaganza on a lake. I sat in the restaurant eating boring food while watching cat-sized rats scuttle backwards and forwards along the exposed rafters and beams. That restaurant was a mistake and for the next few days I paid dearly, with a dreaded dose of Burma belly—similar to Bali belly, Delhi belly and all the other Asian bellies, but far more vicious.

I went to the market and caused a riot. Hundreds of Burmese had heaps of useless junk spread over the ground under the hot steaming Burmese sun. One old lady caught my eye and I sensed she was desperate to sell anything to anybody, especially this foreigner who, like most other foreigners, was probably rich, at least by her standards (from what I could glean of her circumstances, and others like her, an Australian school-child with two dollars in a piggybank would be rich).

I looked over her pile of sad junk, mostly rusted car gears and lumps of metal. I'd almost given up on her when a flash of silver caught my eye. I dug into her pile and pulled out a treasure, a gleaming chrome-plated replica of an old pre-war Western automobile. The car rattled when I picked it up, signifying something was inside. I noticed a little button on the front radiator and pushed it. The top flipped up revealing a lid with an insignia similar to the Chevrolet logo, and a little handle. Under the lid was a little tray with four round pull-up pots and a small octagonal tray about the size of a match box. I looked at the back of the car and emblazoned on the boot was a stylish logo identifying this as a 'Betel Motor Car. Patent no. 75086. Open and close type.' Underneath the logo, the name Y.C. Bham was crudely etched into the metal. The little tray and pots were for storing and mixing the various components used to manufacture betel nut quids. It was an exquisite art-deco curio, a true treasure.

I asked the price and the woman rattled off a figure equivalent to US$10. I knew I should bargain but it was so hot and debilitating that I couldn't be bothered. I simply handed her a kilo of kyats. She almost fainted. She trembled, thanked me effusively, and then manically grabbed other items from the pile in case I could be persuaded to part with another small fortune.

Other stall-holders observed this transaction and became hysterical, grabbing items from their piles and rushing at me, babbling and begging me to please buy, sir, please buy, sir, buy, buy, buy. The woman tried to push them back and she too became hysterical, and in an instant I realised I was being mobbed. I clutched my betel-nut car and ran for it, with several stall-holders holding up old gears or silly bits of metal, screaming and pleading, and chasing after me.

I almost caused another riot at a music concert. I'd seen this advertised on a small poster, and thought I'd soak up a little local culture, presuming the music was Burmese. But instead I found myself inside a soccer stadium with thousands of teenagers watching a naff Cliff Richards and the Shadows cover band. I sat there for a short time, wondering why on earth I was sitting in exotic Rangoon suffering this punishment. But I was also in danger of becoming the main act. Even as I had walked down the aisle to find a seat, I was jeered, whistled and cheered.

After three songs I rose to leave, to more cheers, whistles, screams and catcalls, and a group of teenagers followed me. They said they were university students and one earnestly asked, 'Do you know Mick Jagger of the musical group The Rolling Stones?'

I told them I didn't know Mr Jagger personally but I certainly knew of him, and in fact I had a cassette tape of his group's latest album in my hotel room. Off we trooped to the Strand. I turned up the volume on my cassette player, the Stones' stinging guitars whip-cracked through my room, and there was a party happening.

Briefly. The door burst open and three military police, or 'white mice' as they're known in Asia, in shining white helmets and sturdy, gleaming white leather Sam Browne belts, walked in, brandishing very serious-looking machine guns. They prodded the students out of the room with the guns, pushing barrels into backs, all the time steadfastly ignoring me. Not once, even momentarily, did the police look at me, talk to me or acknowledge me, and they were gone almost as quickly as they had come.

Next morning, the sixth day of my permitted seven days in Burma, I stayed in my room to catch up on my travellers' housekeeping—sorting through luggage, abandoning the unnecessary and lightening my load. I'd collected a pile of newspapers from various Asian cities and I sorted through these, keeping some front pages, clipping interesting articles. I put this material in a large envelope, addressed it to my home address and walked to the post office a few doors down from the Strand. I told the attendant I wished to mail the parcel to Australia, but a man stepped up from behind me, took the envelope and spoke to the attendant, who in turn spoke to me. 'You must go now with this man. He is taking you to the secret police.'

The man led me into the post office, another magnificent and ornate old British colonial building, and down into the bowels, to a large room seemingly half an acre in size, filled with hundreds of unopened mail sacks, many of them covered in dust as though they'd been sitting there for years. I was told to sit on a sack and for several hours I watched sleepy postal workers slit open mailbags, open parcels and remove interesting or valuable contents.

Eventually I was told to get up and was taken to a room where three men sat at a table. There was my envelope, opened, with the contents strewn across the table. But no bamboo spikes were produced, and we commenced what became a long and good-natured philosophical conversation centred on my lifelong fascination with Rangoon and my desire to visit the place of my boyhood imaginings.

I was informed I had been detained for possessing illegal foreign newspapers.

I pleaded ignorance, pointing out the only way to bring these papers to Burma was through customs and I had been rigorously searched at customs, for four hours. The papers had been openly sitting in my suitcase, and they had been seen but not confiscated. This was acknowledged.

The youngest of the trio spoke: 'You are not a spy?'

'No, no.'

'Then what are you?'

Instead of journalist, the occupation I'd entered on my Burmese visa application was marine biologist, based on a smidgeon of fact in that, back home in Australia, I'd just written a book about freshwater crayfish (yabbies). The guy quizzed me. What exactly did I do as a marine biologist? I said I studied freshwater crayfish and added I had just written a book about them. He seized on this and said, 'Ah, therefore you are not a marine biologist. You are a writer.'

They chatted amongst themselves in Burmese and then the

oldest one addressed me, delivering what was in fact the judgement: 'We do not think you have come to harm the Republic of Burma. But you do have in your possession material that is not permitted. We will now take you to the airport. There is a flight leaving shortly for Bangkok.'

He caught my look and shrugged, smiling kindly. 'Your permitted seven days stay in Burma will expire in only a few hours so you are just leaving a little earlier. You can now go.'

'Thank you,' I said.

'But you may not return to Burma,' he added, ominously.

The Myanmar military can really only accomplish one thing effectively. They can engender paranoia, and they do this extremely well.

Paranoia began to insinuate itself into my psyche on that evening in January 2003 when I was on the point of leaving Australia. A strange conversation at Brisbane Airport's immigration counter set the scene for what was to come, confirming my suspicions that my sojourn in Myanmar promised intrigue. Myanmar embassy officials had stapled two sheets of paper into my passport, next to my large, colourful business-class visa. The top document stated that my Myanmar 'guarantor' was Brigadier General Thein Swe of the Military Intelligence Office, Department of Defence, Yangon.

The woman at Brisbane immigration read the documentation, examined my visa and muttered something, sotto voce.

'I beg your pardon?' I said.

She replied, 'I said, are you embassy staff?'

'No.'

'Wait a moment. I need to get someone.'

She returned with a bemused gentleman, who started a patter about how, strictly speaking, Australian nationals were not permitted to work for foreign military organisations. 'I don't work for any military organisation,' I explained. I directed him to another document, which stated my employer and sponsor was the Myanmar Media Company, a private enterprise company headed by an Australian. He turned to the woman and said, 'Okay.'

I exited Australia.

But my paranoia became more palpable at Singapore's Changi Airport, when we changed from an international to a domestic flight. Entering the departure lounge for Yangon meant walking away from the colourful, glamorous mish-mash of excitement that typifies international travel, and walking into a drab room with drab attendants handing out complex, drab forms. As in 1978 Myanmar's immigration forms are still typically hopeless and detailed. The English is awkward, archaic and often unclear, and there are grim warnings printed in bold red lettering.

The passengers themselves were a drab lot, cheaply and colourlessly dressed and serious in demeanour, as though going to a theosophy lecture instead of an exotic port of call. Drama too when the hostess shed her humble child-like pleasantries and transformed herself into a cold, vicious State operative. She'd been ignoring the obviously excessive hand luggage being lugged on board, but when one overladen passenger gave her an arrogant sneer, she switched from smiles to harsh anger as she spat out an order that, because his luggage was overweight, it must be left behind. Two men stepped forward and took his hand luggage, leaving him stunned, rattled and frightened.

There was paranoia too when we were finally seated on the plane and we fished out our Myanmar in-flight magazine, *Golden Flight*, from the seat pocket. Page three carried the bold exhortation that must appear prominently on all Myanmar publications, namely the 'Four People's Desire':

> Four People's Desire. 1: Oppose those relying on external elements, acting as stooges, holding negative views. 2: Oppose those trying to jeopardise stability of the State and progress of the nation. 3: Oppose foreign nations interfering in internal affairs of the State. 4: Crush all internal and external destructive elements as the common enemy.

The behaviour of a young Myanmar male passenger and his girlfriend, dressed in sexy Western fluoro-coloured gear, also unsettled the passengers. He was dressed casually like a hip young inner-suburban professional—good jeans, cool short haircut, expensive street-label T-shirt. This, I later learnt, is the hallmark of many young military officers in mufti. He seemed angry because he'd booked business class, but there was no separate business class on that flight. 'I booked the seats months ago,' he told the steward. 'This is not good enough.'

He moved to the front of the plane and had a steward order the people sitting there to move to the seats he and his girlfriend had occupied. But he was not happy with this seating arrangement either, eventually giving up and moving back to the seats he'd originally been allocated. Unfortunately, I made eye contact with him, and his questioning, arrogant look back at me didn't sit well.

The plane landed in Myanmar and I made my way across the tarmac. By that time I was edgy about my luggage. It contained an assortment of newspapers, magazines, textbooks, documents and a laptop computer I'd been instructed to bring. These may or may not have been permissible. It was difficult to get a handle on what exactly was permissible and what was not.

If I was to believe the paranoid instructions in the guide books, particularly the Lonely Planet guide book (which itself was apparently not permitted in Myanmar, and of which I also had a copy in my luggage), most of what I was about to take into Myanmar was not permitted. In an attempt to clarify this, I had emailed my Australian employer in Myanmar and had received a prompt reply. 'Don't worry, mate. Bring everything on the list. We will have a man inside the airport to usher you through customs.'

I entered the small, quaint, distinctively Burmese Yangon International Airport. I noted that the quarrelsome man on the connecting flight was met by a group of military officers in uniform. He was warmly greeted and the group disappeared through an unmarked side door. A long, shuffling queue had formed at a counter marked Foreign Tourist. But there was no queue at the counter marked Foreign Business, and I figured this was my queue. It was, and the immigration officer cursorily inspected my documentation and visa and slapped down the rubber stamp.

I went inside the shabby wooden customs hall. There was no man inside the airport to meet me, as promised. Instead there was a woman—the beautiful and keenly intelligent Ma Poe Poe, who had unsuccessfully tried to play down her looks with a pair of severe rimless spectacles, inadvertently transforming herself into a thinking man's sex symbol. (Later I learnt she was a 27-year-old virgin and her status was fiercely protected by all senior males within a wide mating range of her working circle.)

Poe Poe welcomed me to Myanmar and chatted expertly as we strolled through the customs area. She nodded and greeted officials effusively, and our passage was unencumbered until we got to the last search point. The woman at that counter, neatly dressed in a sparkling white uniform, was agitated.

Poe Poe said, 'This woman is upset. She is worried that she

is not doing her job and will be reported. Have you anything in your hand luggage that is interesting?'

'Well yes, I've got this snazzy new portable CD player I bought in Singapore.'

'That will do,' said Poe Poe. 'Please show her that.'

I walked over to the lady in white, plonked my hand luggage on the counter, opened it, fished around inside and pulled out my Panasonic SL-CT490 Anti-Skip System CD player and handed it to her. She gravely examined it and pointed to a little red-and-yellow sticker which proclaimed 'No Skip Anti-Skip System'.

'Ah yes, an excellent feature,' I said.

'Very good,' said the now happy officer. 'You may go.'

Poe Poe and I exited the airport. I blinked in the fierce sunlight as I absorbed the sights and sounds of an exciting and modern Yangon, post Ne Win. I took my first bold steps into the city that was to be my home away from home.

It was 25 years, almost to the very day, since I had last walked these steps. Back then I had been expelled for possessing foreign newspapers, but this time I had returned to train young locals in the ancient art of the foreign newspaper.

Nine nights later I am walking along the red carpet at the entrance to the Australian embassy residential compound for the annual Australia Day bash. There is a mood of vulnerable camaraderie at this gathering of expatriates because Asian satellite television services have been leading the news with horrendous images of immense banks of flames burning the Australian capital, Canberra, in the 2003 bushfires. The images of the charred and burned once-white domes of Mt Stromlo Observatory are seared into all our minds. Tragedy has struck the ambassador, Trevor Wilson, and his wife; their tenanted Canberra home has been reduced to rubble and ashes.

The embassy's newly appointed Australian federal copper and his wife also arrived this week, the day after me. They knew nothing about the fire until they landed in Bangkok, checked their emails and discovered that, while fire had destroyed much of Canberra, they'd had a lucky escape. Flames had consumed their back fence and licked across their backyard, but their house had been spared.

I shake the ambassador's hand, his wife's hand, and the hands of several staff members lining the red-carpeted walkway. Then, stepping off the red carpet onto the sumptuous lawn, I slip my gold-embossed-on-white official Embassy of Australia invitation card into the top inside pocket of my newly pressed black lounge suit, take a breath, spot an interesting group to my left and head towards them.

As I approach I see a familiar face and its owner sees me. 'You!' she yells in her drunken hoiky Aussie loudness. 'You're the last person I expected to see here. Weren't you kicked out of this country, or banned or something?'

I make a rapid turn to the right, passing a group of elite Myanmar men dressed in traditional garb befitting their status: a silk Myanmar jacket with a white, collarless shirt studded at the neck with a gem-encrusted gold stud, and a brown longyi, the sarong-like 'dress' almost all Myanmar men wear. The colours or patterns of the longyi can often give clues to the background or allegiances of the wearers. The Myanmar men are standing by the long starched-white-cloth-covered trestles with glinting solid silver cutlery. Official Australian traditional fare is on display and the Myanmar gentlemen peer at a plate one of their colleagues is holding. On it is the famous Australian sausage roll. One man pushes and prods the roll with a fork while another says, 'I think the meat is of some kind of reptile.' I chuckle over yet another example of the many, many cultural differences I have encountered in the few short days I've inhabited this city.

Then I return to cursing my bad luck at encountering the woman who knows about my past. Janette. She worked in the bottle shop a hundred yards from my apartment in my home town, Sunshine Beach, Noosa; about a year ago, before I had any notion I'd ever be returning to Yangon, she told me excitedly that she was going to live in Myanmar with her new boyfriend, who worked in the timber industry. I talked to her about my knowledge of Myanmar and unfortunately recounted my experience of being kicked out. So a few thousand kilometres away from home, a world away from home, I bump into her and I'm publicly outed.

I am introduced to the Russian ambassador's wife, a pretty woman who is legendary for tooling around Yangon astride a pink scooter, wearing a pink jumpsuit and a pink helmet. She has the same prominent cheekbones and hawk-like Slavic nose as I do, but I allow our cutting conversation to bog down into the age-old tedious Polish–Russian argument about who invented vodka.

I adroitly move to another group, composed mainly of personnel from the many and varied non-governmental organisations working in Myanmar. To my dismay, one of the Aussie women says, 'Oh, we've just had a friend here from Melbourne who knows you. He says he voted for you when you were the leader of the Australian Marijuana Party or something.'

An embassy official standing within earshot winces. This is not a good conversation to be having. A messy, hush-hush drug scandal recently swept the Australian embassy staff and

Australian expatriate community. According to gossip, embassy staffers were overheard discussing cocaine in the toilet of a Yangon nightclub, and they were flown back to Canberra for an official carpeting. A Federal Police investigation into the drug-taking habits of the Australian expatriate community ensued and there is ongoing bitter debate about whether or not the Federal Police have stepped outside their sphere of operation by investigating Australians not attached to the embassy.

The embassy party is at full throttle but I decide to quit while I'm still behind, in case I get even further behind. Then I make another gaffe by asking if I can call a cab. Only a new chum who hasn't told his driver to wait for him would ask this question because there is simply no such cab system operating in Yangon. There are cabs galore, but no radio cabs. I'm told to walk down the dusty lane outside the compound for a couple of hundred yards until I come across a main road, where I can easily hail a passing cab.

When I finally arrive back home to my little hotel suite-cum-apartment, I lie wallowing in my bed, wondering if there'll be any ugly ramifications of Ko Ko Chit's pathetically un-successful introduction to Yangon society. Ko Ko Chit is the Myanmar name I have been granted. It means Big Brother Love. I am worrying it may have dubious connotations, but my Myanmar friends keep reassuring me, 'It is a very nice name to have, very nice in Myanmar.'

The moonlight is flooding into my bedroom and, as I lie there, mentally noting that I must track down Janette for a chat sooner rather than later, I contemplate the plant I bought a few days ago in the nearby Bogyoke market, which now takes pride of place on my window sill. It's an intriguing plant with soft, luscious green leaves hiding vicious one-inch-long thorns. The flowers, similar to large geranium flowers, have thick, waxed, fruit-like, pulpy petals which, unlike most Western plants, don't close at night but instead broaden out and come alive, almost visibly pulsating with energy or perhaps even fructifying in the moon's soft serene light. A Myanmar woman giggled when she saw the plant. 'Very good plant, Ko Ko Chit,' she said softly, sweetly. 'Very good. It is our famous Kiss Me Softly plant.'

I love the Myanmar naming process. It is so lyrical, yet so unerringly literal. And I love my Kiss Me Softly plant because to me it's a living analogy of life in Yangon. Kiss softly at first. The surface can be sensuous, sweet and luscious, but under the surface lurks vicious, needle-sharp danger.

A few nights after the embassy bash I spot the redeployed Australian federal copper dining at the popular Sabai Sabai restaurant with a good-looking, classy blonde who, although I can't recall seeing her in Yangon before, has a somehow familiar face.

Later, as I drive across Yangon with some other Australians, sharing a joint, I mention in between long drags, 'Hey, I saw Clive the copper at Sabai Sabai last night with this interesting looking blonde and . . .' At this an Aussie businessman in the front of the car, normally of quiet and dignified demeanour, spits the dummy. He bashes the dashboard shouting, 'Don't mention that fucking prick! He turned out to be a real bastard over that embassy coke shit. He really lost it, trying to investigate the Australian expat community. He doesn't have the right to do that. He even tried to question me, and put out the word that most of the Aussie expats are on drugs. It was fucking outrageous and I'm glad the fucking prick is going.'

He passes me the joint and I inhale, rather futilely because, sadly, Myanmar marijuana is very second rate. Considering that this country is one of the world's most notorious narco states— if not *the* most notorious—it seems unjust that they haven't figured out how to grow primo pot. But such are the vagaries of life.

I report for duty at the offices of the good ship *Myanmar Times*, receiving my orders from the captain as such, CEO Ross Dunkley. He's the man steering the enterprise and the man who holds my immediate destiny in his hands, not to mention my physical safety and liberty. He's a middle-aged maverick Aussie newsman who finds life more sustainable in the far-flung reaches of Asia, and there's a score of colourful stories about him. His shaved head and rotund physique give him a Buddha-like aspect, and while his amiable words are meant to be reassuring, his nonchalance worries me. I have a feeling he is a man who will sail this ship close to the edge of the galaxy.

We talk the small talk Aussie journalists employ to feel each other out. Where worked, who with, what story, who is a prick, who is a cunt, and who fucked whom. Dunkley tells me he is hard-nosed old-school; he is a past winner of Australia's highest journalism honour, the Walkley Award, after having been driven by a hard taskmistress. 'I had a brilliant dominatrix as a chief sub,' he beams. 'She was always sitting at the sub's desk, with a constant menthol cigarette in her mouth. She'd look at my copy, call me over, scrunch up my pitiful little scraps of paper, blow menthol smoke in the air, and throw the ball of paper into my face. "Do this again, it's complete crap," she'd say to me day after day for two years. I still have a fantasy of taking her anally.'

Dunkley's Asian sojourn also began under hard taskmasters, members of the Vietnamese Communist government. He had run an Australian rural publishing company, but in 1991 had moved to Vietnam and been blooded in the ways of the East after teaming up with two other Australians to start the *Vietnam Investment Review* in Ho Chi Minh City. This had earned him the distinction of being the first foreign newspaper editor to operate in Vietnam since 1975.

In 1999 Dunkley had surfaced in Myanmar, teaming up with a printer, U Myat 'Sonny' Swe. The new partners had agreed to publish a weekly newspaper and inked the deal on the auspicious stroke of midnight, 2000. Other partners in the daring venture included a Western Australian, Bill Clough of Clough Engineering, and a Myanmar business heavyweight, Pyone Maung Maung, an associate of the country's number three strongman, Khin Nyunt, Chief of Military Intelligence.

The flagship of the business is the English-language version of the *Myanmar Times*, selling about a thousand copies weekly, and the money-earner is the Myanmar-language version, selling in the low twenty thousands. Plans are afoot to publish this biweekly.

The *Times'* launch in February 2000 had been surrounded by intrigue, especially regarding Dunkley's relationship with the military masters of Myanmar. Dunkley told everyone that, while all publications were censored in Myanmar, he'd had a lucky break by sidestepping the propaganda-oriented, Ministry of Information's 'Press Scrutiny Division', which by law must censor all newspapers published in Myanmar. His paper was deemed a journal, enabling it to be scrutinised by Military Intelligence's elite and intellectual OSS, becoming part of the portfolio of Brigadier General Thein Swe, father of Dunkley's partner, Sonny Swe.

During the launch Dunkley had told a Japanese television presenter, Aiko Doden of Japan's sole public broadcaster, NHK, that censorship was paramount in his mind when negotiating with the military. 'I suggested it would be more appropriate if Military Intelligence was my censor,' he said. 'At least with Military Intelligence you have well-educated, sophisticated, well-travelled people. It was agreed that MI would take on that role.'

One of the few published insights into the inner, secret world of Myanmar politics appeared in the now defunct *Asiaweek* magazine during the launch of the *Times*. In February 2000, journalist Roger Mitton reported:

> Anyone wishing to publish a newspaper in Myanmar must get a licence from the ministry of information, run by Maj. Gen. Kyi Aung, who thinks draconian restrictions and one-sided news presentation are just fine, thanks. But over at the information division of the elite Office of Strategic Studies, they see things differently. Run by the articulate and outward-looking [then] Col. Thein Swe and Lt.-Col Hla Min, the division, like the rest of the OSS, reports to the regime's strategist, Lt. Gen. Khin Nyunt.
>
> Thein Swe and Hla Min have been quietly fuming over the way the nation's flagship paper, the Stalinist *New Light of Myanmar*, undermines their efforts to win greater international acceptance . . . so they authorised the launch of a new paper, *The Myanmar Times and Business Weekly*, part of a radical attempt to revamp the regime's image. The move represents a daring and risky internal powerplay . . . Khin Nyunt's boys have not even bothered to apply to the ministry of information for a license. How are they getting away with that? By playing the old game of semantics. Thein Swe explains, 'Only the ministry can approve a newspaper. So it will be a journal, not a paper . . . because it's a journal they [ministry of information] can't say anything.'
>
> Remember, this is one of Khin Nyunt's inner coterie talking about a key ministry, headed by a fellow general.

Attacks against Dunkley and the *Times* have been constant and virulent since day one, often helped along by Dunkley's confrontational attitude. He wrote a weekly column in the early days of the *Times*, and a broadside against the standard of local journalism caused outcry among Myanmar's journalists. Military Intelligence interceded, instructing Dunkley to give his column a rest. A long rest, because it never reappeared.

Radio Free Asia, beamed into Myanmar from Washington, is one of the *Times*' most fervent attackers; it broadcasts the opinion that Dunkley should be granted the national literary award, because his writings bolster the military government's policy. The network calls him Lorr Dunpli or Mr Traitorous Flattering—in Myanmar *lorr* means traitorous or sly and *pli* means flattery.

The many vociferous opponents of the *Times* claim Dunkley is merely an apologist for the military, and his paper is a pathetic attempt to present an acceptable face for the regime. Proponents say Dunkley is working from the inside to pave the way incrementally for democracy and is producing a paper that, despite its censorship, is better and more informative than anything else produced in Myanmar.

An Australian expatriate told me, 'Look, this is the reality. When Dunkley breezed into town and said he was going to start up a quality newspaper, most people thought he was mad. But he pulled it off. Before Dunkley arrived all we had to read was the Dim Light, and now we've got something else. It may not be perfect, it may not even be all that good, but it's better than what we had.'

Sitting at my new desk, I consult my copy of the opposition, *The New Light of Myanmar*, the State-run daily English-language rag, referred to by expatriates as the 'Dim Light'. It fascinates me because it's a sad product of a 1950s military mind. It is physically difficult to read because of its abominable printing on equally abominable pulpy paper. Sometimes its pages are so smudged they are impossible to read and usually the small-print crossword clues are illegible.

But even when the contents are physically legible, after a quick read I usually wish they weren't. Reading the articles is a slog because of the dense, convoluted style of reportage.

Photos of concrete factories, bridges and mills are obsessively scattered throughout the publication, and an article extolling the natural beauties of a lake is accompanied by a grainy photo of an old bulldozer churning up muck in the middle of the water. Precise circulation figures are published on the front page daily: on 28 November 2002 the circulation was 26 451; on 22 February 2003 it was 24 622.

A typical *New Light* headline reads, 'Strong sense of national unity required in building peaceful modern, developed nation. Tatmadaw [military] members urged to further strengthen unity within Armed Forces and with people.' The travels of senior generals are meticulously detailed. Long lists of dignitaries attending functions and speeches are provided, as well as details of lunches and dinners. The generals are always described as 'offering the necessary guidance and instruction'.

Its xenophobic editorials inevitably warn of outside threats and the need to support and obey the mighty Tatmadaw. Its grim pages are littered with patriotic prose and poetry which suppurate lines such as:

Break the fangs of enemies,
Shun them till their
Kin disappear.

But while poring over the *New Light*, I do unearth a dollop of humour. A report about a 'motivational trip' though rural villages reveals:

Members of the excursion team began to know about one another. They all found Naw Sarinda the most interesting person among themselves. She had a dozen brothers and sisters. She was the tenth child. Others were Spider, Cylinder, William, OK, All Right, All Gone, Standard, Very

Good, Thank You, Once More and Full Stop, the last child. They were a happy family.

I'm given the usual first-day guided tour and meet the small staff of young Westerners whom I dub the 'brat pack'. They're mostly university interns who come and go, and Americans dominate. While they're highly educated, I find them kind of dumb in a naïve way—aggressively opinionated, hostilely and overbearingly politically correct.

I meet the Myanmar staff. Despite language differences, I discover they are a lively, friendly, warm people and, once I get past the almost obsequious politeness and overweening civility, I discover a people with keen intelligence and an enjoyable style of humour centred on sending up the physical attributes and foibles of colleagues in a cutting, accurate manner, without being cruel.

I meet my band of trainees, eight university graduates who look at me with panic because they have difficulty understanding my broad Australian accent. The training program I'm about to implement is funded by a Japanese philanthropic organisation, the Sasakawa Peace Foundation; it's part of the foundation's belief that money for developing countries is best spent on developing the middle-class infrastructures. The biggest program undertaken by the Sasakawa people in Yangon is the training of over a hundred civil servants.

I also meet the editor, Geoffrey Goddard, who has just returned after being stuck a couple of hundred miles north of Yangon on the Chindwin River waiting for a riverboat to collect him. He's also an Australian journalist and he replaced the debut editor, the unfortunately named Australian, Jayne Dullard.

Geoffrey's a tall, crumpled chap with a long-nosed face and a Dickensian pallor; after chatting to him I discover he can be charming. But mostly he exudes an air of quiet desperation that often turns him into a peevish pedant. I sense disillusionment dwells inside him because, realistically speaking, he is the editor in title only; when he does attempt to produce a good newspaper, he is checkmated by the stifling censorship enforced by MI. But he obviously believes his main mission is to push out a newspaper, any newspaper, week after week.

I discover censorship defines life at the *Myanmar Times* and depletes the buzz and excitement that's generally a feature of good newspaper offices where ground-breaking stories are regularly broken. Censorship at the *Times* is absolute and total, but the system itself is quite simple. All articles selected for possible publication are faxed to Military Intelligence and are either accepted in their totality, completely rejected, or partly censored, with words, paragraphs and sections removed. Such information is relayed to the editor, Goddard, usually by an officer named Wai Lin. Sometimes the Brigadier General himself rolls up his sleeves and pitches in, and if big issues, especially political issues, are discussed in an article, Wai Lin will pass the material to him for 'instruction and guidance'.

Inside page layouts and story placements are mostly left to the staff to determine, but the front-page layout is carefully scrutinised and stories approved for publication might not be approved for front-page publication, or the emphasis of such stories might be downplayed.

At times, there can be dialogue about decisions. I am told a story about breakdancing becoming a fad among trendy Yangon youth was axed by MI because they only want to promote traditional dancing. A query, asking if there was any way the story could be saved, resulted in a new ruling that it could be used if breakdancing were not defined as a dance but instead as an American fitness regime.

I discover that Myanmar has a mind-numbing myriad of rules regarding publications. New laws, new variations to new laws, and new amendments to old laws relentlessly emerge.

I don't even try to grapple with this complexity because I am told that ultimately only one law applies—the law of the day as determined by the Brigadier General and his boys at Military Intelligence. If they say no it means no, and there is no burrowing through laws and statutes to find precedents or technicalities to present to lawyers. If the Brigadier General rules it out, it's out and anyone who publishes against his will could well be on the road to Insein prison—which, incidentally, is appropriately pronounced 'Insane' prison.

But the most stultifying aspect of the insidious, all-pervading censorship is that the paper is denied an entity or a voice. All aspects giving a Western paper its character, personality and identity—editorials, letters to the editor, causes and crusades, opinion and analysis—are no-go zones. The term 'political analysis' does not exist in the *Myanmar Times* lexicon.

My first day ends with Dunkley reviewing the procedures and once again discussing the censorship process. The censorship doesn't seem to faze Dunkley, but his nonchalance momentarily gives way to exasperation and he says, 'Mate, I hate censorship.'

She's bugging me because she's staring fixedly in my direction, but her eyes are odd and I can't figure out if she's looking at me or through me. She's extremely beautiful but she's not quite right. She's weird. She's Myanmar but she's dressed as though she's part David Jones fashion model, part grunge adherent, and the clothing combination doesn't gel.

I don't think she's a hooker—she's a tad too classy—so perhaps she's a singer, perhaps a movie actress. All I know for sure is that she's one of the many colourful characters who congregate here, in my favourite late night café, the House of Joy, a Yangon approximation of a bohemian haunt, populated by beer-drinking, cigarette-smoking, horn-rimmed-glasses-wearing, black-garbed inner-city intellectuals, punks, businessmen, hookers and their Wa tribe gangster pimps. And her.

She's sitting at a table opposite me, and I figure if she wants to stare at me, or through me, let her stare. I've resumed reading my *Living Colour* magazine when she speaks in a husky monotone.

'You,' she says. I look at her. 'You are waiting for someone.'

I'm not sure if she's asking a question or making a statement, but I respond as though she is questioning me. 'Actually, I'm waiting for a hamburger,' I say.

Nothing. No response. After a minute I say, 'And you? Are you waiting for someone?'

'I am waiting for no-one,' she replies.

That's it. End of conversation. She resumes staring, I resume reading.

She gets up to go, riffles through her bag and fixes me with another stare. This time she's obviously looking at me and when she has my attention she says, 'She will come to you. She will come to you here in Yangon.'

Then she glides out of the House of Joy. I'm curious so I walk to the front of the café, pretending to poke through a pile of magazines on a bench. I look out onto the street to see in which direction she's heading, or if she's getting into a car, but she's nowhere to be seen. She's vanished, dematerialised, and I return to my table thinking that I don't want to think about it. I don't need any weirdness tonight. I just want to be normal, but I can't help wondering who she is, who she was, where she went, why she said what she said, and how she vanished just like that.

I don't have any answers and that's not unusual. The longer I live in Yangon, the more I come to realise that there are witchy things happening all around me for which there are no logical answers because I'm no longer in Logic Land.

We Westerners are bound by logic and technological wizardry but many Asians, and particularly the Myanmar, are bound by wizards, mysticism and magic. I'm told not to go here, not to go there at certain times because of the ghosts. I'm told the Myanmar avoid visiting the extravagant new Yangon Drugs Museum because it's built on an old gravesite and the ghosts are malevolent. I hear many strange stories, one of the most popular being about a television set in a store that started pouring blood on an anniversary of the 1988 student massacre.

Many trees have spooky little voodoo-like altars attached to them, to appease the nat spirits that date back to the dawn of Myanmar civilisation. Most Myanmar are Buddhist but most Myanmar Buddhists also worship the ancient animist nats. Nat worship is incorporated into many of the major Buddhist rites, just as voodoo worship is incorporated into Catholicism in Caribbean countries.

My hamburger arrives. It looks normal, but when I bite into it I discover that it isn't. The bun isn't quite right because it's loaded with sugar. The meat isn't quite right because it's a sort of powdery, pasty gunk. And the sauce, of course, is spicy and fiery, as is most food in this country where educated locals universally condemn Western food as bland.

But I want Western food. For days I've been hankering after a fix of good old plain ordinary normal Western food, to the degree that I've been hallucinating sizzling steaks; glistening, dripping beef sausages; fat, yellow, brown-edged roast spuds and rich, viscous gravy. Physical cravings grip me as well. My stomach churns and gurgles at the mere thought of such fodder.

The humble Thamada Hotel suite I occupy is comfortable, with its 1970s Soviet décor of white walls and teak fittings, but it is after all a hotel suite, and hotel walls tend to close in after a long spell. The worst aspect of the suite is its lack of basic cooking facilities, which means I have to eat out every night, whether I feel like it or not. I can never whip up snacks in the midnight hour. Therefore, I sometimes have to take risks with what I eat and, because of this, my bowels have been bludgeoned. I just wish I had a kitchen to make up a few snacks and meals that are familiar.

During my first weeks in Yangon I became excited by the sheer novelty of snacks available in the supermarkets, and after my first Saturday shopping expedition my small fridge was stocked with one can of Swallow Nest Rock Sugar Snow Fungus drink, two cans of tamarind juice, one can of Rose Bandung soft drink, one can of Pulpy Jelly Lychee drink, one can of Royal Lipo energy drink, one packet of dried sugar plums, one packet of Vinamit Jack Fruit Chips and two tubs of creaming soda ice-cream. But the novelty soon wore off and I started hankering after normal stuff, like good old Smith's Crisps.

That's why I'm here in the House of Joy, hoping to have a good old normal hamburger. But I persevere with what providence has provided, my non-normal, hot-spiced hamburger. I finish it, pay and head out into the night, walking around the corner to the Nay Pyi Daw Cinema which has a late-night coffee shop, Café Aroma, attached, complete with a cappuccino machine and, blessing of blessings, good Lavazza coffee.

When I left Australia I bade farewell to my friends at my local café, the Canteen, and I slowly savoured my coffee, announcing it was probably the last I'd enjoy in many, many months. But after I arrived in Yangon, I was staggered to discover the inner-city area was dotted with modern, hip coffee shops. I was even more staggered to discover that the most sophisticated coffee shop chain was called Café Aroma, the same name as the most sophisticated café chain on my home turf, southern Queensland. There are about half a dozen Café Aromas in Yangon and the most fashionable of these, and the only one open late at night, is next to the downtown Nay Pyi Daw Cinema.

This has also become a favourite haunt of mine, a place where I meet many people, and it was here that I first encountered Lasheeda, a twelve-year-old street girl who prowls the streets surrounding the markets selling her postcards, a string of twenty in transparent cellophane envelopes for a dollar. Her commission on a sale is 30 cents, and she works from dawn until dusk. But I hardly ever see her make a sale. Her 'office headquarters' are the steps leading to Café Aroma.

Lasheeda stands out because she is such a cute, intense and alive little girl, with the most expressive big brown eyes. But she saddens me because most days her mother, a thin, furtive woman always sidling in the background, daubs her with so much lipstick and make-up that at times she resembles a tragic clown. The effect is bizarre and freakish; it often repels tourists, instead of attracting them.

One morning, as I sat in the Aroma drinking a coffee that probably cost more than Lasheeda makes in a week, she tended to her brother in the street. She put aside her little bag and her stack of postcards, produced a roll of blue plastic, and unrolled it on the side of the road. She stripped her little brother naked, stood him on the plastic and poured bottled water over him, washing him. When this ritual was complete she dressed him, rolled up the plastic sheet, gathered her bag and postcards, and resumed business.

I befriended her after a sad incident that resulted from me carelessly being rude, callous and disrespectful toward her. I was in a bad mood one morning, late and in a hurry, and she zeroed in on me, holding her string of twenty cards in front of me, saying, 'Beautiful card. One dollar.' I tried to dodge her but she was insistent, so I mocked her, offering her five cents.

It was an insult really, and that's the way she took it. She did something I rarely saw on the streets of Yangon—she lost her temper. Her cute little face screwed into angry creases, her large eyes filled with tears of frustration, and she started yelling, 'Commishun, commishun, commishun.' She was letting me know she had to make a commission from each sale in order to eat. Her public outburst was drawing unwanted attention so I looked her in the eye and quickly countered, 'Aggreshun, aggreshun, aggreshun,' letting her know that public aggression was no way for a young Yangon lady to act. To mollify her, I handed over the equivalent of a dollar for the postcards and left.

Next morning, while walking to work, I felt a presence by my side. Lasheeda. She caught my eye, softly saying, 'Commishun.' It was her way of making up for yesterday's outburst and I said to her just as softly, 'Aggreshun.' She wobbled her head like a little old wise lady, making a motion with her hands as if saying, 'Forget about yesterday, it was a bad-hair day.'

From that day on we became good friends and she fulfils all sorts of minor functions for me, for which I pay her K200 or twenty cents. She carries my briefcase to the office, she lets the newspaper boys know I am looking for them, she makes herself useful in lots of ways.

Having her accompany me on shopping expeditions is a great delight. She is like a tiny princess who proudly patrols her dominion, turning what many Westerners would regard as a wasteland into her own wonderland. When I see the streets of Yangon through her eyes, it is as if I am wandering through a slightly dotty auntie's version of a magical kingdom.

Lasheeda knows every nook and cranny, and she knows where anything can be found. I show her a particular type of electric plug and she steers me this way and that way, further and further into the maze of downtown Yangon until I am sure she is leading me a merry dance. But then she stops, points, and there on the footpath is a little old lady sitting behind a plastic sheet containing small mounds of electronic esoterica and salvage, including a neat little pile of the exact plugs I've been seeking.

Along the way Lasheeda takes sudden detours and fishes around in a mound of rubbishy souvenirs spread out on the sidewalk; at last she will hold up a gem, or some interesting medals, or a pair of crazy sunglasses. One day she found a home-modified commando version of a Zippo lighter, that included a thin, lethal switch-blade knife attachment. On another day she stood outside a clothes stall and, almost bending over with laughter, pointed out a peculiarly outlandish pair of jeans featuring British punk motifs.

Lasheeda knows that, as a foreigner, I have difficulty negotiating traffic and crossing the street, so she takes my hand and leads me across the road. It took me weeks of being a resident of Yangon before I began to master the art of being a pedestrian and could successfully cross the street. To be a successful pedestrian—that is, a living pedestrian—a certain technique has to be developed, a technique I call 'sparrow hopping'. Watch a sparrow in a busy street and observe how it skillfully but nervously navigates toward a food source. It's much the same as crossing a road in Yangon. There are yellow pedestrian crossings, but they are crossings only in that they are the point where pedestrians are allowed to attempt to cross the road.

Drivers do not have to give way to pedestrians, but they must not knock them down either. Maiming or killing pedestrians results in instant imprisonment and hospital costs; the loss of wages by the injured party must also be negotiated and paid for. Crossing the road is a gamble: you know drivers have no intention of giving way to you, but you know they don't dare hit you.

There is never really a full break in the traffic. What I do is stand on the edge of lane one and, if I spot a brief break, I hop across that lane and stand on the line separating lane one from lane two. There I stand until my instinct tells me the next car is moving a little slowly and I have just enough time to hop to the next line, separating lane two from lane three. Once I spot a break, I must move forward without hesitation because there's no turning back.

The Myanmar are experts at this, but it takes foreigners some time to build up the necessary nerve. Knowing this, Lasheeda takes my hand, laughing as though she is dealing with somebody who is mentally deficient, and says to me, 'Come, come.' If Lasheeda isn't with me, I often walk a few hundred yards along the road to an intersection with traffic lights, and wait patiently there for the green light.

Recently a traffic policeman stationed in a stall by the side of the road summoned me, telling me I was one of the few pedestrians in Yangon to obey the traffic lights and wanting to know why this was so. I told him it was customary in my country: everybody obeyed traffic lights. When he asked how this is enforced, I told him we executed transgressors. He looked at me in astonishment, and I quickly told him that I was only joking and our streets were regulated by the imposition of fines. He nodded thoughtfully.

In this strange new world that I inhabit, the banal banana has become a bonding agent between foreigners thrown together in an alien society. The mere mention of this fruit—or, more precisely, the buying of it—triggers conversations among expatriates about the quirky differences and peculiarities of life in Yangon.

Bananas can't be bought in Yangon individually, or by the twos or threes, although cigarettes can. Instead, a heavy bunch of about twenty or so bananas must be bought and lugged around town, and this triviality of life drives many foreigners nuts. In turn, the street vendors think foreigners are nuts because we are always trying to buy only a few bananas.

It's a lazy Sunday afternoon and I'm holding court with a group of expatriates who regularly gather here, at the Zawgyi coffee house on busy Bogyoke Aung San Road. I let the comforting Western ordinariness of the conversation wash over me as the teeming Eastern exoticness of Yangon street life tumbles past on the footpath outside the café, giving me a strange sense of disassociation, or perhaps dislocation, as though a surreal, never-ending Asian 3D movie is flickering at the edge of my consciousness.

I come back to the conversation when I hear the buzzword, *bananas*. Margaret has been bemoaning the fact that it's impossible to get fried eggs in Yangon that aren't horribly raw on top, and Christine chips in to say, 'And try deviating from a menu. It's a bit like trying to buy a single banana instead of a bunch.'

Rhonette guffaws. She's a welcome new addition to our regular Sunday afternoon coffee clutch, an American NGO employee who used to work in Yangon but relocated to the Mongolian capital of Ulaanbaatar. She's returned for a social visit and confides, 'You know, when I was living in Yangon, I actually knew a woman who pulled that off. I don't know how she did it, but she actually convinced a vendor to sell her two bananas from a bunch.'

'Forget about bananas,' says Carsten, a young German traveller house-sitting a luxurious mansion in the nearby suburb of

Bahan. 'I've got peacock problems. Two peacocks flew into my garden from the monastery behind the house. My gardener ate both of them, and now the monks are after me. They want me to pay US$150 for the peacocks, or they'll have the gardener put in prison.'

The conversation lazily drifts around the table until it is time for Rhonette to leave. As she pays, I watch her grapple with a fistful of grubby low-denomination kyat notes. She has either never mastered, or forgotten, the basic principles of kyat management.

The humble kyat is pronounced *chat* and, because the Myanmar word for love is *chit*, I've coined a joke that *chit chat* is the money men hand over in local brothels. There are no coins in modern Myanmar and the highest denomination note is the 1000 kyat, roughly equivalent to a US dollar. The low-value notes—the 50-, ten-, five- and one-kyat notes—become so grubby and filthy from constant use that they begin to ferment in their own foulness.

The larger notes, the 1000- and 500-kyat notes, are useful for paying taxis or for goods in supermarkets. But smaller notes are virtually compulsory when dealing with street vendors. If you hand over a 1000-kyat note, vendors simply shrug and try to offload more goods or produce.

The trick to kyat management is to have one wad of high-denomination notes in one pocket, and small-denomination notes in another. But a reasonable amount of currency in 1000-kyat notes—for example, 50 dollars' worth—creates an awkwardly bulging wad, so the well-prepared expatriate also carries either US dollars or the fake Myanmar government equivalent, the Foreign Exchange Certificate, which is supposed to be used instead of the dollar. Really well prepared expats usually carry both dollars and FECs, plus high- and low-denomination kyats.

One skill beyond the grasp of all expatriates, even the most seasoned, is the ability to count wads of kyat Myanmar-style. This involves holding the wad in the heel of the left hand and then skilfully riffling through the notes with the right index finger. I have watched checkout girls in the import supermarkets count their kyats with skill and expertise but, no matter how much I practise, I have never been able to master the art, even though a Myanmar friend told me I should use my right index finger as if it were climbing stairs.

The most crucial element of kyat management is kyat conversion, getting the maximum kyat per dollar when dealing with money changers. Officially the kyat is valued at about seven or eight to the dollar, a nonsensical figure existing only to enable the government to cook the books when buying fighter jets or whatever. Armaments costing US$1 million can be entered as officially costing only US$70 000 or US$80 000 when these dodgy cross-currency rates are applied.

The unofficial official kyat rate fluctuates daily, usually somewhere between the 800 to 1000 kyat to the US dollar mark. The accountant at our newspaper office has told me she phones an authority each morning at around 9.30 to establish the daily rate. But I have never been able to figure out precisely how the daily rate is assessed.

For expatriates to change money it usually means dealing with the theoretically illegal money changers hanging around the Bogyoke Market. If the police and soldiers are absent, money changers will beckon and ask, 'Change money, sir?' Exchange rates are then negotiated, but this doesn't depend solely on the day's official unofficial rate—it also depends on what type of US dollar is being changed.

Torn, battered or dirty US dollar notes are rejected outright, and the best rate offered is for the 'big note, sir'— that's the Benjie, as some Americans call it, the Benjamin Franklin $100 note. But old $100 notes, no matter how mint the condition, are worth less than new $100 notes—the difference is that new notes have a much smaller Benjamin Franklin head.

Having established a satisfactory rate of exchange, the money changer walks at high speed through the jostling market alleys to the stall for which he shills. The money changee is supposed to run after the money changer, but I regard this as ridiculous and too obvious. Whenever a foreigner runs through the market behind a Myanmar man, it can be assumed that a theoretically illegal money exchange is in the process of being transacted. In the past I have declined running and opted instead for obstinate sauntering, but this frustrates the money changers, who hop from one leg to another, trying to hurry me in the direction they're heading, like birds trying to lure intruders away from nests.

I have now given up on money changers and deal exclusively with a friendly woman gem seller. I establish the going rate and slip her a $100 note. She retreats to the rear of her stall, checks the note carefully (to ensure it isn't counterfeit), returns to the counter and surreptitiously slips me a pre-counted wad of kyat bound together with a rubber band.

The one-kyat notes—one thousandth of a dollar—are so useless that most people throw them away. It always intrigues me that I can find discarded money in one of the world's poorest countries, and it always amuses my Myanmar companions when I compulsively bend over and pick up one-kyat notes from the footpath.

'Why you do this?' they ask, and I explain how I am slave to an ancient Western superstition which dictates that, if I am too proud to pick up even the smallest of coins or notes, then large amounts of money will pass me by. The Myanmar superstition is the opposite: if they pick up a piffling one-kyat note, they may use up their luck and never find larger amounts of money.

At the Zawgyi Café this afternoon, the conversation swings around to the exchange rate of the day, as it inevitably does.

I ask, 'Does anybody know of anyone who actually exchanged money at the official official rate?'

George replies, 'Surely not even the most stupid tourist would be that stupid. Besides, where would you exchange money at the official official rate?'

'You could do it at a bank,' counters Maurice, 'but you'd probably have to really insist. And, if you really insisted, there's always the chance you'd be arrested on suspicion of being a subversive element.'

The conversation drifts lazily this way and that, like cheroot smoke in a karaoke nightclub, and my mind drifts off again as I watch Myanmar women walk by in their longyis, carrying their shopping on their heads.

One result of Myanmar's half a century of isolation, which ironically could prove fortuitous in coming years, is that it has retained a strong cultural identity and, while there are patches of Western modernity in the better suburbs, most parts of Yangon are reminiscent of the undeveloped and picturesque Asia of the 1960s. I recall one American matron commenting, 'It's like walking through the Williamsburg Museum.'

Foreigners can only ever have an inkling of what is really going on in the streets of Yangon because the truth as such is always obscured by the cultural differences and hidden behind the language barrier. Few expatriates speak fluent Myanmar, because it is such a difficult language to master. It's a tonal language and its words can have opposite meanings according to the inflection. The words for *beautiful lady* and *ugly lady* are the same, for example, and the meanings are imparted though tonal accent. Their sentence structure is very different from ours and as for the written Myanmar language—The Stoned Noodle Writing, as we foreigners like to call it—well, that is almost beyond the mastery of any Westerner.

The Myanmar themselves can never be trusted to provide accurate translations because they know full well that our ignorance gives them power. A local businesswoman surprised me by telling me, 'Ah, Mr Peter, you don't understand. Your efforts to learn our language don't impress us because we don't want you to learn. If you do, you will only try to colonise us once more.'

Most expatriates are contracted to live in Yangon for relatively short periods, and many view learning the language as a waste of time because fluency in Myanmar has virtually no practical value anywhere else in the world, unlike Chinese, which many expatriates living in China master quite quickly.

It is also difficult to work out who is who in Myanmar because there are no family names, and wives do not adopt their husbands' names. Names are chosen by an astrologer but there isn't a great variety, so two, three or four people in the same office can have the same name.

Even the clothing we Westerners wear sets us apart from the Myanmar and, during the British colonial days, whites were called 'the trouser people'. Almost all Myanmar men and women, except the military, wear part-traditional, part-Western clothing. The women wear figure-hugging longyis and daub their faces with *thanakha*, a sort of Myanmar suntan cream of a golden hue, made from wood paste. It's worn as sun protection, skin coolant and cosmetic, and is mostly worn in wedge shapes on the cheeks of women and children. But the designs can be quite creative and include whorls, whirls, wavy lines, dots—whatever. It's a distinctively Myanmar trademark and, whenever I talk to a Myanmar woman whose face is daubed in this manner, I am acutely aware of our differences.

The men here mostly wear Western shirts or T-shirts coupled with the sarong-like longyi, and the fashion amongst the middle class is to set off the longyi with a wallet tucked in the back of the waistband. The upper middle classes tuck a mobile phone into the waistband.

I bought a Shan longyi, which is basically a wrap-around

longyi with trouser legs, but I wasn't comfortable wearing it because of its lack of pockets. I asked my tailor to put pockets in it, but he baulked. I told him I wanted the pockets so I'd have somewhere to put my wallet.

'But why don't you just tuck the wallet into the back of your waistband like we do?' the tailor asked.

'Because at home the wallet would be stolen within five minutes,' I said.

'Ah yes,' sighed the tailor. 'Robbery. We will have to get used to it when we get democracy.'

I'm snapped out of my reveries about how different life in Yangon can be by a change of conversation around the table at the Zawgyi Café. Serious gossip of the day is being raked over: rumours of a possible impending visit to Yangon by Tom Cruise.

Western celebrities occasionally slip into Myanmar, because they can exist anonymously and unobtrusively. There's no paparazzi to dog their heels, no fuss made over their visits. They just quietly enter and exit the country.

'I'm surprised they're allowed in these days,' says Bob, an Australian seafood exporter and long-time Yangon resident. 'Until recently the military was paranoid about high-profile actors and personalities because they might lobby internationally against Myanmar, as Richard Branson found out. When Pepsi got kicked out and Coca-Cola couldn't operate here, Branson figured he could launch Virgin Cola. But the government refused to give him a visa.'

Bob is a friend of US actor Matt Dillon, who visited Yangon a couple of years ago as his guest. After the actor's departure a very curious Military Intelligence asked about his activities during his stay. 'Nothing was said at the time,' Bob recalls, 'but about three months after Matt Dillon left Yangon, I had MI visiting me, asking what he was doing here.'

Living with Military Intelligence is part of expatriate life in Yangon because operatives are everywhere, lingering in streets, cafés and entertainment centres, listening, watching and reporting, and there are always rumours in expatriate circles about who is MI and who isn't.

I actually operate on the theory that every Myanmar could be, until proven otherwise, and even then I only really relax with those few Myanmar who, having got over their suspicions that *I* might in fact be reporting to MI, have told me things that led me to relax.

One friend, Zin, told me that he still feels strange sitting and talking to me in public. Up until relatively recently, about eight years ago, Myanmar were not allowed to talk to or have contact with foreigners, and Zin's neighbour, an elderly woman, still worries about it. Her son migrated to Perth and obtained Australian citizenship. He returned to Yangon seven years ago to visit his mother, but military officials told her that, because her son had officially become a foreigner, she would be sent to prison if he visited her again. 'That is why I cannot invite you to my home,' Zin said. 'If the old lady sees you, she may collapse with fear.'

I suppose it helps that I am accustomed to paranoia. In the mid-1970s I was leader of the Australian Marijuana Party, which advocated the legalisation of pot; my life at that time was bedevilled partly by the intrusions of undercover narcotics officers, and partly by rumours from rival factions that I was an undercover narcotics officer. The late Peter Blazey, the Australian writer and former press secretary to Andrew Peacock, dubbed me the 'modern poet of paranoia' during those amazing years. Of course, it is well known that marijuana induces paranoia, as does living in Yangon.

Some of my foreign colleagues at the *Myanmar Times* obsess about who on our staff might be MI, but in reality the *Times* is virtually a branch office of the elite factions of MI.

The newsroom has two entrances, an official entrance

through the reception desk and an unofficial entrance in the foyer, which Myanmar visitors inevitably use, despite notices saying not to, thus destroying any notion of security in the office. Opinions were recently canvassed among staff about what signage might be effective in stopping strangers from using the unofficial entrance. One suggestion was to scare people away by putting a sign on the door announcing 'MI ONLY'. But Katherine 'Bo' Hill, a former Australian schoolteacher working on the paper, said, 'Bad idea. There'll be so many MI using that entrance, they'll pile up like grasshoppers.'

Urban myths, or apocryphal tales, abound in the paranoid climate in which we find ourselves living. An American intern informed me a German friend had phoned home, only to have his call interrupted by a Myanmar asking if he could speak in English so his conversation could be understood. But this story circulates among expatriates in any country with a dodgy totalitarian government. I found a variant of it in a 1991 book on Baghdad written by Tony Horwitz, who related the story of an Ethiopian UN worker calling a New York colleague; allegedly when he switched, mid-sentence, from English to Amharic, an Iraqi voice 'quickly cut in, instructing him to "please continue in a language we can understand"'.

Another story that has recently swept expatriate circles concerns a German guy who owned a garment factory that went bust due to sanctions. He put the factory up for sale and wanted to return to Germany to await offers. But at the airport Myanmar officials handed him a tax bill that, according to some stories, totalled almost US$2 million, and told him he couldn't leave until the bill was paid. He eventually caught a bus to the Thai border, swam the river, was jailed briefly for illegally entering Thailand, and then flew home to Germany, cutting his losses.

The Birthday Story is one of my favourites. A senior expatriate celebrated a milestone sixtieth birthday and friends threw a big bash; it involved letting off fireworks, for which the party organisers hadn't got permission, knowing it would be denied. What they didn't know was that their party was being held near a secret ordnance repository. When the fireworks started, a panicked militia swung into action and armoured personnel carriers roared through the Yangon night to the house in the exclusive Inya Lake district. But the troops held back because the lane leading to the house was dotted with official Western embassy and diplomatic corps vehicles.

Several Westerners involved took urgent holidays in Bangkok and Singapore, but the American who owned the house stayed put, and when his house was raided the following day, his wife hid herself in a wardrobe. The American was arrested and charged with several offences, which could have resulted in serious prison time, but the expatriate circle swung into action through its connections and the affair was eventually smoothed over.

Dusk is settling in at the Zawgyi Café and I notice that the power is out, yet again. The erratic power supply throughout Yangon is a constant source of frustration for foreigners. The electricity fails regularly, sometimes for days on end. When news came through of the power failure that crippled New York, people in Yangon wondered what the fuss was all about. 'But they were only without power for a day,' was the rejoinder by locals.

A young Myanmar, Maung Zaw, joins our table of limited knowledge as our conversation moves onto the topic of smoking. George has just returned from Australia and reports on the politically correct mania, as he sees it, of the all-encompassing anti-smoking laws introduced across the length and breadth of our homeland. It's a stark contrast to Myanmar, where smokers rule, as evidenced by the comfort on offer at the smokers' lounge at the Yangon airport.

The airport itself is half an acre of inhospitable hard-plastic seating and grimy floors with no airconditioning. But the smokers' lounge is an airconditioned comfort station, decked out in soft royal-blue lounges, with carpet, television and cold water urns. The only drawback is that it's usually crammed full of smokers creating a dense fug of cigarette smoke.

Maung Zaw listens to our conversation intently. He leans forward and says, 'I have heard this, that when we become a democracy we will be told when and where we can smoke?'

'That's the size of it, Maung Zaw.'

He ponders this strange phenomenon for a moment and says, 'From what I understand, you have those who smoke and then those who don't want the others to smoke, because it interferes with their freedom not to be affected by smoke.'

'That's roughly it, Maung Zaw.'

'But how is this decided?' he asks. 'Who determines which group must have their freedom curtailed? Do they vote on the issue?'

'No, Maung Zaw, the government decides it for the good of the people.'

'Ah, yes,' murmurs Maung Zaw, 'I suppose this is something we will have to get used to if we get democracy. We will have lots of little rules that we must obey. I think it will be quite foreign to us.'

I'm standing in the small, cluttered departure lounge of Thandwe airport in the Rakhine State on the west coast, about an hour's flight from Yangon, and the staging airport to

Myanmar's premier beach, Ngapali, where I escaped the pressures of Yangon for a few balmy days. Now I'm waiting for the flight back to the city.

I'm chatting with a glamorous New York woman whom I met at Ngapali, together with her American husband. They live in Bangkok, where he works at the Arthur Andersen auditing company, and they are very much in love. They spent their days on the beach giggling over the book they were reading, Ian McEwan's *Atonement*.

I'm trying to answer her many curious and perceptive questions about Myanmar and its politics, but we're interrupted by a soldier, who takes me to a cubicle behind a black curtain and frisks me. He pats my pocket, finds a cheap plastic cigarette lighter, confiscates it and instructs me to, 'Go! Go!'

When I exit the cubicle, I find the American woman nervously waiting, concern crinkling the corners of her eyes. 'Are you, uh, okay? Is everything, uh, okay?' she asks.

'Yes. All he did was confiscate my cigarette lighter,' I reply, while putting a cigarette in my mouth and absent-mindedly patting my pocket, looking for the lighter that had just been taken. The soldier appears by my side again, graciously lighting my cigarette with the confiscated lighter.

'How odd,' the American woman comments. 'He takes your lighter, and then he comes and lights your cigarette.'

'Welcome to Myanmar,' I say.

The office had shut down for a ten-day Thingyan Water Festival holiday, so four days ago I embarked on my exodus to Ngapali. I wanted to get out of Yangon because pressure had been building a head of steam as mid-summer temperatures soared to searing heights.

Pressure.

Pressure from the fallout of a potentially dangerous banking crisis.

Pressure from the onset of the water festival.

Pressure from concerned Myanmar men deciding I need a wife in my life or, more precisely, a 'practice wife'.

A bank crisis, the so-called 'Kyatastrophe', kicked in about a month ago. If unchecked, it could trigger bloodshed, although the crisis had eased a little before I departed for Ngapali. Basically the banks ran out of money. Only companies could withdraw cash and they were limited to minuscule amounts. Exchange rates became giddy, credit cards ceased to exist. In the streets I saw the signs of impending strife: extra yards of razor wire installed around some buildings, extra guardhouses erected outside embassy compounds, heavily armed soldiers secreted on upper floor balconies of downtown buildings.

A boggle-eyed American tourist showed me a photo he had taken of a strange sight outside a downtown bank, where about a thousand people milled about, waving useless passbooks. Businesses throughout town were cancelling contracts and battening down the hatches. My boss, Ross Dunkley, had a long and complex phone call with Serge Pun, chairman of the Yoma Bank, and after he put the phone down he said, 'It's a fuckin' worry, mate.'

The coming Thingyan Festival worries many expatriates, and they've expressed fears that the event, coming on the heels of the bank crisis, will cause a boil-over.

At first I paid little attention to this festival because there always seems to be a festival underway in Myanmar, but gradually I understood that the Thingyan Water Festival is the mother of all festivals. Expatriates warned me to wear protective long-sleeved clothing because the high-pressure water hoses used to drench people in the street can be painful on bare skin and the toxic water can infect eyes and ears, and scratches or grazes.

Many expatriates have been leaving town but, on the other hand, the Myanmar have been gleeful, telling me they'll throw lots of water over me as will everyone else. Driver U Tun Htun has been adamant I join the water fight in his street.

Another unsettling development has been that several Myanmar men seem intent on ending my single status. To them I am the most pitiful of creatures, a middle-aged man with no family, no children, no wife. My laundry man, U Ye Myint, has been leading the charge to find me a practice wife, and he told me he'd been negotiating with the manageress of a five-star hotel kitchen, who has a niece who is eligible and interested.

'She has seen you,' Ye Myint told me. 'I bring her to your office in the morning. She sit outside and she see you. She like you.'

Ye Myint has suggested he bring the niece and the aunt to my apartment on a Sunday afternoon so we can talk. If the talks are satisfactory, then the aunt and Ye Myint will exit, leaving me alone with the girl. 'You can try her,' suggested Ye Myint.

After the free trial the aunt would return and negotiations would begin about a satisfactory monthly fee. 'Good price,' assured Ye Myint. 'She will be like wife. Make you very happy.'

Ngapali is the summer haunt for Yangon's fashionable set. It's set on a horseshoe bay and at one end is the Bayview Resort, with its typical Mediterranean-type villa architecture, similar to resorts that have invaded the Australian coastline. At the other end of the bay is the funky five-star eco resort, Sandoways, where I holed up for the duration of my stay, loving the cool, calm atmosphere of the luxuriant teak interior of my bungalow, and the lazy walks through the garden-lined paths alive with exotic butterflies and birds.

Sandwiched between these two major resorts is an array of cheaper accommodation houses lining a beach with paradise written all over it: soft sand, sparkling azure water, no hassles, and graciously curved, whispering palm trees.

In the mornings I'd mount the rugged Challenger mountain bike provided by the resort. I'd cycle out of the gateway, stopping to look at the neighbours over the road and the well they operated in their front yard. A pole was attached to a buffalo which walked in circles, drawing water from the well, while cute kids in traditional garb sat on the pole and waved. Although the heat was intense, the bicycle rides were made more enjoyable by hordes of kids rushing out from the dusty sides of the road to throw bowls of warm water over me.

This, of course, is part of the Thingyan celebration, and I gather the festival here is also a courting ritual. Pamphlets have been issued with official instructions:

> The boys can choose the girls they like and chat teasingly but politely. When the boys invite the girls to join them for water festival, they pour water on the girl's backs and ask for more water saying, 'Please give me some more water, sister.' The Thingyan girls have to enjoy the water festival with the boys whether they like it or not.

Sometimes I'd end my bicycle ride at the Bayview and chat with my boss, who was stationed there, as were several staff members from the Australian embassy.

Most afternoons eased by as I lay on the beach watching French women parade in brief bikinis, or watching the bullock carts creak through the shallows. One afternoon I walked to nearby Linthar village—to Kipling's Bay where, over a century ago, Rudyard Kipling hunkered down in an old bungalow and wrote the first draft of *The Jungle Book*. On such balmy Burmese beach evenings, he brought to life the boy named Mowgli, Kaa the giant python and Shere Khan the tiger.

I'd chat with the old salts, to check if there had been any sighting of the rare whale sharks, or *wai la gna*, which sometimes cruise into these waters. I was told they may come and they may not; as it turned out, they didn't come while I was there. Nature can be a bitch like that.

Late afternoons were spent either waiting for the sunset at a little bar on a small island within wading distance from shore, or wandering down the beach to the thatched-hut fishing village, watching the boats come in. The fishermen would chant, while the swivel-hipped women sorted the catch, putting it in baskets they carried on their heads to the village to sell. Fish, crabs and lobsters for the restaurants.

Evenings were sometimes spent at the Sandoways bar, dodging the Yangon intellectual Dr Min Soe, who lurked in the dim recesses waiting to pounce on hapless Westerners and engage them in detailed discussions about the various forms and guises in which democracy appeared in different parts of the world.

I'd dine at my favourite roadside eatery, the Welcome Restaurant, where I would sit under a moonlit flowering frangipani tree, eating my five-dollar lobster meal with a spicy local sauce and a cucumber and tomato salad, while the proprietor's pet, a baby hissing owl, sat on a branch hissing at me.

I met an English woman, a marketing executive based in mystic Bagan near Mandalay, and we lay next to each other on the soft, sensuous sand one midnight, drinking champagne and watching the big orange moon suspended over the Bay of Bengal. We commented on the various animal and bird shapes the soft fluffy clouds made as they flitted across the face of the full moon. I told her how much Ngapali reminded me of my Australian home town, Noosa, in its layout and overall natural beauty.

I stopped talking when I realised she'd begun a cute snuffling.

'Oh, I'm sorry,' she said in between snuffles.

She explained that she was still getting over breaking up with her boyfriend, who came from Brisbane. He had taken her for a holiday to Australia but their relationship ended when they visited—of all places—my home town, Noosa.

Her snuffles soon subsided and we lay there, side by side, in silence. Then we softly chatted about love lost, love gained, love yearned for, until the night sky turned grey with dawn. We left the beach, walked towards our five-star bungalows and, at the point where our paths parted, we said goodbye and followed our separate destinies.

On my last night I was invited to a banquet organised by the contingent of French expatriates who had been staying at the resort. I enjoy the French. I like their bonhomie and their style. They relax me and I don't have a problem with what is perceived as their arrogance. It's just attitude, and I delight in the cut and thrust of it. I also sympathise with them over their annoyance that English-speaking people always expect them to speak English in their company.

Their exasperation with this arose early during the banquet after it was established that I was not fluent in French. Jean-Luc suddenly turned to me and said, 'But why should we struggle like children to speak your language when you don't make any effort to speak our language? Can you speak any French at all?'

'No.'

They chatted amongst themselves in French and I happily sat back and let the warm Frenchness of it all wash over me. The writer Sarah Turnbull nailed it in her book, *Almost French*, when she described how, during her early days in France, she learnt to become a chair at dinner parties.

After I had been a chair for a while, the sexy woman sitting next to me began to acknowledge me. Jacqueline, with her elegant shawl, her majestic breasts, her cute way of warmly waggling her finger at naughtiness, said to me, in between sipping soup, 'So Pee-tairrr, surely you must know something in French? Do you?'

'Yes.'

'Yes? So what do you know?'

'I know *bouge ton cul*.'

Jacqueline emphatically stopped mid-sip; the soup spoon

she was lifting to her moist, full lips quivered in mid-air. For a moment she almost gagged, then burst out in laughter.

'So. That is very naughty. That is something only a French person would say. Where did you learn it?' she asked, looking at me with bemusement.

'I learnt it from a French woman.'

The women exchanged glances and shrugged in their enigmatic French way.

The banquet segued into a pleasant boozy affair and some Myanmar joined us, including the good Dr Min Soe. 'It is indeed a jolly evening,' he said. 'And what a magnificent resort! Do you know that many senior Military Intelligence officers and their families are also guests here?'

Dr Min Soe had newly shaven hair and he informed us he'd spent the past few days meditating in a monastery. We tried to steer his conversation around to matters Buddhist, rather than the discourse on democracy he was intent on pursuing.

A new bottle of wine arrived on the table and I examined the label: Bulgarian wine. Bulgaria seemed to regularly crop up in Myanmar and I'd discovered that one of the waitresses at the Bayview Resort was a young Bulgarian woman who worked in Myanmar during the tourist season.

Jean-Luc poured the wine, commenting, 'There is a lot of this Bulgarian wine to be found in Myanmar. Some of it is quite good.'

Dr Min Soe picked up the bottle, examined the label and commented, 'Ah yes. Bulgaria. Not only do they produce a range of wines, but they have also produced their own form of democracy and, because they have only relatively recently emerged from the shadows of the Soviet form of imperialism . . .'

Busy chitchat about anything but democracy exploded around the table. Jean-Luc smoothly leant over to the good doctor, relieved him of the Bulgarian wine bottle and poured him a glass of a rich red, seductively twinkling in the candlelight, saying, 'Doc-tairrrrr, try this classic French wine. You will find it much, much better.'

The little commuter plane drones to a landing at Thandwe. I board and drone back to Yangon, where I catch a taxi and look out its window in amazement.

It's as though the entire city has turned into one big street party. Pick-ups full of excited adolescents squirting water pistols whoosh past, an elephant plods wearily by the side of the highway and, every time we stop at traffic lights, water is thrown over the car. Obviously Thingyan has set in.

I decide here and now that I will hole up in my apartment, watch movies, read books and limit my socialising to expatriate circles. Under no circumstances will I allow the driver U Tun Htun to lure me out into these weird streets.

I literally blow the young Myanmar warrior off the back of his truck. Luckily my aim is accurate and I hit him mid-chest. His cool mirrored shades spin off into the distance and he flies backwards. His colleagues, realising they are outgunned, madly bash the top of their truck's cabin, screaming, 'Go! Go! Go!' in Myanmar. Off they speed, defeated and done for, down narrow Daw Thein Tin Road.

This is Kandawlay in Mingalar Taung Nyunt township, a few kilometres from the downtown centre of Yangon, where the fighting has been going on for most of the week.

The guy I blew away caught me by surprise when he popped up from the right-hand side of his driver's cabin, firing his fancy fluorescent *Star Wars*-style water machine-gun at me as I slugged it out at U Tun Htun's pandal (a bamboo and wood street platform) outside his house.

It's Day Four of the seemingly never-ending Thingyan celebration—the world's wildest, weirdest and wettest water festival—and here am I, out on the edge of the god-zone, helping to man the inner-suburban barricades of steamy, teeming mid-summer Yangon during the height of battle. As a Westerner, I am a rarity and as such, I have strategic use as a surprise weapon of mass saturation: warriors from opposing forces are so taken aback to see me they hesitate momentarily, thus losing the momentum of their attack.

No wonder U Tun Htun, my allegedly faithful driver, has been pestering me for weeks to do battle at his pandal. No wonder he engineered a cunning ruse to shanghai me into becoming part of his pandal crew, after I'd vowed to have nothing to do with Thingyan.

Early in the afternoon on the day I returned from Ngapali, he phoned with some confused prattle about taking me to a barbecue that had supposedly been arranged at the Australian embassy by my friends the Gileses, formerly of Western Australia. I wondered at the time why U Tun Htun was phoning me about the arrangements and not Paul Giles or his wife. And when I hopped in his car, I gave up trying to decipher his confusing explanation about why we were heading in the opposite direction to the Australian embassy.

So that's how I ended up here, at the pandal outside Tun Htun's house, joining his mighty fighting force, which comprises his many and varied direct family members, indirect family members, friends, neighbours, acquaintances and colleagues. Indeed, anybody with a passion for water fighting, foul fish-paste-flavoured noodles, fermented coconut beer, and a tolerance for the gut-thumping thud-thud-thud, doof-doof-doof of high-volume modern Western techno music. This insistent beat competes with the whining, grinding, ear-splitting revving of two large, reeking petrol-driven generators, which pump water out of the mains with sufficient force to feed two three-inch water cannons fashioned from old fire-fighting hoses, and about a dozen lighter calibre weapons in the form of plastic garden hoses.

Having helped stave off yet another attack from the opposing forces, I hand the water cannon to a young man who has eagerly and politely been awaiting his turn. Manning the water cannon is hard work. It's heavy and hard to control because it squirms around like an angry Burmese python, and after an hour my shoulders have become knotted and my back is aching.

It worries me that, as a supposedly intelligent middle-aged man, I seem to have regressed. I have spent two days at Tun Htun's pandal, firing a variety of water weapons, thoroughly drenching anyone and everyone who has come near me and in turn been drenched by anyone and everyone who has come near me. Except for the young bloke on the back of the truck, whom I hit full force with the water cannon.

It worries me that I love this mad water fight so much. But then there are times in our lives—and the Thingyan Festival is one of them—when we just have to let go and regress. In doing so, I am simply doing what everyone else in this mad town is doing. Going crazy and regressing, letting off all the tension that has accumulated in everyone's psyche during the long, hot, eventful summer days leading up to the water festival.

Thingyan is four days of collective celebration, building up to one of the most auspicious days in the Myanmar calendar, the Lunar New Year, and we are ushering in the year 1365. The Thingyan concept is quite simple—just spend four days drinking, being happy and being continually soaked with water while soaking everyone else. It's a sensible concept because the Thingyan Festival occurs in the middle of the Myanmar summer, when temperatures in Yangon, often South-East Asia's hottest capital city, hover relentlessly in the high thirties to low forties, making it physically almost unbearable.

The Thingyan Festival is similar to the Songkran Festival in neighbouring Thailand, but the Thai version is tame by comparison. In Thailand there's lots of gentle splashing and throwing of powder, but in Yangon it's an all-out assault by water. As the *New Light of Myanmar* has observed:

> The Thingyan mood is such that even mere strangers treat each others as long-lost brothers, and pranks and light banter abound. The usual thing is to be doused by the bowlful of water, the bucketful, or a squirtful. But with the sophistication that has entered the scene, it has become the usual trend in Yangon, Mandalay and Mawlamyaing, the major cities, to bring out the high-power nozzle jets and let those who want a rough encounter have it.

U Tun Htun's pandal is typical of the dozens that spring up across the city during Thingyan. The yellow padauk flower is the symbol of the festival, and the wooden and bamboo pandals are festooned with its blooms. The pandals are also decorated with advertising pennants from sponsors who have contributed cash to help defray costs. In the centre of the city there is a parade of floats, and talent quests are conducted. The Yangon mayor hosts a showcase pandal, and large companies—such as France's Total oil, and foreign cigarette and brewing companies—sponsor large pandals blaring Western rap music.

But observers have noted that one pandal conspicuously absent in 2003 (or 1365) is the 'Army Brats' pandal, belonging to the family of the recently deceased dictator, Ne Win. Some of the brats, who allegedly operated as nightclub gangsters, cannot be present because they are in prison, under sentence of death.

The action at a typical pandal is frenetic. Men and boys take control of the water hoses and cannons; a constant stream of vehicles—trucks, cars and taxis—scream down the narrow roads, and then stop at the pandals, where the battles rage. The men on the backs of the trucks have their own water hoses and large tanks of water and they try to swamp the crews manning the pandals before the pandal crews can swamp them. Thrill-seeking passengers also come along for the ride, sitting in the backs of trucks or in cars or taxis with the windows wound down. They cringe and turn their backs when pummelled by the sheer force of the water; they scream, wriggle, shake and shriek as the hoses rip into them. Girls are targeted; streams of water peel their clothes back while they desperately attempt to retain the modesty that is all-important in Myanmar.

Modesty during Thingyan has been a political issue in Yangon during the build-up to this year's festival. The dreaded Yodoya (the derogatory and often-used Myanmar term for the Thai people) have allowed girls to become sleazy by wearing Western-style skimpy tank tops that are revealing when wet. This issue, which raged in the Bangkok papers for over a week, spread to Yangon, and many men have expressed concerns that this year 'our' girls might lower their standards and become like their Thai counterparts, or even—horror of horrors!—become as brazen as Western girls who, in their very essence, are considered endemically sleazy.

The Myanmar girls have been good again this year, and they sit in the trucks adequately covered with T-shirts and parkas. But boys will be boys, and they use the cannons and hoses to attempt to disturb as much of the girls' clothing as they can. Even so, customary values reign supreme and, when a girl is so overcome by water pressure that she is in evident danger of losing her top, at the very last second the hoses are switched to the next victim.

And so on it rages in the Yangon heat. Noise, noise and

more noise. The roar of the chugging generators, the shriek of stereo music, shouting, yelling, throbbing and laughing. On it goes incessantly from ten in the morning to six in the evening when, by consensus of the people and by decree of the military, the hoses and music are turned off, and the throngs drift home, ready to re-emerge next morning to do it all again.

In the centre of the city the action is more organised. The pandals are large, commercial affairs. The streets are closed off and hundreds of thousands of people cram the downtown district. Live bands belt out their music from pandals, and council water trucks push through the teeming hordes, dousing everyone with jets of water. People fall off trucks, injure themselves and drown, but mostly the normally sedate and contained Myanmar let their collective hair down and simply go crazy without ever losing it totally. The violence marring many Western New Year's gatherings simply doesn't happen here.

The Thingyan Festival is Myanmar's biggest holiday period and, as the *New Light of Myanmar* explains ever so lyrically:

> The Water Festival starts with youngsters or even grownups throwing water on each other and damsels fair, attired in matching clothes get into an encircling dance around cars as a prelude to the dousing they are asking for.

The build-up to the Thingyan Festival is long and drawn out and intensifies as the starting date approaches. The seasonal blooming of the yellow padauk flower signals time to begin preparations, but for me their appearance triggered an onset of homesickness.

I've now been living in Yangon for two months and one morning I was sitting on a bench in the plaza outside my office, watching the early-morning hustle and bustle of Yangon unfold in all its colourful and bizarre madness.

There is always something different to be spotted. One morning a man came along with two large eagles for sale. Another morning an almost naked man, wearing what looked like a soiled nappy and sporting clay-daubed dreadlocks, wandered past; I noticed he had his mouth pierced and sealed by a small pronged trident he'd pushed through his cheeks on either side of his lips.

But on this particular morning I spotted a woman wearing what appeared to be a sprig of wattle in her hair. Then I saw another woman with wattle. And another. A woman with a bunch of the wattle-like flowers hurried past and arranged the blooms in a little nat shrine hanging from the trunk of the banyan tree that dominated the plaza but I was not sure which nat or spirit was being honoured.

There is a bewildering array of nats in Myanmar—one for every occasion—and my favourite is the *leip-bya*. This is a small spirit with wings like a moth, which leaves the mouth of a sleeping person and flies around. Its experiences are the basis of dreams, but it can only go to places the person it lives in has been to, and it must always return to the person by morning. Hence it is considered unwise to wake a sleeping person prematurely, in case the *leip-bya* spirit has not yet returned home.

The Padaung people, who are also known as the Giraffe Neck people because the women wear brass rings around their neck, believe in a supernatural being known as Big Ball, so called because he has one large testicle. This creature used to destroy trees, but he desisted after a farmer caught him by grabbing his testicle with bamboo tongs; the farmer released Big Ball only after he promised to leave the trees alone.

As I sat in the plaza, I recalled some words from a book about Burma I had just finished reading. It was written by Maurice Collis, an English civil servant turned magistrate, and at the end of his book, when he decided to return home, he observed: 'At times the exoticness of Asia becomes too much and one hankers for the daisies and hedges of a cool, crisp English morning.'

These words summed up my sentiments that morning. Homesickness enveloped me because the yellow padauk blooms reminded me of the wattle, with its attendant jonquils and daffodils, that erupted at the beginning of spring in the usually drab bush surrounding my boyhood home in the central Victorian goldfields of rural Australia.

A chant of *hoya, hoya, hoya* reverberated around the plaza, the sound of a hawker selling his wares—garish pink-and-purple plastic blow-up animals—suspended from a pole stretched across his shoulders.

I was jolted out of my boyhood reveries, back to the reality of bustling Yangon.

Just as the wattle is significant in Australia as a harbinger of spring, the appearance of padauk flowers in Yangon is significant as the harbinger of Thingyan. When the padauk is in bloom, Thingyan is in the air.

The festival, based on ancient beliefs, now has a modicum of western-style commercialisation. Resorts advertise get-away-from-it-all Thingyan retreats, and magazines promote Thingyan fashion spreads ('Myitzu wears 100% cotton F! Series Tank, denim pants with trim and Nina sandals; Sonny wears 100% cotton floral print Tank and distressed jeans'). Music stores release details of the Top 5 must-have Thingyan DVDs, such as *Yae Sa Yar Kaung Lote Laung Par Tai* (We Throw Water Because It's Fun!).

The government issues water conservation decrees, or 'guidance and instruction' about water supplies, because in past years some towns depleted their water stocks during Thingyan.

Garlands of plastic padauk flowers and colourful banners and streamers festoon shops and arcades, and supermarkets feature octagonal cardboard dump-bins brimming with water pistols, although the term *pistols* doesn't really adequately describe super water-guns that look like Darth Vader inter-galactic ray weapons.

While shopping in the trendy Aung San branch of the Citymart supermarket, I mingle with the wives of the high-ranking officials: middle-aged, broad-beamed matrons arriving in their chauffeur-driven olive-green Lexuses, or top-of-the-range Japanese four-wheel-drive vehicles. They have in tow their rich fat spoilt brats, dressed in several hundred dollars' worth of trendy street-label gear such as Mossimo, Ecko and Nike. The brats sport identical crew cuts and some carry mobile phones, for which their parents must pay thousands of dollars in licence fees (which vary from month to month, but are always astronomical by Western standards).

These kids are able to buy the biggest and most complex water guns. While they are examining these weapons in the supermarket, their mothers swan around the aisles, chatting and gossiping. Two young guys man the CD stall at the rear of the supermarket and select the music that's pumped at high volume through shrieking speakers, spewing obscene epithets from Eminem and US hip-hop artists. The elite mothers socialising in the aisles seem oblivious to lyrics such as, 'I'm gonna kill you, you motherfuckin nigger bitch, and then I'm gonna fuck your motherfuckin mother, yo motherfuck ho.'

But Thingyan is not just about water fights, shopping and partying; it's also the holiest period in the Myanmar calendar. There are two versions of the origins of the festival, described by scholars as the mundane and the mythical. The mundane is that royal families celebrated their annual hair-shampoo-ing festivities in the Irrawaddy River on New Year's Eve and participants splashed each other. The festivities eventually shifted into courtyards and the kings allowed commoners to take part.

The mythical legend is that Thingyan is a transition time, when the deity Thagyamin makes his annual descent to earth.

He brings a golden book to record the names of the good, and a dog-skin book to record the names of the bad.

This myth is further complicated by the belief that long ago there was a dispute among the celestial beings over some mathematical calculations. Heads were wagered, literally. The victor, Thagyamin, cut off the head of the loser, Brahma, but was unsure of how to dispose of this grisly trophy. To have thrown it to earth would have caused conflagration, to have cast it into the sea would have made the water boil and to have thrown it into the sky would have burnt the firmament. Thagyamin solved this problem by handing the head to a nat maiden for safekeeping, on the proviso that she pass the head to a new nat woman every year, at the time when Thagyamin visits the earth.

Astrologers calculate the precise hour, minute and second of Thagyamin's arrival on earth and his departure. They also predict whether the deity will be riding a bull or a serpent and whether he will carry a water pot, spear, staff or torch. Predictions as to good or bad harvests, peace and war, etc, are divined from this information and printed in astrological forecasts called Thingyansar.

Like our Christmas, Thingyan is both a religious and hedonistic period. Just as Western children are taught to be good so they'll be rewarded with gifts at Christmas, Myanmar children know they must notch up meritorious deeds during the year or catch up by doing extra deeds during Thingyan. This gives them a better chance to be inscribed in the golden book, as opposed to the dog-skin book. Those displaying anger during Thingyan, and particularly anger at being doused with water, will find themselves instantly entered into the mythical dog-skin book.

Older Myanmar men leave the water-throwing madness to youth and enter monasteries at this time in preparation for the afterlife, because Thingyan literally means transit, the transit of the sun from Aries to Pisces. In the days before the festival started, many of the men at the *Myanmar Times* office arrived at work with their heads shaven, signifying their intention to spend the holiday meditating in monasteries as monks.

Boys about to pass into manhood enter monasteries as novitiate monks during Thingyan. The venerable Yangon monk Thaw Bi Ta claims, 'The best time for ordination, or *shinbyu*, is in the teenage years, when the one to be novitiated, the *shin-laung*, is old enough to scare a crow. This means he is able to carry out the tenfold precepts as is the duty of Buddha's son.'

In the days building up to Thingyan, I looked out of my office window at the processions of colourfully garlanded pick-ups and cars ferrying the teenagers to the monasteries for their novitiation ceremonies.

Back at the pandal, U Tun Htun's cute, boppy, 25-year-old, university-student daughter—a thoroughly modern Yangon Miss Millie, with her funky granny-style shades perched on the end of her nose—cruises over with yet another batch of giggling friends who have come to inspect U Tun Htun's Western foreigner friend and ask chatty questions such as, 'Do you really think our nation is suited to a democracy such as yours and if so do you think we are ready for it yet, at this stage of our development as a modern nation?'

The girls select the music that's mashed through the squeaky speakers placed beside the pandal, and they dance while their mothers tend large pots of noodles heated by charcoal braziers.

Young men taking a break from the water fights dance with the girls and, when I take my break, the girls insist I dance. But when I try to do the Myanmar shimmy to the tune of Queen's 'Bohemian Rhapsody', they shake their heads and laugh. 'No, no,' says one cute woman. 'Your dancing is too aggressive, too Western.' She mimics my stiff-arm jolting style of dancing. 'Do it softly, gently. Do it like a Myanmar,' she says, holding up an arm and beginning a sensuous shimmying that travels from her fingertips, through her arm, and through her body.

I try once again to prove that white men can dance, or at least they can dance Myanmar style. But I can't quite grasp the shimmying, seamless sensuality and, the more I try, the more people crowd around to watch and laugh.

Residing in Yangon as a Western foreigner is like living in the Land of a Thousand Eyes. I feel that I'm constantly under curious scrutiny, that my every move is observed, watched, analysed, dissected, bisected and trisected. I'm sized up, assessed, gauged, discussed, mentally poked and prodded, mostly because there aren't that many Western foreigners in Yangon. My arms are often the centre of attention because they are covered with soft but profuse fair hair, which locals examine closely and sometimes stroke.

There are only about 400 Westerners residing in this city and they mostly mix in their own circles, with some embassy staff advised not to stray too far from their residential compounds. Tourist numbers are small and those who stay in Yangon do so for only about four or five days at most, sticking to a predictable beat.

So a Western foreigner who resides in this city of approximately 5.5 million people and roams the streets at random is a rarity. Especially one who is a journalist, because Western journalists are seldom allowed entry into Myanmar, and allegedly they are officially never allowed to reside here.

But here I am, together with my foreigner colleagues at the *Myanmar Times* newspaper, armed with our precious FRCs (Foreign Resident Certificates), complete with our copy of The Registration of Foreigners Rules Form A (Rules 2, 5, 6, 7, 9, 12, 13, 15, 16 and 17), which doesn't actually reveal what the rules are, but at least we know the numbers of some of the rules.

As for the rule numbers that aren't listed—Rules 1, 3, 4, 8, 10, 11 and 14—no information about them is available, nor is any information available as to why they're not actually listed.

Being a Western foreigner means instant propulsion into a world of high profile, and high profile is not the way I planned to live life in Yangon. My planned strategy of discretion and anonymity failed miserably. I attended opening nights of traditional Myanmar cultural events, usually the only foreigner present and therefore usually ending up with my face broadcast in televised news stories. After one function, the *New Light of Myanmar* published a long list of officials and dignitaries in attendance, and at the end of the list they reported, 'Also present, the foreigner'.

Added to this is the novelty value of my history as an editor of Australian *Playboy* magazine, a fact featured in my lengthy CV which, I discovered, was a document widely distributed through the office and read with curiosity and incredulity. One evening at the Mr Guitar nightclub in Dhama Zedi Road, I was taken to a table and introduced to an urbane and avuncular gentleman, my Yangon 'guarantor', Brigadier General Thein Swe of Military Intelligence, who was there celebrating his daughter-in-law's birthday. He was interested in my *Playboy* past and whether I had met Hugh Hefner. I told him I hadn't, but I had worked with his daughter Christie, who, during my employment, was the power at Playboy's Chicago headquarters.

The Brigadier nodded thoughtfully when I said she was a beautiful, highly intelligent, will-of-iron woman. As he nodded, he assessed me and I realised that behind his kindly features lurked a grim set to his jaw, signalling that here was a man who was never to be underestimated, never to be crossed under any circumstances.

Being a Western foreigner resident of any description creates a wealth of humorous and sometimes intrusive situations.

One Sunday I indulged in a pleasant and typically middle-class Yangon pursuit—an evening walk along the soothing shores of suburban Lake Inya. Hundreds of locals promenade around the lake, enjoying the cool breezes and vivid scenery. Old men sit beside the water smoking large cheroots, kids fly square-shaped kites, and families stop for snacks of the local delicacy, boiled pigs' intestines.

I was introduced to Lake Inya by my trainee Eindra Pwint, who took me there herself. As is often the case with many well-brought-up traditional Myanmar women who share the company of men, a family member, Uncle Dennis, was discreetly trailing behind us, acting as Official Chaperone. I asked Dennis how he came by his very English name and he told me it's a nickname bestowed upon him because he resembles the Dennis the Menace movie character, and the movie was, strangely enough, popular in Yangon.

While I chuckled over this, Eindra put her hand to her mouth in mock horror and said, 'I'm so embarrassed for you. Everybody is just standing and staring at you.' But I explained that this isn't offensive to me. I'm used to it because it happens so often.

While I explained this, a young boy flying a kite in the distance pointed at me and yelled out in Myanmar. Again Eindra put her hand to her mouth in embarrassment, but I said, 'I know what he yelled out. He called me "white monkey".'

Eindra laughed and then, in her typically earnest manner, informed me, 'When the British invaded our country, the only foreigners our people had ever seen were from neighbouring India. So we called the British "white Indians".'

A visit to the quirky Yangon zoo results in my becoming an exhibit. After surveying a series of creatures in enclosures, I sit on a bench in the gardens near the entrance, reading a magazine. Suddenly a couple of hundred screaming, hyperactive school children, dressed in neat uniforms, pour through the entrance; instead of running off to see the tiger, the lion or the hippopotamus, they run and stand in a noisy group observing me, the Western foreigner.

I keep reading and ignoring them until a cheeky boy throws a banana, hitting me on the head. I go ape, jumping up and down, feigning rage. More people are attracted by the commotion, and uniformed zoo guards also gather. The children squeal in delight and rush away in mock panic.

I resume my seat on the bench, trying to read my magazine. The children quickly lose interest and drift off, but several adults come over to shake my hand.

I wander off and stop at a large enclosure containing an odd-looking species of deer, which I suspect are Myanmar deer. A Myanmar dad with his beautiful chubby daughter stands next to me and engages me in conversation. 'Good morning, sir. Are you enjoying our Eld's Deer? Where are you from?'

'Good morning, sir. I am from Australia.'

'Ah, yes, a beautiful country. And, of course, a democracy. Tell me, what do you know of Bulgaria?'

'Well, I know roughly where it is.'

'Very good, sir. I believe Bulgaria, which was a communist country, has now embraced one of the many forms and guises of democracy currently sweeping the world, and I would kindly like to discuss with you, sir, what is your opinion of . . .'

A male deer has created a handy diversion by beginning to shag. So I ask, 'What is that animal doing?'

The Myanmar gent chuckles at my ignorance and says, 'Well sir, it is obviously preparing to begin its family, heh heh.'

His little daughter is transfixed. She is staring at the deer, which is now on its hind legs, stamping its rear hooves and raising small clouds of dust while trying to attain leverage. The Myanmar gent says, 'Sir, I think I will now introduce my daughter to the African lion. I am trying to educate her about the animal kingdom and to let her experience the many forms and guises in which animals inhabit this earth. Not unlike your democracy, eh? Heh heh.'

One evening shortly after Thingyan I dine at one of my favourite restaurants, Singapore's Kitchen, owned by the ebullient Jackson Jang, on the edge of Yangon's Chinatown. I opt for a footpath table, even though half the footpath has been turned into rubble by workmen and an open drain emits sickly sweet odours when the wind blows in my direction.

Because Yangon is still in the grip of a festive mood, there are many people on the street. About a dozen curious onlookers gather on the footpath a few yards away from me, observing the spectacle of a Western foreigner dining.

Four waiters also stand in a semicircle behind me. One looks after my Chinese tea—as soon as I take a sip and put my cup down, he instantly tops it up. Another seems to be in charge of my smattering of little side dishes. He studies their setting and from time to time steps forward and carefully moves one of my side dishes either two centimetres to the left of where it has previously been stationed, or two centimetres to the right.

Another waiter watches my ashtray like a hawk and, as soon as I deposit even a hint of ash, he whisks it away and replaces it with a fresh ashtray. The fourth waiter, the head waiter, is in charge of the overall operation and takes my customary order for the big prawn barbecued with spicy sauce, and steamed Mandalay vegetables.

On my way to the restaurant I'd bought a CD of popular Myanmar tunes and a garland of aromatic jasmine flowers woven onto string. I plop these purchases on the table and my group of onlookers crane their necks to see what the Western foreigner has purchased.

The head waiter says, 'Sir, this gentleman wishes to know if you can speak Myanmar?'

'No, I can't.'

This is relayed to the onlooker.

'Well then, sir, he wishes to know why you have bought a collection of Myanmar songs if you cannot understand the words?'

'Do you listen to Western songs?'

'Of course, sir. Currently I am listening to the Eagles.'

'Can you understand the words of the Eagles' songs?'

'Sir, I am sorry but my English is limited, and it is almost impossible to understand the words on the Western songs. What my friends and I do, sir, is, after assessing the emotion of the song, we then make up our own Myanmar words so that we can sing along.'

'Okay. Well, it is the same for me. I cannot understand the words of Myanmar songs, but it doesn't lessen my appreciation of the beauty or the mood of the songs, and that is why I've bought a Myanmar CD.'

'Yes, sir. A very good answer, sir.'

'Thank you.'

Another bystander catches the eye of the headwaiter. 'Sir, this man wishes to know why you have purchased the flowers?'

'Because I like them. They are very pretty and I love the smell. I take them home to brighten up my apartment, where I have a shrine to Buddha, and I put them on the shrine.'

'But, sir, are not all Westerners Christians?'

'Many are, and I was born a Christian.'

'Then why do you have a shrine to Buddha in your apartment?'

'Because I like many of the teachings of Buddha and, because I am living in Yangon, I think it will help me to have a shrine to Buddha. Perhaps it will bring me good karma.'

'Yes, sir. Another good answer.'

'Thank you.'

'The man would also like to know how much you paid for the flowers.'

'300 kyat' (about 45 cents).

'Sir, the man says that is a good price for a foreigner. But, sir, when a seller walks by, we could buy the same flowers for you for only 200 kyat. And, if you went to the flower-selling area, you could buy the flowers for 50 kyat.'

'Yes. Thank you.'

My big prawn has arrived and the head waiter carefully places it in front of me, steps back to assess his placing and then steps forward and moves the dish about two centimetres to the left of where it was placed. But, just as I start eating, he says, 'Sir, this man would like to be discussing the democracy . . .'

I'm immediately uncomfortable because I know high-ranking military officials in their after-work plain clothes often sit inside the restaurant drinking beer, observing and listening.

The waiter is perceptive. He says, 'But, sir, perhaps instead of discussing the democracy, you would prefer to be doing the eating of the big prawn?'

'Yes, thank you.'

I'm politely left alone to enjoy my dinner. I try to pick up a bean with my chopsticks and the bean scuds away, skittering onto the table next to me. The diners courteously nod toward me, and there's a titter from the gallery.

When I finish my meal, I push my plate aside and immediately there's a commotion from the man who wanted to speak about democracy. He seems agitated. The head waiter intervenes. 'The man is unhappy, sir, because you are not eating the best part of the big prawn. You are not eating the brain. Why do you not eat the brain?'

I've been through this routine in Asia before. In Thailand

one evening I had a happy arrangement with the Thai couple dining at the table next to me—I swapped my prawn heads for their prawn tails. Simple.

But tonight I follow the path of least resistance. I simply pull back my plate and scoop out the prawn head's mushy mustard-and-grey gunk, quickly scoffing it. Then I act out a display of pleasant appreciation for the gallery and everyone is happy. I'm happy, the head waiter is happy and, most importantly, Democracy Man is happy.

It's early Saturday afternoon in the picturesque, lush-green, rustic rice delta country, the food bowl of southern Myanmar, once one of the world's most productive rice-growing regions. The temperature is an enervating 40 degrees plus, and U Tun Htun and I face a two-hour bone-jarring drive back to Yangon. U Tun Htun sighs and, reverting to my Myanmar name, says, 'Ko Chit (Brother Love), I need the sleeping.'

So do I. But I'd like to push on home, to my air-conditioned haven. I worry that U Tun Htun may want us to sleep on straw mats under a tree, sweating and being bitten by insects or nudged by fat muddy pigs. But he has another idea. He leaves the main road, and the car bumps down a dusty lane past thatched huts perched beside canals, where women are modestly bathing. He stops at a village marketplace, disappears into the maze of stalls and returns with a handful of betel nut quids, small parcels about 2 centimetres square, wrapped in green leaves, then wrapped in cellophane. He unwraps the cellophane and stuffs one in his mouth.

He hands me a quid and says, 'Try, Ko Chit. You will not need the sleeping.'

I put the quid into my mouth, suck, enjoy the sensation and suddenly realise that, whereas a few minutes ago I was half-asleep, I'm now wide awake, as is U Tun Htun. Indeed, he has become very chatty. Both of us are chatty in a brotherly, companionable manner. Chat, chat, chat. We chew the betel and shoot the breeze.

Betel nut is ubiquitous in Myanmar. Many people chew betel incessantly, despite half-hearted government attempts to curb the practice, or at least to stop the spitting associated with chewing. The streets are covered with big red blotches because, when locals finish chewing their quids, they hawk red gobs and streams of juice onto the roads and walkways, permanently staining the concrete.

The legendary British colonial chronicler of Burma, Sir James George Scott, also known as Shway Yoe, wrote, 'No one can speak Burmese well till he chews betel'. That's probably because ardent adherents have a quid stuck permanently in their cheek and this impediment affects their speech. It also affects their breath because it rots the teeth, turning them into gruesome reddish stumps, and it's best to stay downwind from chronic chewers so as to avoid a whiff of the rank 'betel breath', as it's called.

Thousands of one-man betel nut stalls are dotted through-out Yangon. Betel quid makers have a stack of small, green betel vine leaves, a pot of white, gloopy slaked-lime paste and an array of herbs and fillings, including cloves, aniseed, grated coconut, cinnamon, camphor, cardamom seeds, cumin and tobacco, plus small, broken pieces of the actual nut.

The ingredients are mixed on the leaf and a stick is scraped through the white gloop, which is liberally daubed over the leaf. The leaf is then carefully folded into a small packet or quid, and enclosed in a small cellophane pouch. Users place the betel nut quid in their mouth and slowly suck. The lime breaks down the ingredients quickly, leaving a pleasant but bitter spearmint-like taste in your mouth.

By the time the betel nut quid U Tun Htun has given me has totally dissolved in my mouth, with the hard nubs of nut softened into a mush, we have reached the outskirts of Yangon and it is time for me to do what all betel nut chewers do. When we stop at traffic lights I open the passenger door, lean out and expectorate a rancid red stream onto the road. Some Myanmar people in the car next to me are watching. They laugh and give me their version of a thumbs-up.

I laugh too, thinking that I've fought at the Thingyan barricades and now I've chewed and spat betel nut. I'm finally becoming a local, turning native. But I'm sad too, because tomorrow I leave Yangon to return to my country to fulfil a university contract, teaching Australian students how to produce and publish a newspaper.

I'd signed this contract at the same time as signing the three-month contract to work in Yangon, thinking that the city would be a colourless, concrete-bunker hellhole and three months would be more than enough of an experience. But a few days ago, when Ross Dunkley asked me if I would return to Myanmar after the university contract and work a much longer stint, I eagerly signed on the dotted line.

I have fallen in love with Yangon and with Myanmar. It's such a beautiful country and the people are so gracious, so warm and welcoming, so fundamentally kind. This country, which has such a grim, grey reputation, is alive, colourful and vibrant. Day-to-day life in Myanmar is in many ways joyous, with more freedoms than suggested by Western coverage—providing, of course, that one does not indulge in politics or overt criticism of the government, or interfere with the mechanics of State.

I recall again Maung Zaw's thoughts, so poignantly expressed a few weeks ago at the Zawgyi Café, when he discussed the West's anti-smoking laws and deduced that the baggage of democracy is lots of little rules. His comment—'I think it will be quite foreign to us'—has stuck in my mind.

In turn, many of the foreign qualities I've encountered in Myanmar have intrigued me. The Western concept of male machismo is non-existent. Strong men in Myanmar are softly spoken and gentle in demeanour, and holding hands is common among men, as it is among women.

I smile as I think back to the times when I have arrived at the office entrance and met up with the journalist Nay, the resident office weightlifter. He'd hold my hand as we walked up the stairs. Or my occasional night driver, Blue Car Honda Harry. Whenever he took me to the Friday night expatriates' piss-up at the Strand Hotel bar, he'd have to park some distance from the hotel for security reasons. When it was time to return home, I'd walk out of the hotel and find Blue Car sitting on the footpath playing cards with other drivers. I'd summon him with the customary kissing motion that is practised in Myanmar and then we'd walk along the late-evening streets holding hands, while he would first chide me for drinking at the Strand, where the price of beer is so high, and then try to sell me on the virtues of yet another 'very beautiful, could-be model' woman whom he claimed he had recruited as a potential practice wife for me: 'She has seen you, I show you to her, she like you.'

Actually, this practice-wife business seems to be a local hustle. Several men have been on my case trying to couple me with a practice wife which, as far as I can determine, means a woman who moves in, taking care of all wifely duties for a fee somewhere between US$50 and $100 a month. It is similar, I suspect, to Chinese second or package wives, but dissimilar to ding-dong girls, who own their own apartments complete with doorbell and phone. But I have resisted the practice wife syndrome. I figure procuring a practice-wife through these contacts will only give rise to further knowledge and gossip about my personal affairs, and I don't need any more eyes in my life. And certainly not Blue Car Honda Harry's inscrutable but obviously disreputable eyes.

Western-style individualism is held in low regard in Myanmar and, while I've yet to find a clear definition or labelling of local politics (other than simply 'military dictatorship'), I've deduced that underneath the mantle of Tatmadaw regimentation lurks a foundation layer of communalism.

I have found scattered references to communalism in the writings of Myanmar's famous martyr, Bogyoke (General) Aung San, revered as the architect of Myanmar independence and the father of the Myanmar Tatmadaw, or military—the same Tatmadaw that now imprisons his heroic daughter, Aung San Suu Kyi, who married an Englishman.

Her father, Bogyoke Aung San, was avowedly anti-British, particularly after a senior but distant relative of his, a governor of three towns, was beheaded by the British. When his head was put on display, people queued to view it after rumours that a mole on his face had shifted in death.

Before the onset of World War II, Aung San was a newspaper man, becoming a sub-editor on the *Burma News* after learning the craft as a university student-newspaper editor. He engaged in printed skirmishes with other notable scribes, including U Thant, a former high-school senior master who became a freelance journalist, then later the Burmese Press Director and Director of Broadcasting, and then the third United Nations Secretary-General, after the death of Dag Hammarskjöld in an aeroplane crash.

One skirmish between the pair occurred over freedom of dress in schools. U Thant advocated the abolition of uniforms, but Aung San countered by arguing that this was a 'flight of fantasy' which might cause a disintegration into the emerging

Western trend of 'Nudism or Sun-bathing, euphemistically'. Aung San believed that the wearing of a national uniform of pinni jacket and longyi instilled the feeling of 'fraternity pledged for the service of the motherland', thereby creating more freedom. So-called freedom of dress only whetted and pampered youth's taste for vanity, he argued.

At the beginning of World War II, Aung San, along with his colleague Ne Win, was one of the Thirty Comrades who slipped out of Burma and trained in Japan, aiding the Japanese to 'liberate' Burma from the British. But the Thirty Comrades quickly discovered the Japanese were worse than the British, so they then did a deal with the hated colonialists: they helped oust the Japanese in exchange for independence.

After the war Bogyoke Aung San became the nation's leader, but in early 1947 he repeatedly said he wanted to quit and embark on a writing career. 'I want to write about politics, history, marriage, child-rearing,' he declared. On 30 May 1947 he held a press conference to announce, 'I'll be in politics until independence. When interparty conflicts arise after independence, I don't want to be part of it. I'll retire and observe all that goes on and write books.' Less than two months later, on 19 July 1947, he lay dead on the floor of party headquarters, his bloody body riddled by assassins' bullets.

I experienced communalism in action yesterday afternoon when I visited U Tun Htun's house to say goodbye to his family. I like U Tun Htun and he has become like a brother to me, helping me with advice and introducing me to the many fascinating aspects of his country.

He is a short, squat, neat man with a perfectly round head and he wears sporty polo shirts, offset by his traditional longyi. He treats his driving job as a small business and in his tenement apartment, next to his Buddha shrine, he has a whiteboard with his weekly income targets listed on one side and his actual income listed on the other. A quick glance at his whiteboard shows that most weeks he is ahead of target, and he is the proud owner of not only a phone but also a computer, which sits on a table in his living room, surrounded by archaeology books used by his daughter in her university studies.

Life in his third-floor apartment is a commotion and streams of friends and family ebb and flow, chattering, borrowing items, using the computer or delivering items that were borrowed. The fronts of the multi-storey tenements around him are connected by a continually moving spider web of cords with clips attached to the ends, which are lowered and raised, carrying items from neighbours' balconies above or below or from hawkers on the street below.

While sitting on Tun Htun's balcony, I watch his neighbours on an adjoining balcony. They yell to a man in the street, telling him there is a call for him on their mobile phone, which is put in a cane basket attached to the clip at the end of the cord and lowered to the man on the street below. When he finishes the call, he puts the phone back in the basket and it is hauled back up to the balcony from where it originated.

Borrowing and sharing resources is big in U Tun Htun's circle and, while I am eating my meal of the traditional noodle and fish-paste dish, *mohinga*, I chat to Tun Htun and some of his male friends about this. I tell them how different life in my country is, where every man has his own house and around the house he has a fence. At the back of each house is a shed and in that shed is every tool that the man may need during his lifetime. I explain that the man who has to borrow tools is often portrayed as a person of low esteem—a loser—and how a television commercial for a chain of hardware stores in my country lectures men to be independent and buy all their tools from the store rather than borrowing them from friends.

Tun Htun and his friends chaffer amongst themselves in Myanmar. Tun Htun turns to me and says, 'But Mr Peter, Mr Peter, but . . . but, but you must tell the men in your country that if they share their tools they will be able to spend more on their children's education.'

The trip to the delta country ends as Tun Htun's Toyota Corolla pulls up at the entrance to my apartment complex. The shimmering orange sun sets and thousands of blackbirds, rooks and ravens circle and dip before descending into the dark shadows of the trees. I shake hands with Tun Htun, promising him that I will email his daughter, advising him of the precise date and time of my return so he can pick me up from the airport.

I walk into my apartment, shower, change and stuff a wad of kyats into an envelope. I walk out into Bogyoke Aung San Road and find Lasheeda laughing with glee and pointing as the finch and sparrow lady opens her wicker cages and releases a flock of birds. They explode in the air, flittering and fluttering, then swoop across the road to perch on the roofs, window sills and balconies of tenement buildings.

During the day, this street lady sells her birds to people, who release them for good luck. I don't know why she's releasing all her unsold birds this evening, but perhaps she's about to embark on a visit to a pagoda or a monastery for a few days.

I hand Lasheeda the money, to compensate her for the income she won't be getting from me for the next three months, and I say goodbye. She stands silently, solemnly staring at me with those big, brown, brimming, spinning eyes. Shyly she says, 'Bye-bye, bye-bye.' The sparrow and finch lady smiles.

I buy a couple of chunks of chicken roasted on a small charcoal brazier by a street vendor, and then at another stall I buy a container of Indian-style curried vegetables before retreating to my apartment.

After the meal I start packing my cabin-trunk-sized Samsonite, but I'm interrupted by the ringing of my doorbell. I open the door and Dee Dha gusts in, accompanied by three of her girlfriends who all live at the same hostel.

I met Dee Dha at the Pioneer Club, a nightspot attached to the Yuzana Gardens Hotel. She is an attractive woman in her early twenties, who dresses alternately in either traditional garb or lively, hip Western-style dress. She's a sort of good-time girl who, like many essentially under-educated middle-class young people in Yangon, figures that working for extremely low wages—seven or eight dollars a month in bars, restaurants, nightclubs or retail outlets—is a 'waste of time'.

So the parents of such girls continue to support their offspring, thus cementing the strong family ties that typify Myanmar society. Dee Dha claims her parents are in the gem trade in the ruby fields of rural Mogok, and she has come to Yangon to taste the delights of modern city life. She lives in the Peony Hostel in Chinatown and says, shrugging her shoulders, that she spends her days mostly smoking cigarettes and watching television.

Tonight she's come to say goodbye and when she walks in she points at my small refrigerator, saying, 'Ka, ka'. This translates as 'cow, cow', meaning she'd like a glass of milk, to which she's taken quite a fancy. The Myanmar aren't dairy-produce people and hard-to-find locally produced milk is a strange, suspect concoction that curdles and sours within 24 hours, even if kept refrigerated. But in the Western-style supermarkets I discovered I could buy cartons of Brisbane-produced milk cheaper than I could buy the milk at home.

Dee Dha sits on the floor with her three girlfriends and drinks from the glass of milk I've given her, then passes it to her friends to sample. Their faces screw up in funny little moues of distaste, and Dee Dha shrugs, happily finishing the milk.

Dee Dha is fascinated by the contents of my cupboards and drawers; tonight she pulls out the drawer from my desk, places it on the floor and the four girls sit cross-legged, carefully taking out and scrutinising every item. One of them holds up a stapler so I give a demonstration of its function. They're not impressed, but when they discover the use of a strip of Blu Tack they become animated. This wonderful Western invention will allow them to stick posters of their favourite South Korean television idols on their bare hostel walls, and so I give them each a chunk of Blu Tack.

After an hour, the busy little chattering group is ready to leave. They're off to a nightspot to see a local rock band. Dee Dha looks curiously into my eyes and makes me promise that I will return to Yangon.

Then, as suddenly as it arrived, the whirlwind giggle of noisy, playful Yangon women swirls out the door and my apartment is enveloped in sad silence, the final silence. Tomorrow I begin the long journey home and I know I will miss the wonderful, colourful array of Myanmar people who have become so joyously entangled in my life.

I'm standing on million-dollar grass in front of a million-dollar restaurant overlooking a million-dollar beach at the million-dollar Australian beach resort, Noosa, my home town.

I'm home, in between contracts in Yangon, and I'm taking part in a media event ushering in the high point of the year for Noosa's well-heeled culturati: the Noosa Longweekend Festival.

Just a few paces away from me is the million-dollar playwright David Williamson, and his wife. Williamson is riding high following the casting of Madonna in one of his plays in

London, and he's here in his role as head honcho of the Long-weekend. The man who once wore romantic leather motorcycle jackets with fashionably long hair now presents himself very much as an establishment figure. He lives a few miles away at Sunshine Beach, the same village housing me, and he can often be seen walking stiffly through the village—tall, imposing, mostly in an establishment-type striped shirt that gives him the air of a retired brigadier.

He, like everyone else, is awaiting the delayed arrival of the star, John Pilger. The messiah of the downtrodden is in Noosa to speak to an audience composed of some of Australia's wealthiest people, people who can afford long, boozy lunches between phone calls to stockbrokers and realtors. Tickets for his shows were the first to sell out in a Long Weekend program featuring a grab-bag of cultural heroes, icons and stars.

Tension is in the air because Pilger is more than fashionably late for his own press conference. The maven of public relations Noosa-style, the professionally blonde Helen Flanagan, a former Sydney television executive, looks distressed, and she's muttering expletives under her breath. She's too polished a performer to publicly bag one of her charges, but she's rattled and lets it be known there are problems with John. She expresses concerns about whether John will even show up to this, his own press conference.

I am waiting for John Pilger because we have a mutual friend, and I've sent the message that I'd perhaps like to have a coffee with him and talk about Myanmar. Pilger is a strong campaigner against the Myanmar military junta, and I figure I can update him on the political machinations and man-oeuvrings.

It's also a depressing time for me. When I left Yangon, there was optimism in the air. Change was being forecast by those possibly in the know, and Daw Aung San Suu Kyi had been finally freed from house arrest and allowed to travel throughout

Myanmar. The government had hoped she would take it easy after her release, but instead she campaigned vigorously until matters came to a head on Black Friday, 30 May 2003, during the Dabayin Massacre as it is now called, or, in the West, the Depayin Massacre.

Nobody in the outside world is quite sure precisely what happened on that dire day because the facts, as usual, have been obscured, but what is known is that Suu Kyi's convoy was attacked and a number of people killed. The government, when it acknowledged the incident, said there had been a stoush between Suu Kyi's belligerent supporters and her opponents, and claimed four people had died and 50 others were wounded. Radio Free Asia, on the other hand, claimed 100 had died and later revised the figure upward, claiming a death toll of 282. More moderate reports put the deaths at about 40 plus.

The government began pushing the line that Aung San Suu Kyi had acted in an aggressive manner, affronting the polite Myanmar, and her convoy had been led by a gang of youths on motorcycles, who had so incensed villagers they brought the violence upon themselves.

Shortly after this event, the state newspaper, the *New Light of Myanmar*, began serialising notes from a diary supposedly written by a disaffected National League for Democracy (NLD) supporter, Maung Yin Hmaing, and I was able to follow the ad hominem revelations from my home via the internet and faxes. Maung Yin Hmaing reported he'd been on the campaign trail and been outraged by the airs and graces of 'Auntie', and he had admonished her for giving chocolates to villagers when 'health tonics or vitamins would be more appropriate'.

In the past, government agents disseminated hateful litera-ture about Suu Kyi—descriptions of her as a slut and prostitute, and terrible cartoons of her fornicating with her *kala*, her white man, her late husband Dr Michael Vaillancourt Aris. Now they are presenting her as a hard-headed nutter, a former ordinary housewife giddy with her own fame, who brought nothing but discordance and aggression into the lives of the millions of happy, peace-loving Myanmar.

Maung Yin Hmaing wrote:

The way she considers the NLD as if she owns it, and acts as sole proprietor of the organisation, is certainly not in tune with the rest of the NLD party members. Auntie Suu is a wilful and hard-headed person liable to rash judgements followed by blind action, in her relations with the present government. Nevertheless, whatever the provocation, responsible leaders of the present government, preferring to act with forbearance, and on the basis of give and take, have always chosen to act in moderation . . .

I, myself, am not a person in the habit of carrying tales about this and that to Auntie Suu like others who wish to curry favour and also benefit from handouts, by going in the front door or sneaking in through the back door. So I am not on close terms with her. What I wish to say is that for us it is more important for the entire NLD party to be active on a higher political standing than for the fame of Auntie Suu's name.

Maung's commentary leading up to the massacre was littered with syrupy concern for his people. On 29 May he wrote:

The shouting of slogans by [NLD] party members of the convoy had now disrupted peace and stability in Monywa. The sound of our slogans had also frightened the people of the town. Is this democracy? One thing sure is that it is an unruly democracy.

He skipped over the actual 30 May incident, merely reporting that four people were killed in a melee and commenting:

> ...NLD motorcyclists escorting Daw Aung San Suu Kyi
> and U Tin Oo hit the protesters with their vehicles, hurled
> abuse at them and beat some and seized and smashed the
> cameras of some photographers. The outbreak of demon-
> stration in Dabayin Township was because the local people
> were not pleased with Daw Aung San Suu Kyi's speeches
> opposing the government, department personnel and USDA
> [the government-supported Union Solidarity and Develop-
> ment Association], her incitement to civil commotion,
> speechifying at cross-roads, her followers shouting and
> blocking the way in public places and causing disturbances to
> people's stable life by breaking the law, rules and regulations.

The last entry in this putative diary leading up to the massacre
was:

> We heard a junior police officer reporting to his superior
> near us. According to what he said four two-inch by one-
> inch rods and one catapult were found on Auntie Suu's car.

I was sickened when I read a first-hand survivor's account,
provided by the National Council for the Union of Burma to
the *Far Eastern Economic Review*, which reported:

> This was when the people from the trucks descended and
> attacked the villagers—who had come to greet Daw Suu—
> with wooden and iron rods, bamboo and iron spears, and tried
> to run them down with their trucks. They flung abuse such as,
> 'You creatures who want to call the kala [white man] your
> fathers, you can die, you can die,' and wildly set on them.
>   The abuse they flung at the girls was obscene. 'We won't
> ask the white man to ravish you, we will do that ourselves.'

PETER OLSZEWSKI

While shouting out like this, and using the foulest of language, they beat the girls, grabbed them by the hair and banged their heads on the concrete road and said, 'Death to you, death to you, wives of kala.'

We could do nothing. Many who were beaten died on the spot and the ground was awash with blood. There was a great commotion . . . I then saw Daw Suu sitting in the car. There was blood on her head and shoulders.

During my Australian respite the *Myanmar Times* Deputy CEO, Sonny Swe, and his wife Yamin visited Noosa, and I gathered Sonny was surprised by the extent of the press coverage and how every Australian he encountered asked him what was going on in his country. I told him the politics of his country frightened me and he laughed incredulously, as though I'd made some crazy joke. For light relief, we began chatting about Australia.

He extolled the virtues of my country but, knowing the Myanmar are exceedingly polite and critical comments can be viewed as rudeness, I interrupted and asked, 'Sonny, you've told me what you like about Australia. Please tell me one thing you don't like.' He smiled because he'd often experienced the crudeness of my directness, but then he seemed to ignore my question. About ten minutes later he turned to me and said, 'I'll tell you one thing I don't like about your country. I don't like the way the fathers spend so little time with their children.'

The American-educated Sonny Swe is a boyish man in his early thirties, who runs the newspaper business in a sympathetic and caring familial manner yet, when crossed or cheated, is quick to hand out harsh discipline. Staff members caught stealing can expect nasty stints in prison. Observing Sonny Swe in action always gives me the positive feeling that if Myanmar is shaped by inventive men like him, then perhaps its future may be hopeful.

As the son of Brigadier General Thein Swe, he represents an interesting microcosm of modern Myanmar society. A dynastic element is emerging among the upper middle classes. The sons of the generals—modern and highly educated young men—dominate the local business and are introducing Western-style influences that appear to be paving the way for a slow, gradual and peculiarly Myanmar democratisation process.

As I've said, a trendy coffee shop culture has emerged in Yangon and the leading chain of smart, modern coffee shops is owned by Ye Naing Win, who is the son of General Khin Nyunt, the Prime Minister and Chief of Military Intelligence. Two of these Aroma coffee shops—the downtown café and another at the smart and fashionable Dagon shopping centre—are as stylish as any Western counterpart.

The Dagon Aroma is attached to a high-tech and very busy internet café, where internet users must initially pay the equivalent of a dollar and register at the counter by giving a thumb print. The fee is comparatively high, ruling out affordability for the poor or grassroots, but modern middle-class kids hang out in large numbers at the café and others similar to it. Emailing has become the new fad, but SMS messaging has not been introduced. Censorship applies, of course; some sites—including all sites critical of Myanmar—are blocked, as are Hotmail and Yahoo!, and most traffic is monitored, although the dissident press has conceded that the easing of restrictions on internet and chat room use could be a sign that the regime is lightening up.

There are two internet providers in Myanmar. One is run and monitored by the government's postal and telegraph services. The other provider is Bagan Cybernet, which is also owned by the Prime Minister's son; the chairman of its board of directors is Brigadier General Thein Swe, whose daughter is employed at the company as a marketing executive. She is a vivacious, savvy young woman with stylish short-cropped hair and an uncanny resemblance to her brother, Sonny Swe.

Bagan Cybernet aggressively markets itself, making internet usage increasingly affordable and attractive, particularly to middle-class youth. Its advertisements feature slogans such as, 'Now the dream is becoming a reality' and, 'Bagan Cybernet will take the people of Myanmar into Cyberspace'.

The company sponsors the annual Bagan Cybernet Music Festival, a two-day event similar to the Big Day Out concerts in Western countries. Safe-sex literature is mostly censored in Myanmar, so I was surprised to discover hip condom promotions at the festival. Two comedians, dressed as lizards, appeared on the stage regularly, making condom jokes and spreading the safe-sex message. Free condoms were available and a condom stall was situated near the main stage.

Meanwhile, back at the million-dollar restaurant in million-dollar Noosa, the star has arrived, scowling and skulking, looking very much like the creative director of a fashionable ad agency. He chats for a while with a fan-cum-journalist. During a lull in proceedings, I slip over and introduce myself.

He looks at me reproachfully and accusingly. He says, 'If you are working for a newspaper in Burma, then you must be working for the military. They own the newspapers.' I explain that some newspapers and journals are owned by private enterprise, including the *Myanmar Times*, which employs me as a journalism trainer. He counters by saying that all press is subject to military censorship, and I tell him how different factions censor different publications and that the *Myanmar Times* is censored by Military Intelligence.

'Military Intelligence! Then you are working for Military Intelligence.'

'No. I'm working for a privately owned newspaper that is censored by Military Intelligence.'

The conversation goes nowhere. Pilger scowls and raises his

eyebrows in an exaggerated manner. He stalks off across the million-dollar grass.

So much for heroes. I admire Pilger's work, but I understand from this exchange that he is not a journalist with an inquiring mind. He is an advocate with a set agenda, a pre-written script. And I'd begun to worry about advocates, understanding that in the new emerging world such black-and-white thinking is outmoded. He stands for good against evil, but in the new world good and evil are often the flip sides of the same coin.

Leftists (and I'm a sympathiser in that house of cant, but not a worshipper) are usually by their very nature infracanino-philiacs—given a struggle they'll almost inevitably, and nearly always emotionally, champion the underdogs, the minorities or perceived minorities, the powerless or perceived powerless. In some cases the stance is merely fashionable, the 'cause of the day' amongst the chattering classes, as they've been dubbed, or the chardonnay socialists. But in the modern world there is no doctrine that is pure, unerringly fair to all, and universally applicable, and the world isn't left or right or even wrong, just as it isn't black or white or always right. It's all sort of shades in between and, at times, as with the attitudes towards such nations as Myanmar, the left unwittingly converges with the right: it virtuously lashes out against oppressive regimes in a manner that prepares the path for the right to invade, invoke regime change, and impose democracy.

On the subject of left and right and what is wrong and what is right, what difference is there really, I wonder, in the day-to-day life of the grassroots people of Myanmar as compared to their counterparts in, say, Cuba? Both are repressed by a militaristic centralist regime, yet the people of Cuba are regarded by many left-leaning thinkers and liberals as beneficiaries of the leadership of a glorious socialist revolution, while the people of Myanmar are viewed as the hapless victims of a cruel military junta.

My stance could be perceived as the stance of a person who is prepared to do nothing but that's not the case; I'm a person who believes we should do something, but something that's different from what we've already been doing with such harrowing consequences.

Saving the world seems so clear-cut when watching world news through the filter of a television screen in the safety of a cosy Western domicile, but I was no longer watching Yangon via remote control. I was up close and personal. Very personal. There were people I knew and loved in Yangon and I didn't want to see them die in a revolution that would prove to be bloody. Or in an invasion that would also exact 'collateral damage', as the Americans so coyly describe the civilian slaughter of war.

I didn't want to sit in front of a TV set in ten years time watching a heartfelt and moving John Pilger documentary about the evils perpetrated by invasion forces entering Myanmar, intent on bringing about regime change and imposing democracy. There has to be a better way, a more subtle way.

A few weeks later I board another midnight jet to Yangon, to do what I figure is the right thing to do—to help bring about change from within in a very small way and a very slow way, and to help the people of Myanmar do whatever it is that they want to do.

Of course, unlike Myanmar, my world is a free world. John Pilger is free to tell his story his way, but I am also free to tell my story my way.

It was the big wet and I sat on two wooden slats perched over an open drain by the roadside, waiting for the key cutter to fiddle with his rasps and files and cut me three apartment keys by hand. His battered, humble mobile stand was next to the drain on the footpath beside a busy road, and he'd thoughtfully provided the planks over the drain for the benefit of his customers.

The monsoon season with its drenching, driving rain had set in well before my return to Yangon and, while I waited for my keys, the deluge stopped momentarily. The drain ran swiftly with foamy sewer-brown water and muck and, a few yards from where I was sitting, it had disintegrated. Water sluiced over the footpath onto the roadside.

A trio of colourfully dressed women tottered and teetered delicately through the water, holding hands, laughing. They were jewels in a sea of shit, standing out against the muddied monochrome of the monsoon's detritus, and they represented the admirable qualities of the Myanmar that I had come to love: the ability not only to make do, but to giggle and pursue life with *joie de vivre*, despite the deprivations dished out by the elements or by the military masters.

Their joy made me conscious of the self-indulgent monsoon blues I'd recently succumbed to, because my return to Myanmar had a sad edge to it. The optimism I'd experienced before my break in Australia was gone, swept away in the wake of international outrage over the Aung San Suu Kyi incident and her re-imprisonment. The Americans had introduced new sanctions, and daily life had taken a grim turn. The newspaper office had lost whatever spark it had possessed, and was undergoing a haemorrhage of resignations and walkouts.

But the most oppressive aspect personally was my dismal living arrangement. I'd agreed to return to Yangon for a long spell on the basis of being given a more practical apartment with a kitchen, but on the eve of my departure I had received a cheery email explaining I'd been given the Baho Road apartment the company rented, and I would only have to share with one other person—even though I had stipulated I didn't want to share.

I had flown to Yangon and complained, but Ross Dunkley pushed aside my protestations with a hearty, 'Give it a go, mate. I know you'll get to love it. You'll probably turn the place into a brothel.'

The bleak apartment was on the third floor of a tenement block and, of course, there was only one key. So I found myself sitting on wooden slats over a drain waiting for the man to cut some spares, watching the women walk through the water, contemplating my options.

A fortnight later, I walked into Dunkley's office on a Saturday morning and declared the arrangements unsatisfactory. I was too old to live in a crash pad out in the 'burbs, and I was happy to call it quits and fly home on Monday. By mid-afternoon I had new digs.

I found I'd moved from one extreme to the other—from a crash pad to a trendy downtown apartment complex, the Grand Mee Ya Hta Executive Residences, dripping with opulence, including a sparkling pool surrounded by Italianate sculptures of semi-naked women. The entrance was a lush hundred yards of curving pathways and luxuriant gardens full of gardeners, and inside the complex the apartments overlooked an interior that made a feature of the second floor—an arrangement of pools, moats and strange staggered stone creations resembling Aztec sacrificial altars, surrounded by a row of stately fake palm trees.

My apartment was of teak—a gentleman's quarters, complete with a kitchen housing that rarity of rarities in Yangon, a real roasting oven. The Grand Mee Ya Hta was in the middle of the downtown action on Bogyoke Aung San Road; it was near the luxurious FMI department store, the fabulous Bogyoke Aung San Market or Scott's Market, and next to the funky French-owned Zawgyi Café.

I moved in that weekend and strolled through the downtown district to familiarise myself with my new neighbourhood, taking care to dodge the numerous nasty holes that punctuated the footpaths. There were hundreds of such holes along Yangon's footpaths. They appeared and grew rapidly during the monsoon, the heavy water simply sluicing through the cheap sandy concrete used to plug the previous year's holes. After each deluge new holes appeared and old holes widened.

I'd noticed a large hole only a few yards from the entrance to my apartment complex. I had taken in its size and depth, noting the jagged shards of concrete and broken strands of heavy-gauge rusted wire protruding from its sides. I had made a mental note to myself not to fall down this hole.

On my first evening at my new accommodation, I celebrated my turn of fortune with a binge at the nearby luxurious Traders Hotel. The rain had momentarily ceased and, as I walked back to my apartment, I gazed at bright stars in the clear, sparkling night sky.

And fell into the very hole I'd vowed not to fall into.

Next day I limped to the office and regaled my trainees with the story. Trainee Minh Zaw promptly wrote a news report about the incident, which he left on my desk. It read:

FOREIGNER & FALLING HOLE EVENT
Mr Peter, an Australian with Foreign Resident Certificate and stay in Grand Mee Ya Hta Executive Residences, stepped down into a hole of footpath and fell down

PETER OLSZEWSKI

immediately and it made him injured left leg after he had dinner at the Trader Hotel, Friday night 9pm, in Yangon.

The securitys from Grand Mee Ya Hta helped him from hole and sent to the doctor during that night. He is a trainer from the famous *Myanmar Times* journal. This is the first falling in hole experience with him in Myanmar.

The doctor said that he get plastered treatment for his left leg and minor treatment for cut in left arm. The doctor arranged all this for him. The doctor payment will be invoicing system for him.

Mr Peter is released a little from pain. He said that he had drunk more than usual. He sent email to his family about happening. His family warned him back to be careful while in Myanmar.

After he has been treated, he would get back his work and not absent for any day. His trainees would not have to wait until his duty on.

He is really angry about the platform hole. He say in his country he would complain about the street to the government. Yangon City Development Council should notice the streets and platform damages not even all but near the surrounding area of the Biggest and High standard hotel, he also said.

The falling hole event is not Yangon City Development Council fault. That night he drunk more and loaded and took careless walk on the way from Hotel. Myanmar people is very helpful. The doctor and nurses are taking care upon him, he added.

It was only an accident on the occasion of his appetising dine out at the Trader hotel.

After treatment, he have to walk slowly. From now on, to be good future, he must have to watch carefully every step in walking on the platform. Unless if he walked and drink carelessly repeated, the another treatment would wait for his right side.

Before the monsoon arrived, I knew I should arm myself with an umbrella but, while lots of women carry umbrellas as sun protection, I simply couldn't find one on sale anywhere. But when the monsoon set in, umbrellas appeared by the thousands in shops and street stalls, and most businesses provided plastic containers for the storing of dripping wet brollies. I had no need to buy my own umbrella because they were part of the amenities provided at the Grand Mee Ya Hta. A large rack of umbrellas was placed by the entrance, and each umbrella locked in an individual slot identified with a number. A staff member ceremoniously gave me my umbrella key, No. 007. Licensed to be protected from the rain.

Umbrella etiquette is an art form on the crowded monsoon streets of Yangon. Thousands of people walk hither and thither with opened umbrellas and yet expertly manage to avoid umbrella bump, umbrella collision and, indeed, even umbrella rage.

Umbrella etiquette took some practice; it was a matter of getting the eye in and wielding the brolly accordingly. I'd gauge that a smaller person was coming toward me from the left so I needed to raise my umbrella a notch to allow it to slip over the smaller person's brolly, but not high enough to get tangled in the brolly of the taller person to my right. So, with tilting, adjustment and constant calculation, hundreds of thousands of umbrellas courteously gave way to each other every day out there on the rain-swept footpaths of Yangon.

I was sort of surfing through the brolly crush one evening, enjoying the zen of umbrella-ness, when—bang!—my brolly was clunked aside by some ill-mannered baggage. But it was only Edwin, a Dutch expatriate working at the Bagan Cybernet internet provider. He said he'd been watching me, aware of exactly what I was doing umbrella-wise, and we chuckled over the shared experience.

Monsoon rain is exactly that. Rain. But it's tricky rain—as tricky as a Myanmar woman, as the Myanmar like to say. It rains every day but not at the same time, not all the time, and there's no advance warning of when it will rain. It's sunny, then black clouds scud across the sun at about Mach 1 speed, and down it comes. Heavy saturating rain.

The rain becomes a sort of entity, stalking the hapless pilgrim. There is no up-side to the rain, in that it doesn't, for example, bring relief from the heat that also constantly envelops Yangon. Living in a monsoon is like living in a laundry.

Traversing town during the monsoon is tricky because inter-sections flood and many cars aren't up to the conditions, slowly chugging out of power or suddenly losing their braking ability. Many of the cars in Yangon aren't up to much of anything, let alone the rigours of the monsoon. Myanmar is often described as a graveyard for Toyota Corollas, an accurate description except that the decrepit cars never actually seem to die and are certainly never buried. They keep on keeping on. Every one of the world's clapped-out Toyota Corollas seems to end up gasping and wheezing on the streets of Yangon.

The Toyota Corolla's utilitarian indefatigability makes it a sentimental favourite amongst the Myanmar, and when I asked a car dealer who drove a Corolla why the Myanmar are so attached to them, he said, 'Our people are crazy. I offer them good cars like the Subaru, but all they want is the Corolla.'

Vintage variants of the Corolla—Toyota brands culled from the four corners of the world—also chug and splutter through Yangon, including the Toyota Crown, Crown Majesta, Sprinter, Carina, Caldina, Grande Mark II, Windon, Vista, Raffine Chaser, Chaser Avante, Cielo, Celsior, Cressida, Avante, Super Lucente, Cresta, Vista Etoile, Levin, Lucida,

Starlet and Suffre Cresta. They endlessly circle the streets looking for a place to die, accompanied by a variety of other battered Japanese cars, such as the Mazda Luce, Capella and Lancer, and a clutch of Nissans: Sunny, Laurel, Cedric, Bluebird, Gloria, Preser, Medalist, Cefire, Sebon Skyline.

Traffic accidents are not as numerous as in neighbouring countries, because most vehicles can't crank up to dangerous speeds. But getting into a Yangon taxi can be a life-threatening experience, especially during the big wet.

On the first Saturday after I moved into my new apartment I set out on a shopping expedition, noticing that an upmarket gift store was festooned with *Monsoon Sale: 10% Off Everything* posters. I caught a cab to the Citymart supermarket on nearby Anawrahta Street, and the cab interior was typical of the genre: a plastic container of petrol tied with twine to the passenger floor, a betel nut quid stuck between the radio and speedo fascias, small-denomination kyat notes stuck in the air vents, ashtray open and containing half-a-dozen cheroot stubs with ash furiously flying forth, cracked windscreen, Buddhist paraphernalia scattered on the dashboard, a cheapo Chinese gewgaw of a cartoon cat suspended on a string from a suction cap stuck to the windscreen, annoyingly placed directly in the passenger's line of sight, a taxi driver ID card (clearly, not of the driver), and fumes wafting from a noisy hole in the muffler.

As the cab set off, the rain belted down in sheets, soaking me because the passenger-side electric window was stuck in the down position. The windscreen clouded over and the airconditioner didn't work, so the only way the driver could clear the screen was by jamming on the heater, which unfortunately *did* work, adding to the oppressive heat. The car's clutch was almost gone and every few hundred yards the driver had to stop and top up the clutch fluid. We jerked and shuddered our way to the supermarket where, because I'd negotiated a two-way trip for the grand total of 80 cents, the cabbie waited for me while I gingerly alighted. Ankle-deep water swirled around the car, creating a moat-like effect, but luckily a tree root had edged above the water and I was able to walk along this to higher ground.

When I finished shopping, the water had risen another six inches, drowning the tree root. But an unstable stack of bricks had been installed as stepping stones, allowing me to teeter back to the cab, where the driver proudly announced he'd been able to raise the stuck passenger window. I sat in the torn, moist, mouldy seat, which was like sitting on a stack of soaked nappies, and off we went—back into the monsoon, back into battle. But the cab's clutch gave out and we became stuck in the notorious Anawrahta Street traffic.

We had been inching forward a few feet every few minutes. This of course meant that a series of gear changes had to be effected, but this was no longer happening in the little Corolla. We ground to a stop by the side of the road, and the cabbie fiddled under the bonnet. The heat was dreadful, like being stuck in a dishwasher at peak cycle, and made even more dreadful because I couldn't get the damned passenger window down. Which was perhaps a small blessing, because a beggar woman with child noted the trapped prey and began tap-tap-tapping incessantly on the passenger window.

I motioned her away, but she was relentless. Tap-tap-tap. Tap-tap-tap. It drove me nuts. I considered abandoning the vehicle, but I realised we were trapped in swirling water about a foot deep, halfway up the beggar woman's shins.

The cabby tried a new ruse. He put the car in gear and started it, taking off in a series of violent kangaroo-hopping spasms, with a weird shrieking noise coming from the gearbox. We were doomed to forward propulsion without gear changes so he veered left, out of the traffic, and became an instant rally driver in the smaller, not-so-cluttered side streets.

He had to navigate without stopping, so we slalomed through the heavy rain and erratic traffic, almost getting blocked by another broken-down cab being pushed off the road. We zoomed through the series of side streets until I was totally disoriented and beginning to believe this extreme shopping trip would never be over, when suddenly we turned into Maha Bandoola Street, the home stretch.

I retreated to the cosy confines of my apartment and looked out of my window at the Saturday afternoon rain, which was coming down in a deluge. I imbibed Johnny Walker and tuned the cable television to a sports channel telecasting an Australian Rules football match from Melbourne, where the Saturday afternoon rain was coming down in a deluge.

My life in Yangon is improving, but a colleague's career has declined dramatically since he landed in Myanmar a mere fortnight ago. I arrive at the office to find him sitting in a chair looking perplexed. 'Mate,' he says to me, 'I've been fucking well thrown out of the country.'

He's the much-heralded Internationally Famous Cartoonist, fresh from the wilds of Washington. He's a mate of Ross Dunkley's, and his profile has been written up in glowing terms in the *Myanmar Times*.

He arrived for a six-month stint to do big things, to produce a fine body of oil-on-canvas renderings, creating a rare Western artistic insight into the colourful streets of Yangon. International exhibitions had been planned by Dunkley, an art lover. There was optimistic expectation that the Yangon work would grace the walls of the fashionable art salons of Paris, London and New York, putting the *Myanmar Times*, modern Yangon and the Famous Cartoonist on the internationally happening map. In the meantime the cartoonist was to help pay his way by producing editorial cartoons for the *Times*.

Preparations for his impending arrival were intense. A stream of delivery boys lugged stretched frames, spare rolls of canvas, boxes of paints and pencils and bags of brushes, and a score of sketchpads up the office stairs and into the storeroom in readiness for the master.

Unfortunately much of this material was never actually touched by the master, because his arrival in town also coincided with one of his legendary binges, instantly and catastrophically causing great concern among the Myanmar.

They were becoming used to the strange ways of the foreigners, but the cartoonist was their worst nightmare. He was the foreigner from hell who did everything they didn't. He was drunk in public; he was loud and aggressive; he was dangerous. When he stumbled down the teeming footpaths of inner-suburban Yangon, swathed in a miasma of stale sweat and beer-fume fug, the Myanmar spun and wheeled away like disturbed angry seagulls, creating a path for him and then closing in again behind him, squawking disapproval.

The first time I saw him he looked harmless. He was sitting on the floor at Ross Dunkley's Inya Road house, clad in T-shirt and longyi, and strumming a guitar, gently crooning cute songs to Dunkley's offspring. Harmony and bliss. I was impressed and wanted to befriend the man, hoping some of his serenity might rub off on me.

The next time I saw him he was reeling in the car park just outside the office at 8.30am. It was already shaping up to be another screechingly hot Yangon day, yet he was dressed in a paint-smeared heavy blue suit over a bright blue, red and yellow Superman T-shirt, with his round sunglasses propped firmly on his bright red, sweaty nose. His wiry, woollen hair stuck out in tufts and he emanated sour fumes. He waved a beer can in the air and demanded I join him for a drink. When I declined on the basis that I was busy, he became stroppy, telling me I was a gutless bastard and a piss-poor example of a journalist.

Later that afternoon he marched into the office like the pie-eyed piper of Dagon, with a gaggle of angry, chattering Myanmar girls trailing in his wavering wake. He'd been dining and drinking at the nearby Sofitel Hotel, and walked out without paying. The girls had followed him to the *Times* office and produced a clutch of hefty bills.

He was housed in a smart downtown apartment owned by Yamin, the wife of Sonny Swe. He trashed this apartment, smearing the walls and polished parquet floors with his oil paints, and when Yamin heard about this she flew into a rage. She sent a couple of Myanmar men to the apartment to assess the damage and they returned with grim tidings. They'd discovered the cartoonist prowling the narrow street outside the apartment, dressed in longyi and dressing gown over the bright blue, yellow and red Superman T-shirt with a turban on his head fashioned from a grubby bath towel. He was abusing the natives and they were terrified.

The driver U Tun Htun, clearly in an agitated state, said to me, 'Mr Peter, Mr Peter, you must do something about Mr Cartoonist. He is drunk and very bad. He is upsetting us all, and the police will put him in jail.'

Sonny Swe issued an edict. The Internationally Famous Cartoonist had to exit Myanmar immediately, if not sooner.

As I arrive at the office this morning and see the Internationally Famous Cartoonist sitting there, I sympathise with him about his enforced departure and then walk into Ross Dunkley's office. Dunkley is not a happy man. He says, 'Ah, mate, I'm going to personally take the bastard to Bangkok, to physically put him on the plane to Perth.'

Dunkley's office is partitioned by glass panels and he looks over at where the cartoonist is abjectly sitting, fixing him with a malevolent glare. 'I've spent close on $10 000 bringing him here and setting him up,' he says. 'I just want to hit the cunt.' Dunkley then grabs his coat, gestures to the cartoonist and they head to the airport.

Hanging on Dunkley's wall is the only legacy the cartoonist has left—a scrunched sheet of sketchpad daubed with a biro sketch of Lasheeda, the postcard-selling street girl.

I look at the drawing, taking in the captivating rendering of Lasheeda's big brown eyes. The sketch is brilliant.

As the monsoon rains lash the streets of Yangon, I come to rely more and more on my little friend Lasheeda. We are an odd couple, but problems arise as we become a fixture in the downtown district. Stern matrons purse their lips, looking at us with disapproval, and I sadly realise how this is being taken the wrong way.

I come up with what I consider to be a cunning ploy. I tell Lasheeda I am going to adopt her as my No. 1 Unofficial Daughter, but she isn't overly impressed. 'Me no baby, you no poppy,' she says.

A few nights later I come home just as another big golden sun is setting, complete with its accompaniment of circling black birds. As I approach the entrance to my apartment complex, I discover a delegation of Myanmar gathered on the footpath, waiting for me. A woman says Lasheeda can't be my daughter because she's not a baby. She adds that I need a wife and Lasheeda will soon become of marriageable age.

She pushes Lasheeda forward. Lasheeda is in her finest tattered dress, with a smeared splodge of violently red lipstick on and around her lips, while her prize possession, a wooden toy machine gun with most of the paint peeled off, dangles around her neck on a piece of twine.

But it is her eyes that move me. She stares at me with her feral, piercing gaze—her eyes big, spinning, brimming, moistening. This is an intense moment of street truth. She fixes her eyes on mine. What will I do? Betray her, humiliate her, mock her, destroy her?

I think fast. The situation calls for face-saving on a very real scale. But how can I extricate myself from this embarrassment while at the same time allowing Lasheeda to save face?

Inspiration. I tell them I already have a foreigner wife and, due to my religion, I am only allowed one wife. This is met with obvious scepticism, because none of these people have seen a trace of a wife, so I tell them that tomorrow I will introduce my wife. I sit in my apartment thinking that all that remains for me to do tomorrow is to actually produce a foreigner wife.

Next day I approach Hanna, a young, lively New York University intern at the newspaper office, and ask her to accompany me and not ask questions. She walks with me to Bogyoke Aung San Road and, although flabbergasted, allows me to introduce her as my mysterious wife.

Of course, everybody understands the charade to be exactly what it is, and everybody understands face has been saved all around. The engagement as such is off. Lasheeda relents and begins to happily call me Poppy. Even the stern street matrons relax and say 'Poppy' when I walk by, holding hands with Lasheeda.

The New York intern who was supplied as evidence of my having a wife writes a cute column about Lasheeda, but this is axed by Military Intelligence with the comments, 'We don't want to hide the truth, but we don't want to have these images', and, 'The style of thinking in our country is different than in the West'.

One Saturday afternoon I set off with my now Unofficial No. 1 twelve-year-old Daughter to shop for fruit and vegetables from the stalls laid out on an old rickety wooden bridge across the railway line just behind the Bogyoke Market. Lasheeda and I are a formidable shopping duo. I pay her about 50 cents—good money for her—to help me shop and she earns her money by vigorously bartering, and demanding only the best quality produce.

We finalise negotiations for fresh straw mushrooms just as the stall-holders begin urgently wrapping their produce in the blue plastic sheets on which it is laid out. Lasheeda points at the skies. Black, angry clouds scud over. 'Water, water,' she says, warning me rain is about to come. I amble off the bridge, but she grabs my hand, stressing urgency. 'Water, water, running,' she says. We run but down it comes, a deluge.

We duck into a lane and sit on stools in front of a market stall selling car accessories. Our stopover becomes a social occasion. The stallholder's daughter brings us a cup of tea, the wife comes over and shows her baby, and the man proudly points at his car, sitting in the rain receiving a complimentary wash.

During a brief respite from the deluge, I tell Lasheeda I want to go around the corner to the Zawgyi Café. 'Running, running,' she advises, so we run. Or at least I try to. But my aptly named slippers—formerly known to me as *sandals*—keep slipping on the slick, wet cobblestones of the market laneways, so I take them off and hold them in my hand as I run.

The street vendors reel at the sight of a foreigner running through the wetness wearing his slippers on his hands. The pig-intestine sellers, the pomelo sellers and some of the passers-by titter as I run past, but the doughty lady selling big mounds of crunchy fried crickets is unimpressed and underwhelmed. She caters to office girls from the nearby Sakura Towers. At lunchtime they rush out of the office block in their Western-style office uniforms and flock to the cricket lady's stall, buying small tin containers of oily fried crickets, snacking on them, scrunching the obviously tasty delights in their delicate, pretty mouths.

As I run past the cricket seller, she shakes her head in disgust at the notion of yet another crazy foreigner let loose. I almost make it to Zawgyi's when an umbrella-wielding Indian gentle-man places himself resolutely in my path and brings me to a sliding stop. 'Your slippers, sir,' he says with concerned gravitas. He points to my slippers, then to my feet, letting me know that the fundamental raison d'être of a pair of slippers is to place them on one's feet, especially in the wet.

He repeats his advice, pointing to the heavens and the rain, which now teems down, drenching me as I stand there with him in my path. 'Water,' he says, re-enacting his charade-like activity once more, again trying to educate me of the fact that, if I put the slippers on my feet, they will be protected from water.

'Sliding, sir, sliding,' I say, indicating how my sandals slip in the wet. The Indian gentleman looks at me sadly and says, 'Sir, why are you not buying the right slipper for our weather?' Lasheeda doubles with laughter. Her foreign Poppy is pro-viding yet another amusing day for her.

Tragedy strikes Lasheeda next morning as I sit at the Zawgyi Café, having a Sunday morning chat with expatriate friends. Usually Lasheeda will lean an elbow on the top of the small wall separating the café from the street, cup her chin in her hand,

and just watch. If she spots new tourists, she'll rush off to stand in front of them, hold up her postcards and capture their attention with her well-practised beseeching gaze. But this morning she is out of action. She can't work. She sits on the steps to the Zawgyi Café in agony. Tears well in her eyes; she squirms. She is obviously very sick; yet the other street people ignore her, letting her sit and suffer.

I've seen such callousness before but still I am stunned by it, because it is out of keeping with the generous nature of the Myanmar. Yet I have come to accept the sad reality of this strange trait ever since the evening I encountered the dead boy.

I saw him on the Sule Pagoda Road footpath on my daily walk home from the office, near the railway line where the Cindy Crawford Omega watch billboard becomes visible.

At first I thought it was just a bundle of rags but, as I drew closer, I saw the brown legs sticking out of the scrunched-up longyi and I figured it was another sick boy collapsed on the footpath.

Then I saw his face. His mouth was surrounded by porridge-like gruel and his fixed eyes, staring sightlessly into the distance, had started to film over. This boy was beyond sick. This boy was dead.

Like everybody else that evening I put my head down and scurried past, pretending I hadn't seen the tragic sight. Yet, though I could avert my eyes, I couldn't avert my mind from the knowledge that I was walking away from a dreadful scene on Sule Pagoda Road. What I really couldn't under-stand was why the Myanmar people also hurried by without helping one of their own. The Myanmar are one of the most gracious and helpful people I've had the fortune to share life with. And yet they rushed by, as heedless as the stereotypical New Yorker.

The morning after I saw the dead boy, I walked along the same road with the journalist Ma Kyaing Pe. I told her what I'd seen and about my shame at my actions. She bit her lip and said, 'We have all done the same. I have done the same; I have walked past sick people and felt the shame. I think here in Yangon we all have done that at some time in our life.'

But why, I asked her? She told me it's an unwritten law that forces people to ignore the suffering. The police do not like people to become involved. She told me her uncle once stopped to render assistance to a man on the road who'd been knocked over by a car that had then 'run away'. For his trouble, the uncle was arrested and sent to jail for several weeks because the police deemed that he had unlawfully interfered.

'This is what we have had to put up with for so many years,' Ma Pe said. 'And for so many years we have had to remain silent.'

But Lasheeda's plight can't be ignored, not by us anyway. I'm reluctant to accompany her to a doctor in case the examination is delicate, so Nicole, a former Western Australian air hostess working in promotions at a major hotel, says she'll take Lasheeda to a doctor.

They disappear for an hour and on their return Nicole says the doctor diagnosed a case of virulent stomach worms, which apparently grow in a ball and cause intense pain. He cured it with an injection in the bottom, charged Nicole four dollars, and Lasheeda was given a meal of rice and boiled egg.

Now Lasheeda is clowning around on the footpath for the benefit of her friends. She pantomimes a syringe being sunk into her bottom and laughs.

Often on our monsoon journeys Lasheeda and I pass an exclusive Catholic school, and one day she looks at the school with those big eyes of hers, then punches herself on the chest with her finger, saying, 'Me. No school. No money.'

It is her eyes that always do me in. Big, brown and expressive, as I've already described, but there are other elements within them—a sort of feral-ness and a glint of vicious cunning when she assesses situations, in much the same way as a mongoose assesses a cobra before attacking.

And Lasheeda can be vicious. I've seen her belting younger street children who have committed some infraction of whatever rules apply on the mean streets. She is a child, but she isn't messing around. She is on a daily survival mission.

U Ye Myint, my unofficial laundry man and Mr Fixit, is always on hand when I need him. Except now. I see him around and about, but he isn't around for me. Finally I run him to ground, hanging out at the Wuthering Heights teashop on 33rd Street, indulging in his ongoing obsession, the search for the ultimate aphrodisiac, which he needs to fulfil his life mission, to make love to his wife every night. I'm dubious about his claim that he has bonked his wife every night of his 30-year marriage, but he is adamant he has and that it is his sacred duty to do so, explaining, 'You must, Mr Peter, you must, or the woman is not happy.'

He adds wryly that 'the woman' may also suspect he has another lover and, from what I know of U Ye Myint's somewhat mysterious life, such suspicions might be on the money.

U Ye Myint is now in his mid-fifties and he fears his powers are waning, although he suggests his long working hours might be a contributing factor. When I drove across town with him about a fortnight ago, en route to the Famous Superstar bar, he stopped the car in the busy Chinatown downtown district and disappeared down a dingy alley, reappearing holding a plastic bag full of a thick highly questionable greenish-brown liquid, which he assured me would make him 'very strong'.

Now, in the Wuthering Heights teashop, he produces a small tin container and opens it to show me a syringe and several glass ampoules of clear liquid which, according to the instruction leaflet that comes with the kit, is pure testosterone. But I'm not interested in this diversion, and I get down to the business of the day. I tell him I have a two-week load of laundry, and another newly arrived foreigner at the office is also desperate for his services. Normally he'd be happy to pick up the work, but his hesitancy gives me the feeling that perhaps he isn't keen.

The next morning my suspicions are confirmed. U Ye Myint has dumped me as a client. Yesterday he said he'd drop by the office to collect my laundry this morning. But instead a man has come to the office and handed me a sealed envelope addressed to 'Mr Peter' from Ye Myint. I open the envelope and read:

Dear Mr Peter,
I am very sorry to inform you that I won't be able to take your laundry at the appointed time because I have already been booked by another business previous your order instead my friend who will introduce you to woman who want to do your laundry.
    Sorry again for my inconvenience. Thank you for your order.
    U Ye Myint.

It takes several days before I run the elusive U Ye Myint to ground again. I see him changing money in the bar next to the Central Hotel, so I approach and do what most Myanmar hate: ask direct questions.

'Ah Mr Peter, Mr Peter,' U Ye Myint splutters cagily. 'You

are looking very young today. Your dress is beautiful. New laundry person do good work.'

'Yes, thank you, U Ye Myint. But, U Ye Myint, you are avoiding me. You are not doing my laundry anymore, and I would like to know why.'

He splutters again and says, 'I am very frightened, Mr Peter. I don't want to work for the foreigners from the newspaper any more. They are watching me, I know this.'

He tells me why he is now frightened of us foreigners, and I understand his fear. The incident he speaks of caused me trepidation as well and it was to do with my boss, Mr Ross Dunkley.

Dunkley had been invited to the legendary Foreign Correspondents Club of Thailand, in Bangkok, to address what promised to be a feisty forum on Burma, as the Thais insist on calling Myanmar. (The Myanmar in turn call Thailand *Yodoya*, an insulting term dating back to when Burmese troops twice trashed and destroyed the ancient Thai capital of Ayutthaya. Sometimes the Myanmar state press ups the insult ante, referring to Thailand as *Siam*.) But Dunkley's presence at the club caused outrage and he was condemned as a 'disgusting' example of a journalist, because of his role at the *Times*.

He gave a measured speech at the forum, but things then fell apart during the question-and-answer part of the proceedings. Some of the comments Dunkley made about the Myanmar military regime were widely disseminated through the Asian media. *Asia Times Online* quoted him as saying, 'I talk to my journalists and editors about ethics, about the law, about corruption and about what a fucked-up government this is.'

It also quoted him as saying that the recent collapse of the Myanmar banking system was squeezing the regime.

The generals are hurting because the generals and their wives are hoarding away hundreds of thousands or millions of dollars of FEC, Foreign Exchange Certificates—which is the so-called equivalent of US$1 each—and the certificate has plunged to 40 per cent or 50 per cent of its value. They are in deep trouble.

The FEC is a monetary device copied from the Chinese as an alternative to the hard-currency US dollar. The government keeps the dollars and instead dispenses the fake-funny-money FEC, which supposedly has parity to the US dollar but, in reality, rarely does. During the height of Myanmar's recent bank crisis, the FEC fell to a low in value of 55 cents, but later strengthened and hovered around its usual 85 cents or so.

The comment about the generals hoarding wads of cash was particularly unfortunate because, according to office gossip, Brigadier General Thein Swe was in the throes of building a new house.

But the comments made by Dunkley that were the most dangerous centred on his claim that the Myanmar people would welcome a US invasion. Radio Free Asia broadcast this Dunkley declaration:

I live in Yangon and I catch a taxi to work every day. And I speak to a lot of people randomly out on the street, and indiscriminately hear opinions from people who don't know who I am and I don't know who they are. But one thing is pretty common—they all want George W. Bush and the UN to come into Myanmar with a whole lot of guns and airplanes and jets and to solve the problem. They believe that's possible.

Dunkley was furious about that quote because he claimed the word 'naively' was omitted, and his comment should have read, 'They all *naively* want George W. Bush . . .' But I'm not so sure that most Myanmar want a US invasion, naively or otherwise.

Most people I speak to are keen on regime change, but understandably afraid of war or invasion.

When the Iraq war started, I spoke to some of my trainees and quoted a piece to them about how the people of Iraq were being liberated from living in terror under a military regime. I said to the trainees, 'You live in a military regime. Do you live in terror of your regime?'

It took some time for an answer to be elicited, but finally some said yes. I continued, 'So do you want to be liberated by America?' The answer was a vigorous *no* because, they said, an American invasion would simply be exchanging terror for horror. I told Dunkley that the Myanmar had come up with new definitions for terror and horror. Terror was living with the regime, and horror was being saved from it by the Americans.

Dunkley delivered his famous speech on a Thursday night and by Friday his comments had caused gossip throughout Yangon, with many expatriates predicting he'd be thrown out of Myanmar and the *Times* possibly shut down. I turned up at the *Times* the following Monday fully expecting soldiers to be in position, with my brief tenure coming to a quick finale; once again I too would be invited to leave the country on the next flight to Bangkok.

The office was subdued, as was Dunkley. I asked him if we were in danger of being shut down. He said, 'I've certainly copped an earful from the general, but a lid's been put on it and everything seems okay. Some of my speech was taken out of context, and other comments, which were made after my speech, were made on my understanding that they weren't an official part of the night and wouldn't be reported. I've been stitched up a bit but, from what I understand, Khin Nyunt actually wants me to publish the text of my formal speech. So we'll be okay, mate. Have you come across anything more?'

I told him I'd just seen an article from the *Irrawaddy Journal*, an informative daily online newsletter and monthly journal published by the dissident Myanmar journalist Aung Zaw, in Chiang Mai, Thailand. Aung Zaw and Dunkley had slugged it out at the Foreign Correspondents Club, and Dunkley had castigated the dissident publisher for being funded by the US to the tune of $US250 000 annually. Aung Zaw claimed the figure was only $US100 000, and that this 'partial' funding came courtesy of the National Endowment for Democracy, a private non-profit organisation backed by the US Congress.

The Bangkok slugfest had grown more heated when Priscilla A. Clapp, the Charge d'Affaires at the US embassy in Yangon, had said that, although she had been critical of Dunkley two years ago, 'he is one of my heroes today'. She turned on Aung Zaw saying, 'I remind him that he is highly supported by the US government and we did notice his editorial in the Thai press saying that America deserved the attack on September 11.' When Aung Zaw tried to deny this allegation, Clapp added, 'That does not go unnoticed in Washington.' A Dutch NGO had then weighed in, saying, 'I think this is a threat from the American embassy. This is ridiculous. Who do the Americans think they are?'

The *Irrawaddy Journal* is, of course, banned in Myanmar and its website blocked, but pertinent sections are emailed to people in Myanmar. I read Dunkley the relevant *Irrawaddy Journal* paragraph, which had just landed on an office computer:

> Last Thursday Dunkley told how Khin Nyunt and the junta's number two, Maung Aye, were conspiring to oust military leader Than Shwe. 'They want to remove this bastard,' Dunkley said. It's gossip that's been doing the rounds in Bangkok for some time, but now the Australian editor is also spreading the rumour.

Dunkley momentarily put his head in his hands, but then began pounding out words on his keyboard.

The incident also caused a flurry of activity among the Military Intelligence officers employed to deal with the *Times*. The official who deals with the paper on a day-to-day basis and who is in charge of the more routine censorship matters made a rare visit to the office. He is Wai Lin, an urbane middle-aged man who has worked with the Brigadier General for seventeen of the 25 years the Brigadier General has been associated with Prime Minister Khin Nyunt. Wai Lin was keen to avoid a flap because he is hoping to leave this job soon for a position in Washington; he said the Bangkok escapade had caused the department, and him in particular, a lot of extra work, because they had to scrutinise all possible outlets to assess the impact of whatever had been published internationally.

But now the fallout has spread beyond the *Myanmar Times* and intelligence circles, and is certainly panicking many of the Myanmar who provide services to the company or its staff, including Ye Myint. I look at my very-worried former laundry man as he tells me the comments that scared him were those broadcast over Radio Free Asia, quoting the taxi driver who allegedly wanted the US to bomb Myanmar. He says a son of an associate of his heard the comments and relayed them to all concerned, especially drivers or taxi-drivers who regularly deal with the *Myanmar Times*. There's a fear of guilt by association, and several taxi drivers have apparently taken unplanned holidays and are lying low.

U Ye Myint says, 'Yes, Mr Peter, I am frightened. I know what they can do.'

He explains that about a decade ago a man who worked for him had signed up for membership for Aung San Suu Kyi's National League for Democracy. The friend was quite public with his opinions, and he was promptly arrested. About two weeks later his wife was requested to collect his body from the hospital. She found the body slit open from neck to groin and, when it was turned over, its back and buttocks were covered with bruises.

The last word on the Bangkok Foreign Correspondents Club affair, at the *Myanmar Times* anyway, is contained in a poem in the staff card given to Dunkley during the party celebrating his birthday. Part of the poem reads:

> Higher productivity, better news stories,
> Or I'll send in the *#@>?! jets, tanks and bombs.

Surprisingly, Dunkley's outrageousness in Bangkok has somehow endeared him to the more moderate faction of the Myanmar establishment. Dunkley followed the Prime Minster's advice and published an abridged version of his official Correspondents Club speech in the *Times*, and then left for a two-week trip to Uzbekistan and Prague. During his absence word came through suggesting that Prime Minister Khin Nyunt personally has given the okay to the notion of a daily newspaper, a permission the paper's proprietors had been requesting for some time.

In a sense Dunkley seems to have created his own footnote in Myanmar history, becoming the only foreign newspaperman in half a century to make such public criticisms of the regime and be allowed to remain in the country. Perhaps he has been able to survive because he made his comments at a time that may prove a turning point in Myanmar history; perhaps he has been earmarked for punishment at a later date.

Certainly political changes have just taken place within the ruling military junta. About three weeks before the Bangkok incident, at the same time as restrictive US sanctions became official, the government underwent a major reshuffle and Khin Nyunt was officially appointed Prime Minister.

Two opposing interpretations of this event were disseminated by experts and journalists via the international media. One view claimed that Khin Nyunt had been promoted and that these changes, officially revealed in the State newspaper in front-page formal lined-box announcements, were a good thing, heralding the beginnings of a new moderate approach and an increased willingness to engage with the outside world.

The other view was that Khin Nyunt had been demoted into a civilian role and had lost his military power-base; that the government reshuffle was a disaster that would plunge Myanmar even further into darkness and leave the UN-sponsored reconciliation process, commenced in October 2000, in tatters.

About a week after his appointment, the new Prime Minister General Khin Nyunt (who still retains his title as Chief of Military Intelligence) addressed the nation and, in a televised speech, announced the introduction of a roadmap to democracy, including a seven-point plan for a democratic transition.

International opinion seemed to have begun to shift. The BBC World Service suggested that perhaps change could be in the wind and that the Myanmar military, obviously prepared to talk the talk, should be given the opportunity to see if they will actually begin to walk the walk.

But just when international coverage was starting to strike a positive note—and within 24 hours of the PM's speech—the US State Department dramatically announced that democracy icon Aung San Suu Kyi was on a hunger strike. Myanmar instantly reverted to Pariah State status.

Throughout the world—in Tokyo, London and Berlin—

protesters demonstrated over the hunger strike, and inside Myanmar, analysts and journalists feverishly tried to verify the claim. Almost a week after the US announcement, the Red Cross announced that a member of its International Committee had visited Suu Kyi and that she had denied she was on a hunger strike. The US State Department said it was relieved to hear that Suu Kyi was not hunger-striking, but stood by its claim, saying that she had been refusing food.

Even stranger was a statement in an Agence France-Presse syndicated news report that an anonymous US official claimed the US ran with the story simply to get access to Suu Kyi. The official was quoted as saying, 'We publicised this to raise international concerns and bring some pressure on the Burmese. I would say that at least that has resulted in the Red Cross being able to visit her and see that she's okay . . .'

Meanwhile, an enterprising Thai entrepreneur, Sunthorn Petchlern, opened a chain of Suu Kyi noodle shops throughout Bangkok, named Suu Kyi Egg Mee Kiew.

The longer I live in Myanmar, the more I become caught up in a curiously contrasting and intriguing cultural crossfire. Yesterday I became a sayar; today I'm being inducted as a hash virgin.

Yesterday, as a newly inducted sayar, I was given a uniform consisting of longyi and shirt. Today, I will surrender my hash virginity while wearing a uniform of black shorts, white T-shirt and aerated Adidas Clima-Cool running shoes.

Yesterday, I sat on a rigid-backed chair while dozens of staff kowtowed and touched their foreheads to the ground to show respect to me and ten other sayars sitting side by side. Today, in the cruel mid-afternoon heat, I will congregate with dozens of Hash House Harriers at a starting point, the Inya Lake Yacht Club, and then we will run like crazy people along a pre-set course.

Yesterday marked the end of the three-month-long annual Buddhist Lent, which the Yangonites celebrated with their usual fervour. For the last couple of evenings, the night skies have been dotted with blazing fire lanterns gently floating on the breezes, and kids have been running amok with fireworks, aiming thousands of shrieking skyrockets across the streets or up and over the roofs of the crowded downtown tenements.

I was aware that the Buddhist Lent was winding up, but I wasn't aware that a sayar ceremony was to take place at the office. During the day I noticed the Myanmar reporters were restless. I kept receiving strange comments about my age and experience, and about sayars. Early in the afternoon, work abruptly ceased and staff began frenetically pushing office furniture out of the way, creating a hall-like space at one end of the office, where eleven tall-backed wooden chairs were then placed against an emptied wall.

The giggling staff congregated in front of the chairs, taking off their footwear and kneeling on the floor. One of the women told me we were about to pay respect and offer obeisance to the sayars, the experienced men in the office, the men who had wisdom to impart.

Several senior men filed in and sat on the chairs. The kneeling Myanmar burst into a bout of frenzied kowtowing— bobbing forward so their heads touched the floor, lifting their heads, then bobbing forward again. Working on the principle of 'when in Rome . . .', I knelt on the floor and copied the kowtowing actions of the person next to me, but a sayar said, 'Peter, get up off the floor and join us here.'

I took my seat as a sayar and the staff began kowtowing again, almost hysterically. It was a strange experience for me to sit there watching people zealously perform acts of worship, but I figured it was something I could get used to fairly quickly. It was perhaps akin to being a lower-order African chief.

A staff member stood and read a letter of homage to us sayars, and then some of the sayars addressed the staff, who nodded in exaggerated and over-obvious agreement at the words of wisdom being cast before them. The experience, or ritual, almost became a parody of itself.

Each sayar was then given a gift-wrapped parcel containing a brown-checked longyi, and a Chinese-style white long-sleeved collarless 'business' shirt. These shirts, which had earlier caught my fancy, are fastened at the neck with a gold stud or sometimes a gold stud embedded with a small ruby.

Sayar Colonel (Retired) Hla Moe, sub-editor and sports-writer, gave some tips about getting on in life, including the taking up of golf. I thought to myself that the Colonel (Retired) could do with some tips himself about preserving life, like refraining from practising his golf swing in the foyer. On several occasions in the past months, I had stepped out of the lift and only barely avoided a beheading from one of the Colonel's whizzing woods. He is, like many of his kind in Myanmar and indeed throughout Asia, addicted to the game.

The Californian surf-and-sportswear label, Hang Ten, has spawned a series of Hang Ten boutiques in the inner suburbs of Yangon. Recently I despatched a trainee to write a story on why a predominantly surfing-oriented company is popular in a city that is hundreds of kilometres from any surf, a city where there isn't a surfboard to be seen. The trainee wrote that the label is considered prestigious among hip young people, and that there is a big demand for the polo shirts and sports slacks among military officers, who proudly don the Hang Ten uniform for their weekend golf games.

To conclude the sayar ceremony, the office Buddhist mentor, sayar Dr Saw Win, who doubles as the photo librarian, offered a list of prayers to help free the staff from 98 causes of death.

That was yesterday, sayar day. Today is hash day, a strange cultural proclivity perpetrated by mad dogs, Englishmen and caucasian foreigners of many persuasions, occurring in the blazing mid-afternoon sun.

Many years ago I vowed to steer clear of these mad bastards. Over the decades I've come across packs of them rampaging through Asian cities, bedecked in stupid T-shirts, chanting, blowing trumpets, drinking, sweating, crowding locals off the footpaths. I wanted nothing to do with them.

But in Yangon I have realised that the most effective way to expand my circle of expatriate acquaintances is to succumb to a hash run. And so, kitted out in running gear, I catch a taxi to the Inya Lake Yacht Club, the gathering ground for the Yangon chapter of the Hash House Harriers, ready to obey the trumpet clarion, ready to drink beer and run along a pre-set shredded-paper-marked trail though the outer reaches of Yangon, but not quite ready to wear a daggy T-shirt.

The Hash House Harriers was started by an Englishman, Albert Stephen Ignatius Gispert, in Kuala Lumpur in 1938, and the name was derived from the Selangor Club Chambers, known as the 'Hash House' due to its stodgy food. The custom, once restricted to Asian expatriate groups, spread throughout the world and there are now, unfortunately, about 1500 clubs in almost every major city in the globe.

The significance of the Yangon hash has become very evident this year because it has usurped a sacred American expatriate tradition, the Marine Ball, honouring the contingent of US marines posted here as embassy guards. The annual ball is held around the world, wherever US marines are stationed, on a set Saturday in November and this year, 2003, it is set for November 10. But, because this will coincide with what is called an inter-hash run, with runners from all over Asia coming to Yangon for the weekend, our local Marine Ball has been pushed to another weekend. This will put it out of kilter with the rest of the world's Marine Balls, a development that, for true adherents of the US Marine *esprit de corps*, borders on the sacrilegious. But such is the power of the hash.

Luckily the monsoon rains have desisted and the weather is clear and sparkling when I arrive at the Yacht Club grounds. I discover about 50 expatriates and a smattering of Myanmar milling around, so I mill towards a group that included an official from the British embassy who is, according to gossip among some Western women that I overheard the instant I alighted from the cab, accompanied by a Myanmar woman suspected of being a hooker.

Myanmar women are a constant temptation for Western men because they are mostly so beautiful and gracious and, although they are strong-willed and strong-minded, they are also gentle in their dealings with men. This makes many Western women secretly fear them, often dismissing them as subservient Third-World victims of men, and in urgent need of feminist re-education.

Hopefully Myanmar women will withstand the confusing mish-mash of knee-jerk dogma espoused by the many earnest Westerners who drift into the nation, often employed by NGOs and aid agencies, intent on one hand on preserving the traditional cultural values in their host countries, and yet on the other hand, intent on 'saving' the local women by exhorting them to think and act in mirror image of themselves. It's a sort of unwitting cultural imperialism practised by Westerners who regard themselves as the antithesis of imperialists. It usually doesn't fool the locals.

Asian women are much misunderstood by many of their Western counterparts. The politeness of Asian women, their reluctance to act against family wishes and their social acquiescence to traditional authority figures is the opposite of how many educated Western women comport themselves.

Perhaps it is the Asian women who can in fact liberate the Western women. Rather than being weak, Asian women are often strong and at ease with their roles, and it's no accident that there are and have been so many powerful women in Asian politics, in India, Indonesia, Sri Lanka, Pakistan, the Philippines and so on. And of course Suu Kyi in Myanmar.

Myanmar women in particular are noted for their strength and independence, and there's a strong feminine element to the country, but not in the way Western feminists view matters. One of Myanmar's leading women writers wrote a tract on Western feminism, opining that while women like her respect the aims of Western feminists they do not necessarily agree with the methods, particularly the erosion of the traditional female nurturing aspect, the denial of positive aspects of masculinity, and the confrontational nature of the process. She derided the notion of a battle of the sexes, saying that change should not be war but mutual accommodation.

But perhaps the aspect of Asian life that most angers Western women is the overt prostitution and the pornography of sex shows in bars in seamy parts of Bangkok and other Asian capitals. Once again, this is a nest of oft-misunderstood seething cultural contradictions. The attitude toward sex in Asia is more practical. While officially Asian nations are far more 'prudish' about sex than the West, the unofficial practicalities are more accommodating.

The *Times*' resident women's rights journalist, Kyaing Pe, told me, with great amusement, that, 'In public we are like the Western women and we say that we hate sluts. But privately we are different to Western women. We thank the sluts, even respect them, because they keep our men from pestering us until we are ready to have sex with them.'

While prostitution is regarded by Westerners as endemic in Asian cities, the number of brothels in many Western cities, particularly Australian cities, is surprising, and newspapers feature hundreds of sex-for-sale advertisements.

Little wonder then that Asians become a tad perplexed when Westerners, especially women, rail against Asian sleaziness and female exploitation. The real reason that Asian cities attract Western sex tourists is not always because there are more hookers; it is simply that they are cheaper and often kinder toward their clientele.

I approach the hash group containing the embassy official and his putative prostitute at precisely the moment some of her female friends approach from the opposite direction; among these I spot Thet Tha, a slim, swivel-hipped, dark-skinned beauty from Mandalay, with satsuma breasts and full, fleshy, pouting lips which she coats with glossy pale pink lipstick. I met her one evening in the ABC Pub in Maha Bandoola Street and we struck up a friendship based on flirtation. I enjoy her insouciance and the mellifluous modulation of her voice, and she seems to enjoy my cheeky sense of humour, so we chat and laugh until the hash trumpet intervenes, messily and wetly blurting like the farting of a diarrhoeic donkey. This is the signal for all us hash participants to gather in a circle, receive our instructions, team into small groups, and jump into cars that ferry us to the official starting point of today's run through a poor part of town, the slums areas on the outskirts of Yangon.

Once we have congregated at the starting point and are shuffling on the spot, the strident trumpet blurts again and off we set. I keep pace with hashers in the middle of the pack until we come to a series of rickety wooden bridges crossing drains.

Downtown Yangon in all its busy funkiness—just mind the holes in the footpath!

Unofficial Daughter No. 1, Lasheeda, and her apprentice practise the look of a thousand beseeching eyes.

Beautiful postcard sir, only one dollar, only one dollar, very beautiful.

Spray that again—getting wet is the way to go during the Thingyan Water Festival in Yangon.

Living in a Yangon monsoon is like living in a laundromat.

School's out: pupils stroll along a country lane deep in the heart of the Shan State.

How exasperating! There's no accounting for the gossip to be heard during the hill tribe women's weekly shopping expedition at Kyaing Tong central market.

Peace and calm prevail on the waters of Myanmar's extravagantly beautiful Inle Lake.

The wood is still slick from the morning monsoon deluge and chunks have rotted away, leaving ragged, gaping holes. I've already undergone my seemingly obligatory Yangon falling-hole-event, so I gingerly pick my way across the teetering bridges, slipping to the back of the pack until I am the last runner, plodding in the wake of a small, pudgy, neurotic woman reluctantly and tentatively shuffling herself in a forward direction, like an overstuffed agoraphobic guinea pig.

As we run and stumble through isolated poverty-stricken villages on the outskirts of town, with the braying trumpet brazenly urging us forever onward, I become aware of the stunned reactions of the locals, who rarely see foreigners at all and *never* see mad foreigners running through their villages en masse.

As word spreads of our pilgrimage, villagers line the narrow, rutted streets shrieking with laughter—except for the kids, who shriek in terror. Mothers giggle while protectively cuddling their kids.

In one village the kids stand transfixed, staring, and when I make a move towards them they shiver in fear, looking like rabbits caught in a spotlight. In another village I am astounded to see a familiar face, one of Lasheeda's young street-kid friends who also sells postcards on the road outside my apartment. Now, as he proudly waves at me, pointing me out to his parents, I understand the poverty that necessitates his working all day every day to earn a few cents from foreign tourists.

I see two women dressed in elaborate costume. They are proudly walking along a dusty village boulevard, dodging pariah dogs scratching furtively for food, stepping around scrawny, long-legged chickens pecking desperately in the dirt, and avoiding slothful pigs reeking from their wallows in the nearby nauseating open drains. At first I figure they may be from an exotic hill tribe but, as I draw closer, I realise they are university students in their graduation gowns performing a walk of honour through their village.

I see groups of women sitting on the footpaths processing empty soup cans. One group of women soaks the cans, peeling off the paper. The next group in the production line cuts the tops and bottoms from the cans, while another group cuts the cans along their length, flattening them and stacking them so they can be collected by men on bicycles and taken to town to be sold. So much industriousness for so little return. But that's poverty.

The run finishes at a predetermined gathering point under a bridge, where all participants 'circle up' for club rituals, mainly involving 'downings'. A variety of people nominated by the Hash Master—who refers to them by their hash names, such as SpermStopper, Kiss Me Hardy and Deep Throat—are compelled to down, or skol, beers to a chant of 'Down, down, down!' Visitors from other clubs have to down a beer as a form of greeting. Club members leaving Yangon have to down a beer. I have to down several beers. I have to undergo a virgin's downing, obligatory for all people on their first-ever hash run.

Then I am 'outed' because I'd been spotted buying betel nut at a village stall. 'The only official drug on a hash is beer,' declares the Hash Master, who is bruised and bleeding from badly lacerated legs after falling through a hole in one of the rickety bridges we crossed. He makes a ruling that I have to down another beer, but this one causes a sharp stitch-like pain to momentarily burn across my stomach. It's happened before and I figure maybe I should take it easy on the beer.

The downing rituals, speeches and announcements drone on and on until the sun suddenly plummets from the sky. We are mobbed by kids desperately holding out their cute, grubby little hands for the cans from which we are drinking when we aren't downing the official pots of hash beer. At first I think the kids are desperate for a drink, but no—they crave the empty cans because, like the women on the footpaths, they can sell them for the equivalent of about one seventh of a cent.

Eventually the mad rituals come to a close. A club news-letter, parodying the language of the *New Light of Myanmar*, is passed around. It contains possibly the only topless photos of women published in the length and breadth of Myanmar. The hashers disperse into the Yangon twilight, their invitations to each other for drinks gatherings yodelling through the dark grey velvet evening air.

But I decline all such invitations because there's a nagging worry in the back of my mind about the strange pain that insinuated itself into my side toward the end of the hash run. It's still there, niggling away, coming and going as it has for the past few days. Actually, make that the past few weeks. Perhaps I should consider doing something about it.

When it finally happened, it happened quickly. The brief stomach pains that had bothered me for weeks suddenly increased in severity and duration until the pain was so intense I couldn't bear it. And, unlike before, it didn't go away.

Hardly able to stand, I fell into a taxi, which took me across Yangon to the International SOS Clinic, where I was referred to a Myanmar surgeon, Dr U Nyan Thein, an American- and Irish-trained medico with an outstanding reputation. Within an hour I was rushed to Yangon's Asia Royal Cardiac and Medical Care Clinic, where I was diagnosed as suffering from an acutely infected gall bladder and a secondary infection of the bowels, which required immediate attention.

The checking-in process was torture. I was in intense pain, and a sulky, churlish male orderly added to my grief. He asked for a list of my attendees. I didn't know what he was talking about, but I was told 'attendees' are the family members and loved ones who move in with the patient to provide care, to cook, to monitor. There is great shame in Myanmar in not having family members to care and nurture, and the orderly became judgemental when I couldn't produce one solitary member of my clan or any clan connected to me.

He waffled on with a diatribe about abandoning families and in turn being abandoned by them. He invoked the name of Aung San Suu Kyi, who only recently had been in this same hospital with gynaecological problems. He said that, because she had abandoned her mother to live in England with her foreigner husband, the karmic consequences of her action now doomed her to exist in her large house on Inya Road by herself, without family.

I didn't bother to argue that Daw Suu had in fact returned from England to look after her mother and it was then that she became politicised and embarked on the heroic path that had such dramatic consequences for her. I didn't bother explaining that Suu Kyi was no longer rattling around her mansion by herself, but was sitting in a prison cell. I simply told the guy to finish the forms and get me help.

While waiting for whatever was to happen next, my mind dwelt on the nightmarish stories I'd heard about Myanmar hospitals. One of the biggest fears harboured by expatriates in Yangon is to be carted off to a local hospital. If expatriates become ill they quickly flee to Bangkok or Singapore, as do many of the generals. The horror stories about Yangon hospitals are embellished as they travel the rounds in expatriate circles.

A French restaurateur who'd been involved in a bad accident on his motorcycle, injuring a Myanmar pedestrian, had told me of his ordeal. He had to be admitted to the casualty section of the public hospital, the Yangon General Hospital, as part of the officially dictated, lengthy, drawn-out, time-consuming and expensive procedure expatriates involved in such incidents must undergo. He said he lay on a gurney in a corridor where bedlam reigned. People with horrific injuries died in front of him, and the side door of the corridor was left open so that he looked out at a dusty, filthy alley. An accident victim had been wheeled in and parked in the corridor. Blood and gore from the man's wounds had seeped through the steel gurney holes onto the floor, and several pariah dogs slunk in from the alley to lick and slurp the gore.

The restaurateur smiled wryly when he said he had noticed patients occasionally being rushed though a door that displayed the sign, 'Reincarnation Room'.

A *Times* colleague, Paul Giles, who had also been hospitalised in Yangon, had warned of the reluctance of staff to use effective painkillers. A stoic Buddhist attitude of toughing it out is expected of patients, and medication containing opiates is unavailable in Myanmar, a strange anomaly considering the country's dubious status as the world's second largest illicit-opium-producing nation.

But before I could worry too much about what might happen, a hospital crew suddenly arrived and swung into action. I was hooked up to tubes and jabbed with needles.

Treatment commenced, but language difficulties and pain left me disoriented and confused until the staff showed mercy and produced a small vial containing a powerful Bangladeshi painkiller, which was administered via an intramuscular injection into my buttock.

The pain was gone, but a hitch arose. IV line infection set in quickly, caused by my hairy foreigner arms. After the airtight tape was in place, those cunning little hairs rose like bean sprouts, pushing up the tape, breaking the airtight seal and letting infection set in. 'Not good enough,' deemed the female duty doctor. 'I will give the job to my most experienced hand.'

Enter the Head Night Nurse, a strong, powerful, good-looking woman who knew how to take charge and now had the job of figuring out how to stop the foreigner's arm hair from breaking the airtight seal. She left the room momentarily and returned with her angelic nursing aide, Krapit Phaw. Her name means Christmas Flower in the Karen language, and she was given it because she was born on Christmas Day. Earlier Krapit had left a little note for me: 'Nice is Krapit Phaw'.

Christmas Flower and Head Night Nurse stood beside me, grinning mysteriously, and then Head Night Nurse revealed the surprise: a little plastic shopping bag containing one cheap, bright yellow Chinese razor and one blade in a packet. 'Shevvin' arm,' she said.

I finally started to heal and one early dawn, the time when souls traditionally leave the body, I became bored with being hooked up to the Plop Plop, as Krapit Phaw and I had named the IV drip. I unhooked myself from the device, lay back, and basked in newfound freedom.

The Head Night Nurse popped her smiling head into the room but, when she saw the disassembled IV tube, her face hardened. She strode forth like a leopard hunting prey, closely examining the removed IV line. Emotions flitted across her face: amazement, disbelief, seething anger. 'You,' she said, pointing at me. 'You do this?'

'Yes,' I muttered meekly. She was about to blow her stack. She paced the room to cool off, then grabbed the discarded IV line, snaked it through the air and threw it in the bin, informing me that the whole IV line now had to be replaced.

Next night was cannula replacement night. But when Head Night Nurse unhooked me, she explained in sign language and the few words of English she knew that I could have one hour of freedom before being hooked up again.

I stretched languorously, but she shook her head. 'No, no, get up, walking,' she commanded. She led me to the back of the ward, opened a door and pushed me out onto a narrow landing. 'Look,' she said, pointing at the magnificent night vista of Yangon's Shwedagon Pagoda bathed in an ethereal golden haze created by the monsoon's mists. It was beautiful but, after ten minutes of contemplation, I returned to the ward, intending to take to my bed again. But Head Night Nurse was stationed at her desk writing notes, and snapped, 'No bed, walking, walking.' She pumped her arms, indicating active physical motion.

Aha, she wants me to walk briskly, I deduced—no big deal. But when I set out to stride forth, it was a big deal. My right leg, weakened from several intramuscular injections, gave way and I almost fell over. I hobbled a few laps of the ward and gradually began walking normally. After several circuits Head Night Nurse took me back to my bed, ready to be hooked up to the IV again.

I started feeling much better and looked forward to getting out of hospital and returning to work. Krapit Phaw stopped by to tell me I could soon go home. She gave me her address and made me promise that I would visit her on her birthday, Christmas Day.

After my fourth night in hospital I was declared healed, but the male duty doctor said I needed to stay another night and do physical exercises so I could walk properly. 'The Head Night Nurse has already done that for me,' I said. The Head Night Nurse nodded assent. 'And I showed him the Pagoda,' she added.

As I walked out of the ward and headed to the elevator, the duty doctor gave me a tip regarding a healthy future. He said Head Night Nurse was, like me, unmarried.

The 2003 monsoon season officially ended at 8.38am on Friday 24 October, when, with my 007 key-tag in hand, I tried to liberate my brolly from the umbrella stand.

But the doorman was wheeling the stand away, and said, 'Putting umbrellas in storage, sir. Rainy season is finished.'

I walked to the office and, just as I crossed the bridge on Sule Pagoda Road, black clouds scudded over, blocking out the sun and unleashing a torrential outburst that drenched me.

It's twelve days since I was discharged from hospital. The monsoon has gone, but the pain has returned, and now I'm writhing in agony on a small bed in the casualty ward at Asia Royal.

This morning, Sunday morning, I was having coffee with friends at the popular J's Donut café and telling them how I was looking forward to flying to northern Thailand tomorrow to start my holiday, when the pain came back, worse than before, if that's possible. I was on the verge of collapse so I excused myself abruptly, staggered from my chair, hobbled across Bogyoke Aung San Road to my apartment and threw myself onto the bed. The pain was so severe I contemplated getting a razor from the bathroom to slit myself open so I could remove the offending gall bladder and throw it against the wall.

I rang Doctor Nyan Thein and he told me to get to hospital as quickly as possible. So here I am in Casualty—surveying the scene through a haze of pain—when I spot Head Night Nurse. She's obviously clocking off from her night shift and she's just changed out of her uniform into a colourful longyi.

But when she sees me on the bed and realises I am in a bad way, she pushes up her sleeves and takes charge. She leans over me and says, 'You. You remember me, eh?' I smile briefly. How could I not remember her?

When I checked out of hospital a dozen days ago, I optimistically declared myself cured to the world at large via an article I wrote about my experience for the *Myanmar Times* English-language version. The article, complete with a cartoon of me in my hospital bed with my foreigner's long nose obviously protruding, was also translated into the widely read Myanmar-language edition.

But the curse of journalism is that words nonchalantly committed to the word processor during a day's work have a habit of coming back and biting the journalist on the bum, as the saying goes in Australia. The article I'd written, complete with the line about the doctor recommending I marry the Head Night Nurse to ensure a healthy future, appeared on the streets this very morning and now here I am this afternoon with Head Night Nurse administering to me once again.

My embarrassment about this is quickly overwhelmed by another wave of searing pain. A small brown bottle of the potent Bangladeshi painkiller used sparingly at the hospital is produced, a syringe prepared and the long intramuscular needle is buried in my bottom.

The surgeon arrives and his news is grim. The quick return of the infection means that there is no option other than to remove the offending organ, and there is no out from Yangon for me. The infected gall bladder rules out air flight, due to the dangers presented by air pressure dynamics. I am due for the chop, and I am due for the chop in Yangon.

It's early in the evening and a procession of nurses and orderlies files into my room. 'Come. We take you to operation,' a nurse says gently. I am wheeled down corridors, thinking, this is how death-row prisoners must feel en route to the lethal injection. I enter a brightly lit operating theatre, am briskly strapped down in crucifix form, and before I know what is happening I am well beyond knowing what is happening.

I emerge from this nothingness some hours later to gradually comprehend that I am enmeshed in a bizarre, horrible nightmare. My eyes are gummed together and, when I can manage to open them slightly, bright lights hit them and make them water and close again.

And then it hits me. Pain. Searing pain. 'Pain, pain,' I gasp. 'Painkillers, please, painkillers.'

A woman doctor leans over and looks me in the eyes. 'Relax, you must relax. Relax and pain will soon go away.'

'No, no,' I reiterate. 'Painkiller, painkiller.'

The doctor says, 'It has been a very long operation. It is early in the morning. Surgeon tired. He go. There is no instruction for painkiller.'

I don't care what she says. I want painkillers so I start chanting loudly, 'Kill me or kill the pain. Kill me or kill the pain.' The woman doctor vanishes into the pre-dawn, saying she will phone the *Myanmar Times* executive, Ma Thin Thin, at her home. The doctor returns and says, 'Okay, we give painkiller.' My new friends, the small brown bottle of Bangladeshi painkiller and the long, thin intramuscular syringe, are produced and soon I am swathed in a cocoon of sweet, marvellous, cosy painlessness.

My recuperation is quick, successful, relatively painless and at times even pleasant. The surgeon pops in to see me, and he is accompanied by a nurse carrying a small plastic bag full of green glunkish liquid and small objects: 351 gallstones from my removed bladder. 'I am thinking of entering you in the *Guinness Book of Records*,' says Dr Nyan Thein. 'I have never even heard of someone with so many gallstones.' He hands me a computer disc containing digital photos he took of my dissected gall bladder.

During the nights my constant companion is a young, good-looking intern, who's only recently graduated from university. Having been weaned off the powerful Bangladeshi painkiller, I am now on the only analgesic normally administered for pain if stoic Buddhist meditation is beyond the patient. This is a useless, low-dose paracetamol, administered as an anal suppository, which the hospital staff continually insist is a method far superior to oral administration. No matter how vociferously I try to beg off this embarrassment, my night companion insists she must obey the instructions, as she slides on her latex glove. On my last night in hospital she chides me about my strange Western squeamishness regarding anal suppositories. She hands me a parting gift: a handful of suppositories and a dozen latex gloves.

A few days before my holiday leave ends, I unlock the door to my downtown Yangon apartment, lugging my holiday-in-hospital souvenirs: an invoice stating, 'Medical equipment & supplies and skill services, for the best services with our sincere and experienced person, we are to bill for US$1000'; a neat four-inch scar; a preserving jar containing 351 gallstones, plus a computer disc with holiday snaps of my dissected gall bladder.

And, of course, my dozen latex gloves.

The monsoon rains are easing and on days like today, when the sun pushes apart the cloud curtain, I recuperate from my operation by lazing beside the pool at my apartment complex, reading the *Bangkok Post*, the *Bangkok Nation* and the *Straits Times*, filling in crosswords, and swimming. The incision across my stomach is stiff and painful when I move, and swimming helps make it supple and soft, relieving the pain and aiding the healing.

I'm doing a lot of deep thinking too, which friends tell me is natural after a brush with mortality. My Buddhist mentor, Dr Saw Win, visited me and gave me meditation tapes, which I listened to today, before I came to the pool. Now, sitting by the pool, I copy the cadence of the tape. I am sitting, sitting, sitting. I. Am. Sitting. And. Thinking. I am sitting, sitting, sitting and I am thinking, thinking, thinking.

I begin the journey to the centre of my mind and, as I mentally travel, I think back on what I've just been through. And, even though I know it's a Hallmark greeting card cliché, I think about the meaning of life. Or, more precisely, the meaning of my life.

I'm fast coming to the conclusion that at present my life lacks meaning, that I'm aimlessly drifting through the world and, whereas I once celebrated the aloneness of the long-distance traveller, now I worry that I might simply be becoming lonely. And whereas once I only thought single, now I'm thinking double. Like double as in two for life's tango. Like love. Like maybe I should fall in love? Like maybe that's the purpose that my life is lacking.

I joke in my head that operations do weird things to the

psyche, but I know I'm not fooling myself. Yesterday I lay here by the pool watching a French family—a young guy, an adorable brown toddler, and a beautiful wife of Polynesian descent wearing a brief sparkling yellow bikini over a dangerously curved brown body. They were all caught up in each other's radars. They only had minds for themselves. They were lost in each other's company, they swam in their love, and I envied them.

I recall the American couple I met briefly at Ngapali, who read an Ian McEwan book together and who were obviously so deeply in love. I envied them too. I want to be like them but, for that to happen, *me* has to become *we*. Shit! Suddenly I realise I sound like a new-age self-help book title.

Besides, what am I on about? I've got a good thing going as a confirmed bachelor.

Except that, as a bachelor, maybe I'm no longer so confirmed. The peace by the pool is rent asunder by a group of Myanmar women buzzing to the water's edge like a small swarm of colourful bees. They're here for their swimming lessons—a good thing, considering most Myanmar can't swim.

But, spotting me, the women come to a faltering stop. They lift their hands to their mouths and titter. They surprise me by jumping into the pool fully clothed, and then removing their blouses and skirts, which they've worn over their blue Speedo-style swimming costumes. They slosh their sodden raiments over the side of the pool onto the concrete where the garments will quickly dry, and while they do this they glance surreptitiously at me, once again holding their hands to their mouths and tittering when they realise I am still watching.

Modesty, Myanmar-style.

Modesty rules this nation. When I first came to Myanmar, I thought such modesty was old-fashioned and foolish, but now I've come to regard it as an endearing quality. Women cover themselves basically from neck to ankle, although the covering is close-fitting and quite sensual. Breasts, however, are never accentuated, and brassieres are thick affairs that not only flatten but also ensure there is no hint of nipple.

Women with large, prominent breasts are in danger of being regarded as sluts, and yet, despite this banishment of the bosom, breast-feeding in public is common throughout Myanmar. Many Myanmar regard Western women as sleazy because of their immodest dress, but I enjoy confusing the Myanmar by telling them that until quite recently Australian women were not allowed to breast-feed in public.

A perhaps unwitting (but I suspect not) result of the modest dress worn by Myanmar women is that I, like many men, find it compellingly and compulsively exotic and erotic. While breasts and bare flesh are de-emphasised, attention is drawn to the derriere, which is invariably shapely, perfectly formed and encased in a caress of curve-hugging, silken longyi. Myanmar is a callipygian paradise, and many times I have discreetly watched Myanmar women walking away from me, their cute bottoms swinging lazily like palm leaves blowing in a soft breeze, their long black hair twitching pony-like over the buttocks, and their parasols dangling over their shoulders, protecting their delicate, pretty complexions from the sun's intrusion. A further febrility-inducing feature (among Western men at least) is that those shapely, longyi-encased female Myanmar derrieres often seem devoid of even a hint of, ahem, lingerie lines.

Modesty in Myanmar is a two-way street. It is expected and it is accorded. A woman breast-feeding in public is deemed natural, and her privacy is guaranteed in that no-one looks. The same when people squat to pee by the sides of the roads—no-one looks. When I visit the tailors to have my trouser legs measured, the changing room is in people's minds. When I strip to put on my untailored trousers, the entourage of half-a-dozen seamstresses—on hand to measure and pin—simply turn their backs and chatter until I give them the all-clear.

At the *Myanmar Times* I share an office with the legendary writer Chit Thein Oo, known as CTO, who, like many veteran Yangon journalists, has undergone a stretch in 'the can' for the crime of being an outspoken 'Christian communist', as he puts it. Often he'll take time out from examining English magazines featuring topless women to rail at the immodesty of the dress worn by a couple of the female American interns employed at the *Times*.

One morning he blew his stack. 'Look at her,' he said, taking a puff from the battered oxygen tank his medical condition dictates must be constantly by his side. 'She is showing her breasts. She must want us to look at them, but if we look at them she gets angry. I don't know where to look. I don't know how you Western men put up with it. If that is democracy, then we don't want it.'

'Please, CTO,' I demurred. 'Don't expect me to explain the ways of young American women.'

He showed me an influential essay he had written, a reflection on a parody of Kipling's famous 'On the Road to Mandalay' poem. Incidentally, Kipling never actually visited Mandalay, although another famous writer, George Orwell, did visit the exquisitely named city, giving it a bum rap. He wrote, 'Mandalay is a rather disagreeable town—it is dusty and intolerably hot, and it is said to have five main products all beginning with a P, namely, pagodas, pariahs, pigs, priests and prostitutes.'

The parody of Kipling's Mandalay ditty was, according to CTO, written by a patriot and circulated in the 1930s, when Myanmar was striving hard to defend and protect its culture from the infiltration of—as well as the outright invasion by—'alien cultural traits'.

The parody read:

On the road to Mandalay
She was smoking her saybawlay;

From a tiny hleyin cart
She alighted prim and smart;
With Acheik Htamein and velvet slipper
She had no bacon nor kipper;
No khabab, khauksway nor parata;
Her simple food was dein-nyin-thee
And toe-za-yar;
Look here, meinkhalay,
Why can't you do the same today?

CTO claimed that during the period the parody was circulated, an upsurge of nationalism called on all Myanmars to wear only locally produced clothes, known as pinni eingyi and yaw longyi. He wrote:

Earlier, young monks in Mandalay had moved around brutally 'admonishing' young ladies wearing blouses made of imported, thin transparent materials—by beating them with pin-tipped canes in the Zegyo and other public places.

It has been about 70 years since then and from today's point of view the poem itself is out-dated, the sentiments it expresses no longer in accord with the times. Myanmar ladies still wear Acheik Htamein and velvet slippers, but the designs are totally different and the way in which they are worn fashionable and up to date. Myanmar meinkhalays (young women) no longer travel by hleyin cart and do not smoke saybawlay. Of course, they still like eating dein-nyin-thee and toe-sa-yar, but this is not their sole food—today, they enjoy all kinds and no one would admonish them for eating khauksway or parata; these have become Myanmar food.

The patriot's poem represented the milder form of reminder to young ladies and girls of the need for them to protect the Myanmar mode of dress and to eat only

Myanmar food as part of the struggle to regain national identity and independence, waged under the slogan: 'Myanmar is our language; love our language. Myanmar is our land; love our land. Myanmars are a master race.'

The mistresses of the master race who have been swimming in my apartment's pool now, perhaps emboldened by their immersion, flop out of the pool, gather their clothes, look at me, hold their hands to their mouths and titter, and run off to the privacy of the locker room area.

It's silent again and my thoughts return to ruminations about relationships. I'm enamoured of Myanmar women and I wonder if a meaningful liaison between oriental and occidental could be established. A voice suddenly clicks into my thought process like a Microsoft pop-up window. It's the sibilance of the witchy woman from the House of Joy, saying, 'She will come to you in Yangon.'

I detect a near-at-hand susurration and glance toward a clump of green by the back wall of the apartment complex. A shiver travels through the grass. I step over to look and glimpse an elegant, small cobra slithering in the growth, then disappearing into a hole in the wall.

I bounce out of bed on the first Monday of December, recuperated and ready to go to the office to begin my third, and last, training group. I grab my briefcase and walk out of my apartment complex, exchanging cheery greetings with the staff, past the gardens still full of gardeners and out onto Bogyoke Aung San Road. Where I walk slap-bang into the unexpected: Christmas.

I hadn't expected to experience Christmas in this predominantly Buddhist stronghold, where the government goes out of its way to not officially recognise Christian activities, but Christmas has exploded into life all around me, with the precision that marks Myanmar's beginnings and endings of festivals and seasons. The first Monday of December is obviously officially the first day of Christmas.

Everywhere I look I can see bursts of green tinsel and red holly, but I also notice that the Christ has been taken out of Christmas. There isn't a nativity scene or a Baby Jesus in sight, but the commercial hoopla that surrounds Christmas in the West—the décor, the Santa Clauses, the gift-giving and the merry-making—has been enthusiastically co-opted and gleefully embraced by the festival-mad Myanmar.

I walk into my local supermarket at the La Playt Wun Plaza to be assailed by displays of Christmas decorations imported from neighbouring Thailand. In typical Asian fashion, the decorations are over the top—flashier, gaudier, larger than those I am used to in Australia. I leave the supermarket and walk past the Grand Plaza Hotel, where a dozen labourers are erecting a giant plastic blow-up of a rather sinister-looking Santa Claus with Asiatic features.

A row of roadside stalls near the *Myanmar Times* office has, overnight, been converted from Buddhist trappings to Christmas kitsch. During the last few weeks these stalls have been festooned with Buddhist offerings to the monks, complete with ornate decorations made from carefully folded low-denomination kyat notes. I had admired the bank note origami, with the notes folded into intricate shapes, and I had been intrigued that the paper-money sculptures, which tallied to a tidy sum, had been left out overnight and never stolen. But, come the first Monday of December, the Buddhist décor has disappeared and been replaced with Yuletide glitter.

Back in September I sighted a Christmas card, a lavish but used German card given to me as a present by Lasheeda. But now the footpath stalls in frenetic Maha Bandoola Street stock a variety of locally made Christmas cards, some with traditional Christmas motifs and others made of plastic hearts and flowers.

Most evenings now I sit on the balcony of my downtown apartment overlooking Bogyoke Aung San Road. To my right is a mosque which, as the sun sets, emanates an electronically amplified wailing muezzin call, adding exotic chords to dusky evenings. To my left is a Hindu temple, where strange activity is often on the agenda, usually accompanied by frenetic gong-banging, cymbal-clashing and eerie singing. To add to the religious cacophony, a snaking line of maroon-robed Buddhist monks chanting sutras often threads its way through the throngs. But this evening, on this first Monday in December, a new element has been added to this Asiatic discordance: the Laser Disc and CD shop opposite my apartment has started pumping forth a loud, upbeat version of 'Frosty the Snowman'.

Major department stores and Western-style supermarkets are stringing up Christmas decorations; hoardings are announcing festive season sales, fashion shows and music concerts.

Just as in the West, a winding down is becoming evident as the holiday period approaches. But while the pre-Christmas period in the West becomes a grim jam of surly, battle-weary shoppers in crowded malls and department stores, punctuated by boozy office parties, the Yangon experience is pleasant. The shops are busier, but there is no surliness. Instead, an atmosphere of almost childish glee prevails, with the added buzz of perpetual and persistent gift-giving.

Just as the Myanmar are addicted to festivals, they are habitual gift-givers, and flurries of cards, flowers and small tokens flutter backwards and forwards butterfly-fashion during any event, circumstance or happening that can be deemed an occasion—an endemic generosity that flourishes in this poorest of nations.

At first I was disappointed about this outbreak of Christmas, thinking that it diminished the exotic aspect of my Myanmar experience, especially the constant squawking of 'Frosty the Snowman'. But then I decided to get with the spirit. I stocked up on cards and gifts to give to people; I purchased a Thai creation compounded from green tinsel and golden bells to hang on the door to my apartment; and I stocked my fridge with Christmas cheer, in preparation for an outburst of goodwill to all men and women and peace on earth.

I'm sitting on the steps of a building in Nawaday Street, a block from the office, with my trainees who, as I have told them, are in luck because today they will be paid for simply sitting, watching, observing and taking notes.

So we sit and observe, much to the bemusement of the street vendors who in turn observe us.

At one end of the street, workers are busily decorating the Yuzana Garden Hotel with yet more banners, ribbons and Christmas greetings, and erecting signs announcing yet more fashion shows, music concerts, and a ten per cent discount on everything.

Street commerce unfolds in its typically relaxed manner and, although the majority of street vendors spend their days engaged in earning only a dollar or two, there is no anxiety, no urgency, no desperation. Just an adherence to the Buddhist philosophy of accepting one's lot in life, of living life without having one's guts churned by the bitter worm of envy because, if this life is lived well, the next life will propel the adherent one step up the ladder of fulfilment.

Nawaday Street is a street of contrasts. One side comprises the buildings and grounds of No. 1 State High School, or No. 1 B.E.H.S. Dagon, as it is officially known, Dagon being the downtown suburb. This No. 1 school caters for the No. 1 kids from the ranks of the middle and upper-middle classes of Yangon society—No. 1 kids who are dropped off and picked up daily by family drivers in sleek modern tinted-window saloons, by mums in more modest vehicles, and by taxi-drivers.

The cars simply park on the adjacent four-lane Sule Pagoda Road, which is a feeder route into the city proper. Cars are parked and abandoned in two lanes of the road, while parents chat, socialise and eventually gather their children, creating a higgledy-piggledy traffic jam. Occasionally a traffic cop, resplendent in white jacket, white helmet and snappy sunglasses, will inspect this tangle, scowl, scratch his forehead in exasperation, and then simply disappear.

Some of these traffic policemen attain legendary status in Yangon. Only recently the well-known writer Ma Thanegi related the story of the retired traffic cop, Inspector Let Kaut (Inspector Stiff Arm) who used to administer his own idiosyncratic justice on the spot. If motorists hit and injured a tree, he'd make them physically kiss it until he was satisfied the tree had forgiven the motorist. Unruly and inconsiderate motorists were ordered to do push-ups on the side of the road, or to hold their earlobes, squat in the dust and jump like frogs. Careless women drivers had to run around the nearest post several times. His legend grew when a rich kid was ordered to lick the tarmac. The kid threatened to call his influential dad and Let Kaut told him to do it so they could both lick the road.

On the other side of the street from the school are vendors who cater to the school kids' needs for snacks, stationery, small toys and cute stickers for school bags and books. These are all laid out on patch sheets on the footpath. One of my new trainees, the poised Su Myat Hla, says, 'This type of vendor's stall was my favourite spot during my school days and a place that my mum, who used to pick me up from school, hated most.'

In Myanmar, family businesses, including the humble street stalls, are exactly that—family businesses with the entire family pitching in, including the children, who they often cannot afford to send to school. So, while on one side of Nawaday Street rich kids are in a playground performing physical exercises to the shouting of 'one-two-three' from a loudspeaker, on the other side of the street children are helping to set up stalls, helping to light the charcoal braziers, helping in whatever way they can.

Another of my trainees, Maw Maw San, also ponders this discrepancy in lifestyle and destiny, writing in her exercise book:

I see two young girls selling palm fruit, oranges and papaya. They are gazing at the children playing in the school park. At their age, they should be at school. I feel sorry for them. They are the same age as my nieces, but how poor they are. At the same time I am proud of them because although they are poor, they are not asking anyone for help. They stand on their own feet. I learn from this and make up my mind to try my best and not cry over the spilt milk like two young grocers.

But while open envy is largely absent on the colourful streets of Yangon, hope persists that the present life may somehow be miraculously enriched, and for most grassroots people, the only way such hope is manifested is through gambling. My fellow countrymen, the sunburnt Australians, are said to be so gambling mad they will bet on flies crawling on the wall, but I'd wager the Myanmar could give them a run for their money in the gambling stakes. Gambling is a mania in Yangon, and one of the more common, affordable forms is two-digit gambling: simply guessing what the two lucky random numbers of any day will be.

Sitting on the steps of Nawaday Street, I watch a woman, dressed in a brown longyi, with thick wedges of thanakha on her cheeks, stirring fried cockroach-like creatures called *payit* in a battered, well-worn wok. It is heated on an old charcoal-fuelled brazier, kept alive by the lazy waving of a small wicker fan. Another woman stirs noodles in an old aluminium pot, while her companion serves deep-fried tofu to a customer.

The tofu-seller asks the customer, 'What is the good digit? Do you have any idea?'

The customer replies, 'According to the monk, the probability is five. More likely is that it will be the first digit.'

A fat apple-seller with yellow and white flowers laced through her hair overhears the gist of this conversation and waddles over to confirm details of the lucky digit.

My attention is diverted from this scene by a woman gracefully walking past, balancing a shopping basket on her head. The basket is covered with a cloth, but a big fish tail protrudes. I saw this same woman the day before, when I was sitting on the same steps in Nawaday Street during my lunch break. The woman came around the corner carrying an enormous wooden crate on her head. The crate was so heavy that two men struggled to lift it from her head and lower it to the ground. When the crate was removed, the woman took off the coiled head cloth that cushioned the load, arched her back, stretched, and smiled proudly as if to say, 'Another job done well.' She walked over to a group of men sitting by a wall; one of the men handed her a baby and she sat against the wall breastfeeding the baby, smiling at the passing crowd.

Meanwhile, another vendor is taking up his station in the street. He arrives with a wooden yoke balanced across the back of his neck. Two wicker panniers are suspended from the yoke, and the panniers are full of luscious guavas and palm fruit. He sets the panniers on wooden crates and, while waiting for customers, sprinkles the fruit with water to keep it fresh.

Another woman arrives with panniers of flowers. These will be bought by the students as part of their daily ritual of gift-giving to their teachers to pay their respects. The trainee Su Myat Hla tells me, 'Whose flower will be worn in a woman teacher's hair is something that preoccupies the students most of the mornings.'

A vendor switches on her ghetto blaster and a discordant 'We Wish You a Merry Christmas' echoes along Nawaday Street, as a Snow White toilet tissue truck pulls up in front of us. The driver hops out, looking curiously at the foreigner with the group of young adult Myanmar earnestly scribbling in notebooks. A Shan Star jeep parks behind the truck. The jeep is a rather unfortunate-looking open jalopy, decked out as an ultimate boy's toy, complete with dinky outdoor accessories strapped to its sides. It is one of the few Myanmar-manufactured vehicles and it tries very hard to be the epitome of sporty four-wheel-drive fashion, but somehow it fails to make the cut.

The trainee Nyi Nyi Soe tells me controversy surrounds the vehicle because it is fitted with a Toyota engine that has not been authorised by Toyota. Toyota is influential in neighbouring Thailand, and stern instructions have been delivered to the Myanmar government to cease manufacture of this vehicle.

To date, the government has been silent about the issue, and Nyi Nyi comments, 'Silence has many meanings in Myanmar.'

Christmas parties proliferated in trendy Yangon circles, and I met her at a cocktail soirée at the Strand Hotel. It was like a chorus from a Doris Day song: I saw her across a crowded room, and fireworks exploded in a dazzle of instant attraction.

She was beautiful, dressed in a shimmering green satin jacket with white Chinese-style trim and knotted cloth buttons, and a green ankle-length dress in the style of a traditional longyi. Her skin was a natural tan that Western women would envy: a velvet glossy sheen setting off a smile bursting with sparkling white teeth.

As fate would have it, we had a mutual friend in Nu Nu Nweh, a bubbly young woman who worked in one of Yangon's few advertising agencies. Nu Nu introduced me to Queen Saroya, as I'd already dubbed the oriental beauty. She told me her name was Ma Pan Cherry and she was a scriptwriter with a company trying to produce a Myanmar television soapie to compete with the national television obsession: subtitled soapies imported from South Korea.

We chatted amiably and at length. I basked in her keen, witty intelligence, and our conversation quickly plumbed depths because of her precisely perfect English. As the conversation meandered towards its conclusion, I told her where I lived and she said she walked past my apartment on her way home from work nearly every evening. 'Maybe we can accidentally bump into each other one evening,' she said.

Her attention was diverted by a stumbling Nu Nu, who clutched her like a young koala clinging to its mother. Myanmar women rarely drink and consequently their tolerance to alcohol is low. Nu Nu was living dangerously. She'd had two glasses of wine and was wobbly. Then she self-destructed.

A waiter walked by with a tray of drinks and she grabbed another red wine, theatrically downed half the glass, and within seconds she was gone. Ma Pan Cherry and another woman steered her in the direction of the toilets, and that was the last I saw of any of them that evening.

During the party I bumped into the journalist Ohn Mar. She said she was rounding up some people to drink snake wine at her friend's father's former restaurant, the Rooftop, which had recently been closed down after a flurry of bad international publicity.

The Rooftop, which billed itself as a seafood restaurant, was Yangon's leading ye wei restaurant. Ye wei—Chinese for *wild taste*—is a mania among the Cantonese, who believe that eating wild or exotic animals imparts social status and invests diners with the qualities of the animals dined upon, qualities such as long life, bravery and, of course, sexual powers. This custom is also the basis for the popular adage that the Cantonese will eat anything with legs except the kitchen table and anything with wings except an aeroplane.

Thousands of ye wei restaurants dot southern China and soak up wildlife to the extent that many Asian species are verging on extinction. Yangon's Rooftop was a mild version of a ye wei restaurant; although it did serve bear's paw and viper stew, it offered mostly seafood and culinary esoterica such as durian coffee and deep-fried mohinga.

The restaurant once attracted foreign embassy staff and expatriates. At the height of its popularity, the *Myanmar Times* reported, 'Rooftop is a successful dream come true for owner U Tin. Expatriates head there quite often, where they usually dare each other to try the snake-soaked wine.'

Its popularity proved its undoing, and in mid-2003 the Myanmar police raided it, shutting it down amidst a flurry of Western news agency reports. After the scandal, the restaurant staff transformed themselves into wholesale suppliers of morally acceptable seafood. One of its specialities, fish sausage, became a new food fad in Yangon's well-heeled quarters. The owners had been allowed to keep the stock of vintage snake wine, stored in barrel-sized glass urns in cellar-like conditions, and this was permanently on tap.

After the Strand soirée I headed off to the Rooftop with Ohn Mar and Douglas, a former Los Angeles mohawked punk librarian, who had reinvented himself as a subdued *Myanmar Times* sub-editor sporting a suburban haircut. I'd wanted to sample snake wine for some time, but I also had an ulterior motive for going: I knew that Ohn Mar knew Pan Cherry and I wanted to glean some information from her.

As we wended our way through the rooftop maze of connecting ramps, rails and stairs at Yangon's Thein Gyi Market, past dodgy beer halls where chalk messages on blackboards promised the forthcoming delights of Miss Tiger, Miss Snow Leopard and Miss Python, I peppered Ohn Mar with questions about Pan Cherry. But Ohn Mar resorted to inscrutability, telling me, 'You are being too obvious. All I will tell you is that Cherry does not have a man in her life.'

Shadowy figures flitted across our path. Indistinct features of curious onlookers peered at us through the gloom as we walked into the large hall that used to be the Rooftop. Faded photos of the restaurant's recent heyday hung on the walls, showing rows of chefs slicing up cobras. The crowning glory was a moody, exotic photo that had appeared in *National Geographic* magazine.

The owner's daughter, Daphne, also a friend of Ohn Mar, showed us rows of large glass urns housing the wine her father so lovingly made. One urn contained the bodies of several snakes bathed in a yellowish liquid, but Daphne said this was just average, run-of-the-mill snake wine. For a real kick she indicated another urn containing fermented liquid, the body of a cobra and hundreds of thin, elongated, mushroom-shaped objects. 'Cobra penis wine,' she explained. 'Very popular with Chinese because it make them strong for their women.'

An urn of fermented snakes' heads stood next to urns containing two types of fermenting scorpions: the odious giant black scorpion and the even-more-odious giant black and orange scorpion. Or, if we preferred, we could opt for the urn containing hundreds of fermenting snakes' eggs. 'My father is one of Myanmar's best snake-wine makers,' explained Daphne. 'Care must be taken in the preparation because of the poisons. Some people die from snake wine, but my father has been making such wine for ten years and no customers have died.'

She produced the house specialty, a cocktail of bodies fermenting in a thick, opaque yellow liquid with lots of floating herbal matter. The urn contained a cobra, a Russell's viper, part of a python, both types of scorpion and, for good measure, a small bear's paw. 'And if you look carefully, you can also see the lizard,' Daphne said. 'This mixture is very good and several traditional rare and expensive Chinese herbs are also included for health and long life.'

The concoction was decanted into a sake-like porcelain container, and thimble-sized porcelain cups were filled to the brim. I gulped my thimbleful and spluttered. It packed a punch, tasting like spicy sake or perhaps tequila, and, after the liquid burned its way down my throat, there was a rather distinct, rather nauseating aftertaste of flesh.

A group of Myanmar students joined us, and we chatted

about Californian democracy during our meal of the famous fish sausage and assorted piquant delicacies, brought to a table that had been placed on the top of a market building. There we were observed by Daphne's slobbering boxer dogs, a rarity themselves in Yangon, where the humidity, parasites, strange insects and airborne pestilence dish out death sentences for most pure-bred Western dogs.

Daphne apologised for being unable to offer snake curry, which apparently goes well with snake wine, but her father now didn't dare serve anything more exotic than a prawn. She said her family was saddened by the scandal and couldn't fully understand why it had happened. 'Many foreigners come here—ambassadors, diplomats—and no-one complains,' said Daphne. 'A few tourists did complain about a pet bear we kept here, but most foreigners say nothing.'

We finished our meal and, heads spinning from snake wine, called it a night. As I headed back to my apartment I thought about Pan Cherry, and the news Ohn Mar had given me about her single status.

Two evenings later I was chatting to the betel-selling lady on the footpath outside my apartment when I successfully accidentally bumped into Ma Pan Cherry.

We diverted to the nearby Zawgyi coffee house. We chatted in an easy manner for a couple of hours, and then she said she must go because her mother would become worried, or even suspicious. 'My mother and my aunties worry about me working at the television company because we are in contact with foreigners. My eldest auntie told me foreigners meet the girls, ask them for dinner, then take them back to their hotels and take advantage of them.'

'Before you go,' I said, 'Let me ask you something. Can I take you out to dinner one evening?'

'Yes,' she replied.

'Okay, great. What night would suit you?'

'What night would you like?'

'How about this Saturday night?'

She begged off, saying it was her mother's birthday and she'd have to celebrate at home.

'Okay, so when?' I persisted.

She made a show of counting on her fingers and then came up with a night five weeks hence, in mid-January. It was a long way off, but it was a date. Maybe.

The doorbell rings. It's 8am, Christmas Day. I open the door and there's a newspaper boy standing there holding out a batch of papers: yesterday's *Bangkok Post* and *Nation* and the *New Light of Myanmar*. I pay him, walk to the lounge room, sit down, and out of curiosity I flick through the Dim Light to see how the men from the Ministry of Information have covered Christmas.

They haven't. The lead story is text from guidance given by Senior General Than Shwe, and the headline reads, 'Forces of national construction and national defence are to be mobilised and strengthened'.

The only reference to Christmas is featured in what appears to be an advertisement placed by Sotero Phamo, Bishop of Loikaw, and there is a slight politically correct edge to the message: 'His [Jesus's] only gesture was a parody of imperial claims. He entered Jerusalem riding a donkey!'

The Myanmar press might offer relief, albeit dull, from Christmas hype, but it seems there's no escape from Christmas indulgence, and I didn't escape it. Yesterday the office held its Christmas party, which was unnervingly similar to standard Western Christmas parties but, luckily, during the middle of the afternoon I was able to wrest a reprieve from Christmas drinking. I headed off with a couple of Myanmar women from the office to a day-night bash hosted by the FMI Centre, Yangon's most luxurious department store, which is located next to my apartment block. The owners had erected a large stage for a musical concert to be held in the evening, and during the day the centre's parking lot had been turned into a fairground. I strolled around for a couple of hours with the office women, eating ice-cream and buying an entire large barbecued fish skewered by a thick sliver of bamboo thrust through its mouth and body.

After a couple of hours I bade adieu to the women and took my fish and myself back to my apartment, where I showered, trying to rid myself of the grimy sort of hangover headache that accompanies midday drinking.

When the concert started I sat on my balcony overlooking the stage, watching the wild performance of a woman who sounded like a Myanmar version of Bonnie Tyler until, entranced, I decided to leave my balcony and join the action. I walked downstairs, crossed the gardens and took a seat in front of the stage, sitting next to some Myanmar people I knew from the FMI Centre.

The concert was being stage-managed by a cool Myanmar dwarf in shades, and a series of 'chick singers' took the stage; each one belted out three numbers and then, collecting their sheet music, left the stage. An almost sickly cute girlie band then appeared. One singer was in yellow: tight yellow T-shirt, tight yellow trousers and a white tennis visor. Another was dressed in white, with a white lacy band around her midriff and also a white tennis visor. The third singer was dressed in gym trousers and a T-shirt emblazoned with hard-rock slogans. The trio belted out a medley of Myanmar-language versions of Christmas songs such as 'Jingle Bells' and 'We Wish You a Merry Christmas'.

A geeky male singer in jeans, white T-shirt and a daggy patchwork leather jacket started crooning. I turned to say something to the woman sitting next to me, but she muttered, 'Filmin', filmin'.' I turned the other way and, sure enough, there was a man standing to the side filming me with a video camera.

The concert finished at ten and I returned to my apartment, feasting on the remains of the skewered fish. I lolled in bed listening to the chiming of the bells from the nearby Catholic cathedral.

I don't like those bells. They're dolorous, depressive and deleterious. They're sobbingly mournful Catholic bells of burning hell, and they elicit dancing demons that have haunted my psyche ever since my boyhood Catholic school days. Those days ended quite dramatically and traumatically, with the head nun, the cruel, beak-nosed, rimless-spectacled Mother Aden, banishing me from the sacred confines of St Augustine's. That was after standing me in front of the classroom, pointing a finger at me and declaring to the other pupils, 'This boy, Peter Olszewski, will become a communist and break down church doors with an axe.'

Catholic guilt—it doesn't get any guiltier than that, especially during the guilt-fest called Christmas—and the muted clangour of those damned reverberating bells resurrected almost-dead memories from my mind's morgue nearly as unerringly as Mother Aden's whistling leather strap bit into the flesh at the back of my bare calves during those long-distant convent-cold winter mornings of overt rebelliousness as I devolved from head altar boy to communist in the period leading to my public unofficial excommunication, following my refusal to accept the supposedly scientific theory of transubstantiation. My adolescent argument was that if we Catholics literally consume the flesh of Jesus and drink his blood during our communion rites, then we are simply members of a cannibalistic cult and no different from the pagan flesh-eating tribes of the South Sea Islands whom our missionaries so earnestly saved from their barbaric practices and brought into the fold of gentle Jesus—who now, every Sunday at mass, we eat.

The bells of Yangon rang on, twelve times, heralding the arrival of Christmas Day 2003.

As I lay there in the Christmas night, with spectral light spilling through my windows from the incressant moon outside, I recalled the guilt-ridden depressive writings of Orwell that I have been reading lately, and the lines from his Burmese poem 'The Lesser Evil' sprang to mind:

I thought of all the church bells ringing;
In towns that Christian folks were in;
I heard the Godly maidens singing;
I turned into the house of sin.

I tossed and turned, but that brought no respite. The fingerlings of existential guilt continued to slither, and I figured the only way to banish the onset of this depression was to turn to my faithful help-me-through-the-night companion, cable TV, and ease my way into a Christmas by watching the late-night movies.

The movies piped into my apartment were made all the more fascinating by the English subtitles unnecessarily given to the English-language movies. But the Myanmar translators' grasp of the language wasn't quite up to speed, or perhaps the translators were on speed. Thus strange phrases appeared on the bottom of the screen, such as, 'That you fuck what here', 'Your man is who what, call vegetable', 'Seeing you can still be on the hoof to walk out' and 'My name is Plain West, he exactly this elephant inside so'.

On this Christmas dawn my friend, the cable TV, delivered a movie called *Hollywood Homicide*, which featured a re-enactment of a scene from *A Streetcar Named Desire*. When the actor was yelling, 'Stella, Stella', the subtitles said he was yelling, 'Sand Tile, Sand Tile'.

I push aside the newspapers and pick up the phone. It's close to midday in Australia so I try to call my mother, but there's a glitch and every time I dial I get an angry Myanmar voice yabbering at me. I put the phone down and walk over to the balcony, thrusting open the French windows, seeing the ghost of myself shimmer in the glass sheen, and letting the heat and sounds of downtown Yangon sweep past me to permeate the apartment. I stand looking out over the road, watching Myanmar life parade by, listening to the many delightful sounds of a busy morning where commerce continues, unhindered by the arrival of the sacred Christian Day.

My phone chirrups. I pick it up and my tour-guide friend, the Chinese woman Xiao Lee, chirps that she is on her way to my apartment.

She'd promised to accompany me on my surprise visit to the Karen Baptist Mission compound to see the adorable nurse Krapit Phaw, Christmas Flower, who had been so nice to me in hospital, and who was celebrating her eighteenth birthday today. I'd promised this visit while in hospital but I'm sure she doesn't think I will actually visit.

After Xiao Lee phones, I duck into the handicrafts store behind the Zawgyi coffee house to buy some gifts. Two Myanmar women are stationed at a large handloom, intricately weaving a Mandalay-style longyi and softly singing along to pop songs on the radio, setting the scene for a Christmas Day with a difference.

Xiao Lee and I take a taxi to Krapit Phaw's address, a large sprawling compound hidden off a main road. We stroll along tree-lined paths, past large wooden cottages, looking for 121, the number of Krapit's house. But every cottage is number 121— number 121e, number 121d, etc. We knock at two different houses, and two different women give us two different directions. Another woman points to a small dusty path, telling us to follow it until we come to a big tamarind tree and then turn left. So we walk, find the tree, turn left and still can't find the house.

A group of young guys are playing chinlon, the traditional Myanmar game where boys stand in a rough circle and kick or head-butt a ball made of woven rattan. The idea is to keep the ball in motion as long as possible, and it's a game of communal co-operation rather than individual victory. There are no teams, no sides, in street chinlon.

We talk to the boys and at first they are wary, speaking only with their eyes, which tell me they are suspicious of the strange foreigner asking questions. But I smile, adding my English version to Xiao Lee's translated version, and eventually one of the more senior boys gestures for us to follow him.

A few seconds later he points to Krapit Phaw's house, where two women with children sit on the stairs and smile shyly. They direct us into a small wooden house made of wooden slat walls with a roof that is a mixture of woven cane squares and corrugated iron. A shy girl in her early twenties greets us, explaining that Krapit Phaw is having a bath. But we are made welcome and asked to sit at a low table. We are given bowls of noodles, a small dish of tangy salad and glasses of orange cordial.

Finally Krapit enters the room, looking stunned. She mumbles over and over that she never really expected to see me, but she is so proud I have come to her home. We chat and reminisce about my time in hospital, and she talks about how everyone at the hospital liked the article I'd written about my experience. Krapit Phaw then puts her hand over her mouth and bends her head shyly. She looks up at me, giggling. She confesses she'd tricked me and that her nurse friend at the hospital wasn't really her twin sister as I'd reported in the newspaper article. But, because the both of them went everywhere together, the hospital staff jokingly referred to them as the twins, and she had decided to play the joke on me.

'Do you mind?' she asks me sweetly. I tell her she is very naughty to trick a foreign journalist like that. But I quickly add that I very much enjoyed being tricked in such a playful manner and it only adds to the beautiful memories I already have of my stay in hospital and the tender care and special treatment afforded to me by my Karen angel, Miss Christmas Flower.

A man walks into the house and Krapit introduces me to her uncle, a Baptist pastor. Krapit's family lives in a traditional Karen rural village, but she came to Yangon to find work and was recruited as a trainee nurse by the Asia Royal Hospital. Krapit's uncle is her city protector and he isn't too happy with my presence, probably suspecting I am courting his delightful niece. Conversation is not forthcoming and he distractedly waves his arm, saying he cannot spend any more time chatting because he is busy. He exits.

Krapit Phaw, Xiao Lee and I natter on for another half-hour or so, and then I notice the time. We have been here for almost three hours and it is time to go. The three of us walk outside and I admire a plantation of thin, graceful, palm-like trees in neat, ordered rows. Krapit says these are areca palms, betel nut trees, and help supplement the mission's income.

A mother hen and a brood of chicks scratch around in the dust near us, and a cheery, cute little spectacled man in a longyi and jacket and furled umbrella busily walks along the path. Krapit introduces him as the mission's main man, the head pastor. We exchange pleasantries and he asks, 'What is your country?' I tell him and he smiles approvingly. 'Ah, a very beautiful country. And a democracy,' he says. 'I worked in your country for three months in 1987. I was in the city of Adelaide and I was the pastor of the Knightsbridge Baptist Church there.'

In the cab back to downtown, Xiao Lee says to me, 'She is very pretty, Peter. But very young.' I explain there is no hidden motive to my friendship. Xiao Lee laughs and says, 'You know she tell me that you coming for her birthday is the most amazing thing that ever happen to her.'

When I return to my apartment, I part company with Xiao Lee and stroll through the city. Many spivs hang out on the busy corner outside the Traders Hotel and, sure enough, a new guy on the block attaches himself to me, an Indian-looking guy who introduces himself as Hilary and goes through all the usual patter before getting down to business. 'Hello, sir, how are you? What is your name? You are looking beautiful today. What is your country?'

Finally he gets to his sales pitch, and his specialty is a new one: organising dangerous interviews. 'Yes, sir, I can organise the dangerous interviews for you. I can take you to people who the government does not want you to talk to and they can tell you many stories of our country.' He recites a long list of major international news organisations for which he has arranged dangerous interviews. I am almost tempted to go along with it, just to see what unfolds, but from experience I am sure what will unfold will be a lot of stuffing around, a lot of fruitless waiting around and shuffling. He will run me all over town to meet people who never turn up because something has gone wrong or because it has become too dangerous even for a dangerous interview.

Sensing my deliberation, he quickly adds, 'I have been doing this for years, sir, for many reputable organisations and there is no trouble. Is safe, sir.'

I reply, 'If it's safe, it can't then be a dangerous interview, can it? I'm not interested, I am busy.'

He gives me a curious look and disengages quickly, 'Thank you, sir. I am always here, you can always find me, I am Hilary.'

I walk through the downtown district for half an hour until I come to another of my favourite haunts, the 50th Street Bar and Grill. This is a homely, pub-like venue that was popular with expats during the 'gold rush' of the mid-1990s, when there was a lot of foreign money in town. These days the bar is largely deserted, but I find it a nice cosy retreat with a superb pool table, lots of magazines and daily editions of the *International Herald Tribune*. The walls are festooned with old black-and-white photos of Burma and many old metal signs such as, 'The Statesman. India's Largest Selling Newspaper on Sale Here', 'Drink Biscuits Brandy' and 'De Souzas Dak Remedies'.

I am known here as Mr Frap Jack for my habit of ordering flapjack breakfasts on Saturday mornings. But tonight I'm eagerly anticipating a traditional Western Christmas Day dinner of turkey and vegetables, plus a rum sour, plus ice cream, for US$10.

They've been promoting this dinner for weeks, but when it is placed in front of me, it is far removed from what I presume a turkey dinner to be. The turkey is served as two-inch cubes of undercooked, fatty meat, and the vegetables are edible but incongruous, cooked in the Hokkein Chinese style popular in Australia. A chunk of dry white bread and a small plate of dubious pesto sauce accompany the meal. Suddenly loneliness and mild depression sink in.

Afterwards I leave and, on the way home in a cab, the streets seem darker and smokier than usual. The night is an inky smudge rendering the lights of oncoming cars so bright I have to squint. As the taxi wends its way through the narrow, rutted, downtown streets, I watch the shadows of Yangon families flit across the headlights and I feel far from home—a stranger in a strange land.

Back at my apartment complex an irritating Chinese version of 'Jingle Bells' is still being piped through the public address system. I look forward to not hearing it again.

I board a small prop jet at the airport, and settle back in my seat to enjoy my holiday flight to Kyaing Tong, the capital of the Golden Triangle. Once we are airborne I chat briefly to an engaging hostess with a name tag introducing her as Charlotte. She says her mother is Myanmar and her father French, hence the name.

I look out the window as we land at Heho an hour after leaving Yangon, but there is nothing to see except dry and scrubby reddish earth, reminding me of central Queensland. Twenty-five minutes after leaving Heho we descend into Mandalay and again I look out the window, and again there is nothing to see except caked grey dried earth. An hour after departing Mandalay, we descend into the Myanmar–Thailand border town of Tachilek. Looking out the window, I discover the scenery is now a little greener, a little more exotic and Asian.

I'm sitting in the front seat, C1, and at Tachilek all the seats around me are vacated. Suddenly there's a ruckus and the seats are filled with senior military personnel. Sitting across the aisle from me is a sleek general with several rings on his fingers, including an expensive nawarat ring, which tradition-ally imbues masculine wearers with power and glory. It is made of nine gems that are always set in the same order: ruby in the middle, diamond at top centre, then, clockwise, pearl, coral, topaz, sapphire, moonstone, zircon and emerald. The individual gems must be set at auspicious times and days calculated by an astrologer.

But there's a touch of incongruity to the general's uniformed appearance—a pair of soft, shiny-black, trendy boots with clip-on side straps. One of the heels is unevenly worn, the only flaw in his impressiveness. I also note he is studiously oblivious to my presence. On his hip he wears a small silver pistol in a holster. There are about six other uniformed senior officers, most wearing side arms also, and several sidekicks in plain clothes. I catch one of these guys looking at me thoughtfully and decide to avoid eye contact for the rest of the short twenty-minute hop to Kyaing Tong.

I look out the window and can clearly see the road from Tachilek to Kyaing Tong. It's a magnificent piece of engineer-ing, snaking its way through densely forested mountain passes. It looks like a clichéd picture-book scene of a remote Chinese mountain highway, which in a way it is, because we are only about 100 kilometres from the Chinese border.

On the ground at Kyaing Tong, we mere mortals have to wait while the general and his entourage slowly parade past a welcoming committee of soldiers snapped to attention. Then I proceed into the dim, rudimentary airport building to wait patiently in a queue while immigration officials painstakingly enter foreign passengers' passport and ticket details into an old-fashioned ledger.

Outside the airport I hail a pick-up truck and within minutes I am in my hotel in downtown Kyaing Tong. The agent I used in Yangon recommended the Old Kyaing Tong Hotel and booked me into what she called a large, self-contained 'junior villa suite', with a 24-hour electricity supply, hot water, television and breakfast. I emphasised the need for hot water because I know Kyaing Tong is chilly at night, and because I know hot water isn't always on the agenda at accommodation in the Myanmar sticks.

But I discover the only accurate description I've been given about the Old Kyaing Tong Hotel is that it is old and it is in Kyaing Tong. It is not really a hotel, and the junior suite is not in fact a villa or anything approximating it. It is a small old cottage divided into two, and in my half there is no power and no hot water. The room reminds me of an outback Australian pub room with its old, mismatched furniture, cheap wooden fittings with faded cracked gloss, and a general air of having seen better times.

The only thing going for this alleged hotel is the management and staff. A sad, sleepy-eyed manager oversees the running of the place, and the staff seems to consist of an extended family: softly spoken, gentle women, cute kids and easy-going, courteous men. I like them instantly and they are already greeting me with 'Hello, Mistar Pwatarrr', 'Good morning, Mistar Pwatarrr', 'Are you happy, Mistar Pwatarrr?' The Pwatarrr comes from Piotr, the Polish spelling of my name. Because Piotr is on my birth certificate it is therefore in my passport and, while in Australia I am Peter, when I travel internationally I become Piotr, or a mispronounced version of it.

Shortly after my arrival I wander over to the reception to begin a series of drawn-out negotiations. The manager says, 'Ah, Mistar Pwatarrr, you are happy?'

'Well, yes and no,' I reply. 'There is no electricity and no hot water.'

The manager looks at me, sadly shaking his head.

'Ah, Mistar Pwatarrr. Electricity supply is bad here. All of Kyaing Tong is the same. We are not given supply until about

4pm, but after that there will almost always be electricity in your room until the morning. None of us are happy with the situation, but there is nothing we can do. We are only poor people in a forgotten corner of Myanmar.'

'I see. And the hot water?'

'Not working, Mistar Pwatarrr. None of the hot-water makers are making hot water anymore. It is because of the electricity. It is always going off and on and it is ruining the insides of the hot-water makers. None of us are happy about this, but we are only poor people in a forgotten corner of Myanmar. I may be able to arrange for some women to bring you hot water from a solar heater.'

'Hmm, yes well, the electricity is obviously not your fault. But as for the hot water, this is essential. Take a look at my booking slip. See, here it is says hot water and this is what I have paid for. Can't you fix the hot-water system?'

'No. But we will look at it for you. In fact, I will look at it myself later in the day.'

I return to my junior suite and self-contained villa for an afternoon nap, but no sooner do I start to drift off than I'm snapped to alertness by a banging and thumping reverberating around the room. I look outside to see several men energetically hitting the water pipe outside the room with small pieces of pipe.

I figure maybe they are fixing the hot water and, when the banging stops and the men are gone, I venture into the bathroom and turn on the taps. Nothing. Now I have no water at all. Back to reception.

The manager is standing in the same spot he seems to stand in most of the day.

'Ah, Mistar Pwatarrr. Are you happy in your room?'

'Not really. Now I have no water—hot, cold or otherwise.'

'No water?'

'No water.'

'Are you sure? Have you turned the taps all the way?'

'There is no water at all, absolutely none.'

A group of concerned staff gather and begin speaking at once. The manager says, 'Come. We will look at this problem now.'

About a dozen men, women and children gather in my bathroom. The manager slowly and theatrically turns the taps. Not a trickle of any sort of water. The men who had been banging the water pipes with small pipes rush into the room and slowly and theatrically turn the taps. Still no evidence of anything resembling water.

The people crowding the bathroom begin jabbering. The manager looks at me sadly. 'Mistar Pwatarrr, there is a problem with the water. Something is not right. I will have to make investigations.'

I am about to lose my temper. I feel ratty and grimy from the long flight. I haven't been able to wash, let alone shower, and I haven't been able to nap. I decide to go for a walk and calm down.

As I leave, I notice that the men who had been banging the pipes are now furiously digging a large hole in the ground just outside my bathroom.

I wander through the narrow streets of Kyaing Tong fantasising about a voluptuous hot shower. Dusk is encroaching, but the electricity obviously hasn't yet come on. People are firing up small charcoal braziers and lighting lanterns and candles, creating an eerie flickering in the dim, smoky atmosphere. I figure this is what Paris must have looked like in the thirteenth century.

I decide that if I can't have a hot shower, at least I can have a hot meal. There are only two or three restaurants in Kyaing Tong catering for foreigners, and I'd heard the best was the Golden Banyan restaurant. I have a tourist map giving the location, but the map's neat, straight-lined roads and streets have absolutely no recognisable relationship to the higgledy-piggledy maze of streets and lanes I'm walking through. I come to a corner where a pod of scooter 'taxis' are congregated, and the drivers are sitting at tables inside a well-lit tea shop.

I walk in and an interesting bespectacled old man, who looks donnish in a Myanmar way, hurries over and greets me: 'Good evening, sir.'

I say, 'Do you serve meals?'

'No. This is a tea shop.'

'Yes, but in Yangon some tea shops also serve food.'

'Ah, yes, but we are not in Yangon.'

I tell him I am tired and hungry and looking for a restaurant, but I am lost because my map is no good.

He surveys me with bemused concern and says, 'There is a restaurant near here which caters for the foreigners. It is called the Golden Banyan restaurant. It is famous.'

He tells me to hop on the back of his scooter and he whisks me around the corner to the restaurant himself. I thank him and ask him to share a beer with me. We chat and he tells me a little about himself, how he came here from Yangon 25 years earlier.

He sits with me while I eat my meal, and he chuckles good-naturedly about what he regards as the impossibility of my situation, wandering around a strange city with no idea where I am and without friends. He kindly draws me a map showing the route back to my hotel and then takes his leave, shaking my hand and saying, 'Come back to Kyaing Tong. But next time come with a better map.' As he hops on his scooter he adds laughingly, 'And bring some friends.'

I finish my meal at the Golden Banyan and pick up a copy of the *New Light of Myanmar*. I read that Myanmar is the cradle of civilisation, as reported by Senior General Than Shwe in his Armed Forces Day message to the nation. The general said:

The finds of the fossilised remains of the anthropoid primates have proved that Myanmar is the place where human beings originated. Thus, independence is the inborn heritage of the Myanmar people. Therefore, no matter how the colonialists change the practice of colonialism, it is incumbent upon the entire people of the Union to collectively defend and safeguard the independence, the inborn heritage, as a national duty.

I ponder why, if the Myanmar were the first people on earth, they are among the last to conquer electricity.

I return to the Old Kyaing Tong Hotel which, incidentally, is next to the New Kyaing Tong Hotel, a characterless and contentious hotel built by the military on the site of the old teak Kyaing Tong Palace, erected in 1905 by the fifty-third chieftan or *saopha* and British knight, Sao Kawng Kiao Intaleng. The palace's last inhabitant was Kyaing Tong's last saopha, the Australian-educated Sao Sai Long, nicknamed Shorty. Ne Win's men imprisoned Shorty and seized the palace, which quickly fell into disrepair until it was declared unsafe. In 1991 it was demolished, despite protest by monks and residents, and the New Kyaing Tong Hotel was built in its place, retaining only some of the palace walls and a small tower.

I tentatively enter my junior villa to see if any progress has been made on either the electricity or the water front. The electricity is on and, when I turn the tap, the pipes groan and clatter. A sickly coughing comes from the tap, and mud and dirt splutter into the sink. After about half a minute clear water flows, but only cold water and the night is chilly. I whisk some water over me and retire to bed, only to discover that the partition between my junior villa and the adjoining junior villa is flimsy plywood and a noisy group of people have settled in next door.

One man shouts non-stop, so after half an hour I abandon

the notion of sleep and turn on the television. I can only get Myanmar TV, but fortunately the channel is broadcasting an English soccer match live, with English commentary. I settle in to watch this, but the man's braying grows louder. I think he's drunk, and I decide to retaliate. I turn the TV volume to full. The commentary booms through my room but it does the trick. The man shuts up.

I eventually sleep, and wake next morning feeling optimistic. I walk to the dining room, which reminds me of my youth in the Australian bush. It is a large former dance hall, with a stage at one end festooned with the ratty remains of once-plush maroon velvet curtains, forlorn reminders of the grand days.

A lone table has been set up in the centre of the hall and my breakfast is placed on it. Cutlery, salt, a slice of toast, and a pot of coffee. A concerned woman brings me a plate with two fried eggs, but the eggs are cold and congealed.

The manager appears. 'Good morning, Mistar Pwatarrr. You are eating the egg. I had the woman cook it early this morning so it would be ready for you.'

I hate to churlishly put the brakes on such enterprising endeavours, but I need to appraise him of some realities. My experience with many Myanmar men is that they use the hopelessness of their political situation as an excuse for their own dysfunctionality, and the only way to get them going is to seriously put the skids under them.

'Look, the eggs are no good if they are pre-cooked. We foreigners want hot eggs, just as we want hot water. And speaking of that, you said yesterday that the women could bring me some hot water from the solar heater. Could this be done now, perhaps, while the woman is cooking me hot eggs?'

'Ah, Mistar Pwatarrr, sadly all the solar hot water from yesterday has been used. Now we have to wait for . . .'

'The sun to heat up more water?'

'Ah, Mistar Pwatarrr, you understand the working of the

solar systems. I am very happy.'

I've had enough and say, 'Look, you may be happy but I am not. This hot water business is not good enough. I am sorry, but that's the way it is. I paid for hot water and I want it, so during today I will inspect other accommodation. If there is no running hot water in my room by tonight, unfortunately I will be moving out tomorrow.'

Later that morning, while having coffee at the Golden Banyan, I find another interesting passage in another tattered ink-smudged copy of the *New Light of Myanmar*. This reads:

> True to a Myanmar aphorism that goes, 'Visitors come when the house is pleasant,' a continuous stream of precious visitors from foreign nations come to Myanmar. The precious guests and other tourists visiting Myanmar, where stability and tranquillity prevail owing to the absence of the smell of cordite as well as destructive acts and armed insurgencies, witness with their very own eyes how peaceful and pleasant Myanmar is to travel.

I figure I can do without the smell of cordite, but I hope I have impressed upon my Myanmar hosts that I love the smell of freshly cooked eggs in the morning.

I take time out to explore Kyaing Tong, which was opened for tourism in 1993. The tourism trade has yet to be developed beyond a small trickle of slightly more adventurous travellers, and Kyaing Tong remains an atmospheric, torpid old town composed of narrow, twisting laneways and small streets running erratically through the downtown district. A peaceful silence prevails, interrupted only by the soft droning of masses of monks and the buzz of hundreds of Chinese motor-scooters scuttling through streets in surging packs, like startled cockroaches.

A brisk market bustles in the centre of the town. Dressed in their colourful finery, hill tribe women mingle with the more modern town locals. The writer Somerset Maugham rested in Kyaing Tong and devoted two chapters to this marketplace in his 1930 travel tome, *A Gentleman in the Parlour*. Like Maugham, I enjoy disappearing in the twisted maze of the crowded market alleys, savouring the exotic sights and evocative smells, surveying stupa-shaped piles of slithering silver fish, bargaining for ornate bead-and-silver studded Akha woven baskets, and buying a small, primitively elegant jungle hunting bow.

Kyaing Tong is ancient, dating back to the great Buddhist Lanna kingdom of the thirteenth and fourteenth centuries, which encompassed much of Thailand and some of Burma, particularly the Shan state. The inhabitants were known as Khun people. King Mangrai, the Thai king who founded Chiang Mai, encircled Kyaing Tong with a 7.5-mile wall with seven gates, and later kings added other fortifications. Only one gate or arch, reportedly the site of executions, still remains. In grand old days noisy rockets were fired from the parapets to frighten and stampede war elephants.

Kyaing Tong means The Walled City of Tung, and the Tong refers to the town's legend, allegedly prophesied by Buddha. A Moses-like mythical hermit, Tunga, or Tungkalasi, drained an inland sea with his magical staff, and the devout city that rose in the wake was named after him. In its centre there is still a natural lake, supposedly a remnant of the sea.

Kyaing Tong in time became a strategic trading town, the first Burmese destination for mule caravans travelling from Thailand to southern China and to the coast of Thailand. An Englishman, Holt S. Hallet, searched for a rail route between Burma and China, and described the caravans arriving in Kyaing Tong in his 1890 book, *A Thousand Miles on an Elephant in the Shan States*. He reported that thousands of mules arrived in Kyaing Tong every year from Chiang Mai, carrying dates, walnuts, silk, tea and camphor, and returned with cotton, gold and silver, tobacco and laquerware.

But the last big caravan that passed through Kyaing Tong carried a much more contentious cargo—opium. In 1967 the feared warlord Khun Sa brought an opium convoy to Kyaing Tong, a single-file column of 500 men and 300 mules, stretching for over a mile and laden with more than sixteen tonnes of opium.

Later in the afternoon I check out alternative accommodation at the Princess Hotel, and it is pleasant. It is a real hotel, along the lines of what Westerners call a boutique hotel. Rooms are well equipped and hot water is available 24 hours, but the electricity is erratic. I am tempted to move in immediately, but I have a soft spot for the staff at the Old Kyaing Tong, and I am aware my American dollars are helping the extended family stave off the economic vicissitudes of modern life in the Myanmar provinces. Plus I'd issued the manager with a challenge and, if he manages to get the hot-water heater going, which I very much doubt, I am honour-bound to stick with him.

Come evening, when I return to the hotel, the entire extended family gathers around me and the manager proclaims, 'Ah, Mistar Pwatarrr, happy news. Today I am consulting with the official plumber at the New Kyaing Tong Hotel and he is looking at the hot-water maker. Mistar Pwatarrr, it only needed small part which he have. He kindly put the part into the maker, and there is now hot water in your room.'

'Fantastic! I will have a hot shower right now.'

'Ah, Mistar Pwatarrr, please allow me to be present when you make the hot water. I want to make sure that everything is now satisfactory for you with this hot water.'

The entire extended family, which seems to be perpetually expanding like an amoeba, crams into my bathroom, including excited kids. I am about to turn on what I believe is the hot-water tap, but the manager gently restrains me. He wants to do the honours, and does so with slow, dignified ceremony.

Water commences flowing. I whisk my finger under the flow. Damn. Cold water.

But wait. I can feel a little warmth—yes, definitely—and the warmth is slowly increasing. Until we have it—hot water.

I extend congratulations to the manager. The women titter, the children giggle and the manager solemnly stands with his hands behind his back, his demeanour suggesting this feat is nothing out of the ordinary, just another challenge in his busy and complex working life.

He conspiratorially pulls me aside and says, 'Today I am also speaking with the professional manageress of the New Kyaing Tong Hotel. She tells me that the hot water is very important for the foreigners. However, please do not expect me to be fixing the electricity. This can only be done by the government in Yangon. Actually I believe we will never have good electricity until we have the democracy, because I have been told that good electricity is very important for the democracy.'

I'm in the hills a few miles from Kyaing Tong, sputtering through the jungle on the back of a sturdy trail bike driven by my new local buddy, Sai Zoom, guide and organiser. Sai Zoom has proved great value because, when I met him on my first day in Kyaing Tong, I realised he wasn't an official guide as such, just an enterprising 30-year-old picking up some extra money and making contact with foreigners. I had a good feeling about him, so I engaged his services, and it's a decision that's paid off.

Except perhaps for now.

Sai Zoom seems convinced we are on the road to the village of the black teeth people, but I think we're on a treacherous trail that may have once, in ancient times, seen use as a goat— or perhaps buffalo—track. Branches, vines, tall grasses and bamboo whip my face as we bump along from one rut to another, but when we come to a swampy, messy patch, the trail peters out.

There's a crashing from the swamp reeds and coming towards us is a turbaned hill-tribe chap astride a sleek, big-horned buffalo. We look at each other with incredulity. It's a meeting of disparate cultures. Up to now we've been separated by thousands of miles and aeons of time; yet today here we are, in the jungle, staring at each other. The man smiles and talks in the Shan language.

Sai Zoom translates. The laughing man is telling us we can go no further because this is the buffalo track to the village of the black teeth people, and from this point on, only buffalo can venture. We need to go further down the mountain to find the alleged road to the village.

I grit my teeth as Sai Zoom and I turn around and head back along the many miles we've already traversed on this bone-jarring track, with the branches, vines, tall grasses and bamboo once again whipping my face.

Further down the mountain we find a larger track which, Sai Zoom assures me, is definitely the alleged road. We hurtle down hill, up hill, then round a bend. Large red rhododendron-like flowers explode by the roadside, framing a view of green stepped-terrace paddies lurking behind wisps of mist. And there, just down the road, is a collection of strange-shaped bamboo dwellings inside the confines of a sort of palisade fence. The village of the black teeth people.

They are called the black teeth people because they have black teeth and gums. Many Myanmar people have red teeth and gums as a result of chewing betel nut, but the black teeth people chew their own version of betel, a black version that gives them a distinctive and rather creepy black smile.

As we approach the village, a woman tending a vegetable crop launches into a strange, crazy jig, which is a form of welcome. I think. We pass through the palisade fence and enter the village. Noisy baby black pigs squirm towards us; a group of solemn children approaches. Young women come forward, holding lengths of striking hand-woven cloth.

We are led up the hill, past men weaving cane baskets, to the back of the village to meet the power-brokers, the old ladies, and to give them the large bag of medicines we have brought. I bought these medicines—mostly analgesics and cough concoctions—at Sai Zoom's insistence. Apparently such medicines are an appropriate and expected gift or offering.

Half a dozen old ladies drift out of the dim recesses of their huts and wander around in small circles, seemingly oblivious of our presence, stooped over with their heads nodding like a bunch of hens picking through sawdust. One by one they acknowledge us and the eldest lady examines our medicines approvingly.

Visits to villages such as this constitute the main tourism industry of Kyaing Tong, and almost every day Sai Zoom and I set off to visit yet another village. Akha people, Wa people, White Wa people, Lahu, Shan, Khun—I see them all and, early in the piece, we abandon the small, beat-up trail bike for a more powerful beast that enables us to extend our range and travel further off the beaten track.

Now, well off the track, we ride through the jungle again, dismount and walk through the forest to a remote Wa village. We encounter a desperate-looking chap in quasi-military garb, armed with a battered machete and shouldering the long, strange rifle I'd spotted here and there during my travels in the district. It is, I discover, a World War I musket and our friend the Wa warrior is happy to show how the musket works.

He produces a small glass full of misshapen grey lead slugs similar to those I've seen on sale in the Kyaing Tong markets; he demonstrates how these are tamped down the six- or seven-foot-long barrel. He aims at a small stub of a broken branch on a nearby tree, fires, and blows the branch away. Clouds of smoke roil from both ends of the musket. He loads the weapon again and hands it to me. I miss the tree I aim at and hand the weapon back, my ears ringing, and the smell of cordite tickling the inside of my nose.

We press on and come to the scraggly Wa village. I stoop so I can enter the doorway of a dimly lit hut, where I see an old man resting on a dais. An old lady shuffles forwards and places a cushion at the side of the dais, indicating I should recline. The old man lies down, and a younger guy armed with a machete enters the hut and sits impassively near the doorway.

The woman carries paraphernalia to the old man, who fishes amongst the bits to produce a small lamp. He heats a nub of opium and uses a pin to push a black, sticky glob into a bamboo pipe with an onion-like bulb at one end. He puffs on the pipe, a wisp of smoke curls upwards, and the pungent, sweet smell of opium seeps through the hut. He sizzles more opium over his little lamp, packs the pipe, and hands it to me. Smoke trickles down my throat and into my lungs. More pipes are packed until I mutter that I am happy.

Sai Zoom suggests we journey to the monastery of the fasting monks, and I'm amenable to anything. So it's back on the bike and more clattering along a confusing maze of paths through the bush until we come to the monastery, an ornate white multi-storeyed building with steep red-tiled gabled roofs, which look more Chinese than Myanmar, and of course China is just a few miles away, over the mountain passes.

The approach to the monastery is lined by long rows of primitive huts made of grass and bamboo, and festooned with flags and long, colourful cylindrical pennants. The thatch at the crown of the roofs has been fashioned into topiary menageries of other-world animals—monkey-man gods and bizarre sentient beings. The fasting monks sit on colourful mats outside the huts, receiving guests and offerings. Their chanting pleasantly permeates the air, massaging my opium-calmed mind. I am being transported to another, magical, time and place, far from the West; but as I walk past more huts that house fasting monks I realise the West is never that far away, even here. The young monks, dressed in flowing bright yellow robes, wear woollen hats emblazoned with the sacred labels of Timberlake, Reebok and Mikasa.

The afternoon fades and Sai Zoom reveals another surprise on the agenda: tonight there will be a Shan dance out in the foothills, a dance famous for its gathering of Shan village dancing girls.

We ride for almost an hour and as we near the venue we become part of a scooter cavalcade. Dozens of locals buzz toward the dance with girlfriends sitting side-saddle on the scooters, chatting and gossiping with girls on other passing scooters. We stop at a clearing where hundreds of people have gathered, surging around stalls selling snacks, fruits and strong Chinese liquor.

At first most activity is centred at a row of gambling stalls, but then people mill around an old truck parked at the far end of the gathering. Large stereo speakers perched on the truck's tray belt out sinuous, evocative Myanmar traditional music as a circle of girls—the legendary Shan village dancing girls—dance seductively and nimbly in the shadows, with soft light cast by four candles placed on each corner of a small table. But as the night unfolds, the tempo cranks up and the eerie Shan music gives way to the doof-doof of Western dance music, inescapable even here in the remoteness of outback Asia.

The dancing also becomes a curious but practical courting session. The district's young studs buy tickets that permit them a two-minute dance with the girl of their choice. The girl must always accept the first ticket, but can then do as she likes. An old, turbaned Shan lady doubles as ticket-seller and time-keeper. Every two minutes she vigorously blows her whistle and the line-up on the dirt dance-floor changes. Young Shan village girls congregate at these dances and earn a little pocket money while assessing the merits of the district's young men. Talking and flirting is permitted, but touch the girl and the dance stops immediately. Kiss the girl, and the consequences are serious.

Sai Zoom and his mates buy a wad of tickets for me and push me into the dancing circle. I thrust a ticket at the first girl who makes eye contact and, luckily, she is a college student who can speak English. Chinese liquor and opium have made me loquacious, and I launch into the flowery, poetic conversation the Myanmar love so much. I regard the Myanmar as the Irish of Asia because both countries have been locked in long, bitter civil war, both countries are deeply religious, and both peoples will wax lyrical at the drop of a turban. The overriding ethos seems to be: why use ten words when a thousand will do?

Flattery in Myanmar is an art form of which I am a keen student, so I say to the Shan dancing girl, 'Your eyes are so beautiful they make me sad. Once I have looked at your eyes, I know I can never look at a star in the night sky again because that star will no longer shine for me.'

The Shan dancing girl, who tells me her name is Nang Twe, says, 'Ahh, you speak very beautiful. I like what you say very much. I would like to listen to more of your beautiful words. Would you like to have an appointment with me tomorrow?'

I tell her I'd enjoy a date, but I will need my guide and friend Sai Zoom to accompany us. I ask if there's a girl who would accompany Sai Zoom, and she points to a friend who likes Sai Zoom.

I tell Sai Zoom about the arrangement, but he laughs. 'You are dreaming,' he says, 'You have too much opium at the Wa village. Here you must talk to a girl for one year before you get an appointment, and then it takes another year before you even get a kiss.'

I shrug, but one of Sai Zoom's friends confirms my version of events. Sai Zoom rushes over to the girls to make the necessary arrangements for tomorrow, and then we leave. But the prospect of an appointment, or date, has rocketed to Sai Zoom's head and he becomes dramatic, spinning the back wheel of the motorbike in a wild arc. When we hit the paddy field levee-top road, he throws his hands in the air and yells into the chill black Myanmar night. 'Ayieeeeee, my first appointment with a girl ever, and it is because of a foreigner!'

Next morning Sai Zoom borrows a car, and we drive to a monastery to collect the Shan village dancing girls. We head to the scenic Bang Doaw waterfall for lunch, and on the way back to town I sit in the back seat of the car with Nang Twe, talking about her career as a dancing girl. When I ask her if she ever kisses any boys she dances with, she shakes her head vigorously, telling me that even touching is out of the question. 'If I touch man in public it means I am to marry him,' she says. 'But better not to touch man in public until after marriage. I never touch men.'

I say to her, 'But you are touching me now. Your leg is touching mine.'

'It is inadvertent,' she says without hesitation.

'Inadvertent? How can it be inadvertent?'

'I must sit this way because of the moving of the car,' she says.

I tease her until Sai Zoom takes charge from behind the steering wheel. 'If a girl says the touching is inadvertent, then you must accept that the touching is inadvertent.'

Silence settles momentarily, then Sai Zoom yells, 'Ayieeeeee! You must marry Shan girl and come to live in her village. Then we can open business for tourists. It will be very good, you will see.'

Ah yes, I think, how simple it always is in such moments of magical madness. I ask, 'But Sai Zoom, where can I find a Shan girl who will marry me? Maybe Nang Twe will marry me?'

Nang Twe is silent. Sai Zoom asks her if she would marry me. 'I would consider it as a possibility,' she replies. 'If he was serious. But he is annoying me because he is just messing around.'

We deliver our appointments back to the monastery at sundown and, after a meal, Sai Zoom suggests we visit the Saing Tang Ya Karaoke and Night Villa for a 'beauty massage'.

The Night Villa is well out of Kyaing Tong, so once again we hop on the bike and roar through a black night until we come to a series of shacks lit with rows of fairy lights and tucked back off the road, behind a small lake. The largest shack, the karaoke room, is a chintzy, large bar-cum-lounge overseen by a bulging, bellicose Chinese mama san. Customers drink alcohol, smoke tobacco from yard-long bamboo pipes, shriek loudly in poor tune with the karaoke songs, or chat with the girls who specialise in the famous Myanmar body massage.

I'm an enthusiast of the non-sexual Myanmar massage. It's a thorough going-over: vigorous, exhilarating, at times painful, and the process usually reaches it climax, as such, when I lay on my back with the masseuse standing on me, digging her feet deep into my groin, thus cutting off the blood flow. She stands motionless for about a minute, then steps back and a warm rush of blood pelts through the body.

Here at the Night Villa a tall, gracious massage girl, her fingernails painted in lurid lolly pink with black spots, wafts over to our table and starts chatting. This exasperates Mama San, who clearly likes to keep the cash registers ticking over. 'Go, go,' she says to me, after demanding a dollar for a massage.

The girl takes me to a large room with about a dozen mattresses on the floor, and curtains that can be drawn to form a sort of cubicle. She goes to work and, although she is slender, she is strong.

The trial by massage also becomes a social occasion. A Myanmar man being massaged next to me parts the curtains between us and engages in a limited conversation. Various massage girls pop over to observe and to say *mingalabar*, the Myanmar greeting for foreigners. Sai Zoom and some guys he's been drinking with come and sit on the floor next to me, and he tells me that the massage girl has just told him that she is too frightened to fully stretch me because my legs are so stiff, probably the result of hours spent on the back of a motorbike.

But the massage has its effect. After it's finished, I bid farewell to the Night Villa and its intriguing denizens. I return to my room at the Old Kyaing Tong Hotel, snuggle into the cosy bed and drift into a deep, dreamless sleep.

I assigned Sai Zoom the task of organising the necessary government paperwork and permissions to travel to nearby *zhongguo de gangmen*, the arsehole of China, as international reporters have begun referring to the isolated city of Mongla, allegedly built on the proceeds of drugs and gambling in the hill country wilderness that straddles the Burma–Chinese border, 80 kilometres from Kyaing Tong.

I was curious about Mongla because a procession of outraged journalists passing through the city outdid each other in detailing the decadence to be found in this out-of-the-way destination, and all unfailingly suggested that such decadence was further proof of the inherent evil of the Myanmar military regime. As feverishly as the journalists tried to paint a picture of vile, government-sponsored decadence in Mongla, the decadence they claimed to have uncovered, while perhaps quaint, fell far short of what has become standard issue in the fleshpots of Bangkok, southern China and indeed the red-light districts of many Western capitals.

The editorial board of the glossy magazine *Myanmar Perspectives* seemed to agree. They visited Mongla and reported, 'You can enjoy a good Chinese restaurant-cum-music-and-dance-theatre with the fascinating name of Foreign Amorous Feeling Place. There are even transvestite dance-and-song shows in some of the big theatres such as the Recreation Dance Hall.'

I was more curious about the political status of Mongla and its surrounds because it is part of a group of autonomous zones run by the Wa people, an ethnic minority living in both Myanmar and southern China, and ruled mostly by former rebel leaders from the Burmese Communist Party and former Chinese Red Guard revolutionaries.

The Wa people are the unofficial traditional bogeymen of Myanmar, former lawless headhunting warriors who inhabited what was once tiger-infested wild country and who believe they originated from tadpoles in a sacred lake. They were infamous in nineteenth- and early twentieth-century Britain as 'Boys' Own Adventure' archetypal wild jungle men. The cover of a 1913 British adventure book titled *In the Grip of the Wild Wa* featured a comic-book-style painting of two turbaned, loin-clothed, furtive Wa villains carrying off a bound white man.

Now the Wa are modern bogeymen—gangsters said to run the opium and methamphetamine industry in the north, and to control nightclubs and prostitution in Yangon. An anonymous Wa official told a Bangkok newspaper, 'Wa is now a dirty word. Everybody is afraid of us and they say we are the scum of the earth.'

Many influential Wa are wealthy, and their leaders have become powerful rulers of their own fiefdoms. The autonomous zones are curious creations, almost countries within a country. They have their own flags and car licence plates, and can levy taxes; armed Myanmar military do not enter the zones.

There are several autonomous zones in Myanmar, but the two largest are controlled by the most powerful force in the region, the United Wa State Army, and its political wing, the United Wa State Party.

Mongla is officially known as Special Region 4, and is controlled by the National Democratic Alliance Army, also sometimes referred to as the Eastern Shan State Army. This organisation is secretive and is led by the former Communist Party of Burma heavyweight, 54-year-old Lin Mingxian, or Sai Lin. He took control of the 5000-square-kilometre zone with a population of 75 000 on 30 June 1989. By the early 1990s his group was reported to be producing 2000 tonnes of pure heroin annually and he was named near the top of the US State Department's blacklist. He was removed from the US blacklist in 2000. He suffered a stroke in 2003 and curtailed much of his business activity, but still patrols his patch in a distinctive white Rolls Royce without number plates.

I also wanted to visit Mongla because of my fascination with the case of Rachel Goldwyn, a young English activist who had been sentenced to seven years prison in Yangon for singing democracy songs in the street, but was released after two months and given a free trip to Kyaing Tong, together with her parents, by the government. She and her family were also sent to Mongla to see the Drug Elimination Museum as part of her 'research'.

Goldwyn's story gives a rare insight into the workings of the Myanmar regime and the overriding sense of old-fashioned paternalism permeating this society, of the need to punish sternly and then offer compassion to those who are seen to have learnt their lesson. It also demonstrates the belief by the Myanmar rulers that the world misunderstands their country and the military regime.

Rachel Goldwyn, the daughter of an English television producer, first met Myanmar people at a Thai border refugee camp. Later, back in Britain, she decided to travel to Myanmar itself, telling her parents she was going to Germany. On 7 September 1999, shortly after arriving in Yangon, she chained herself to a street railing near the Sule Pagoda, unfurled a banner and sang pro-democracy songs. Thirteen minutes later she was arrested and taken to a police station where, according to an account she later wrote, 'I kept trying to break the tension by sticking my tongue out.'

On 16 September she was sentenced to seven years hard labour for 'undermining the stability of the State'. She was taken to Insein prison, where she received many visits from high-ranking Military Intelligence and Psychological Warfare officers. Colonel Hla Min, the son of a former ambassador to the US, and other intelligence officers introduced themselves as 'VIP visitors,' gave her books on Myanmar and discussed the politics and history of Myanmar with her. Her parents arrived to plead for mercy and were befriended by Military Intelligence officers, especially the high-ranking Major Myo Khaing, who became their 'host'.

Goldwyn's parents were allowed to visit her ten times in six weeks, and she later wrote, 'Myo Khaing ferried them around Rangoon and beyond, even introducing them (and later me on my release) to his family. They were taken to container ports and airports under construction, pagodas, even "new towns".'

Following dialogue with intelligence officers, Goldwyn

(later claiming, probably quite accurately, that she was in a confused state) asked if she could research the effect of sanctions on the poor. A table was provided outside her prison cell, and she was given use of a pen and paper. But Hla Min said Myanmar's drug eradication program was a more suitable topic for research and it was suggested she should return to her UK university to prepare the work and then return to Myanmar to do the research.

She was released from jail two months after her conviction, and signed an acknowledgement that her acts had been 'erroneous' and that she would agree to not 'violate the existing laws of Burma in the future' and to not 'disturb any interest of Burma'. Her parents also had to sign undertakings. The family was then taken by Myo Khaing to Kyaing Tong and Mongla. Goldwyn wrote that at the time she was terrified of making a wrong move and ending up back in jail, but she also wrote of the 'inevitable' friendship that developed between her and Myo Khaing.

The Goldwyns then returned to Yangon, where Rachel was offered free lodgings by Serge Pun, who is actually my landlord at the Grand Mee Ya Hta Executive Residences, where I live. She wrote, 'I was summoned by one of the country's leading industrialists, Serge Pun of Serge Pun Associates (SPA), to talk about my research. He offered me accommodation for my return, and flattered me on how important this research would be for the good of the Burmese people.'

Rachel Goldwyn returned to the UK to discover that another strange and sad twist awaited her. She was denounced by leftist organisations, and publicly condemned for her perceived 'betrayal' of the Myanmar people by activists who have no inkling of the reality in Myanmar nor of the subtle psychological interaction Westerners have with the Myanmar elite.

Goldwyn's failure in the eyes of earnest activists was to

not denounce the Myanmar government. On her arrival in London she said, 'My world is a very confused place right now.' She said she could not make critical comments for fear she would break her bail conditions. The director of the London-based Burma Campaign Group, Yvette Mahon, described Rachel as 'selfish' and her actions as 'utterly shameful'. Mahon said Goldwyn had, '. . . shocked human rights activists by refusing to speak out against Burma's brutal regime . . . having sought and gained media attention she has since failed to use the privilege of her position to tell the story of Burma's suffering.' Mahon said Goldwyn's priority seemed to be her project and 'ensuring her return to Burma is utterly shameful'.

Shortly afterwards, Goldwyn wrote her version of her story in vivid and at times harrowing detail, highlighting the fear and dread she felt while imprisoned in Yangon. She won a British Press Complaints Commission submission against the *Daily Mail* newspaper, and the Commission reported: 'Miss Rachel Goldwyn complained that an article inaccurately stated that she had agreed to help the military government in Burma with research on human rights activists.'

But her version also upset the Myanmar government officials, who felt she had betrayed them while under pressure from English activists. The final word from Myanmar on this odd saga appeared in the Information Committee's Information Sheet No. B-1223 (1) published on 18 January 2000. A cheery headline stated, 'The Government of Myanmar Wishes the Goldwyns All the Best Happiness for the New Year.'

The bulletin read:

The Myanmar Government does not feel disappointed but it feels sorry for Ms. Rachel Goldwyn that she has to change her ground so suddenly. It is quite understandable that she is under tremendous pressure from people with vested interest. The Government of Myanmar realizing that she has been victimized by a certain group of people while recognizing the love and affection of the distressed parents on their daughter decided to release her on humanitarian grounds.

The Government has no regrets for the leniency and clemency it had granted to Ms. Rachel Goldwyn and continues to wish her all the best. Taking this opportunity the Government would also like to extend the Goldwyns a very Happy New Year.

Oddly, whenever I accessed Information Sheet No. B-1223 (1) on the internet, my computer broke out into a loud, lush and irritating string arrangement of 'Heartaches by the Number'.

Early in the morning Sai Zoom and two mates he'd rounded up arrive in a battered Toyota, driven by the owner, and off we head over the mountain pass on the new road to Mongla.

As we trundle toward Mongla, the straggly Kyaing Tong suburbs slowly give way to a countryside that is home to buffalo, ducks and large, stub-nosed, slate-grey Chinese pigs. As we climb, towering stands of dense lush-green bamboo groves screen the jungle and for the first time I understand the accuracy of the term, 'bamboo curtain'. Occasionally we pass a hill-tribe village set back off the road, and the subdued colouring of the dirt surrounds and thatched huts is punctuated by blazes of brilliant kingfisher blue: women strolling around in traditional costumes.

At the top of the pass the vegetation thins, and Sai Zoom points to a row of collapsed dilapidated straw huts on a nearby ridge. 'That was opium village,' he says. 'Now no more. The opium villages are now over the ridge so they cannot be seen from the road.'

We travel on and soon reach a checkpoint at Tarpin, consisting of a small wooden office, a boom gate across the road and a thatched hut which serves as a shop. The word 'welcome' is spelled out in white stones on a green grass bank opposite the checkpoint office and gives me the feeling that we are entering another country which, in a sense, we are. We are entering Wa Land, or 'Wa Vegas', as I have dubbed it in my mind.

The driver pops into the office to have the paperwork checked and then we're on the road to Mongla again, down the mountain pass, onto the flat lands and through fields of rice. Soldiers march by the side of the road in the uniform of the National Democratic Alliance Army. Some carry modern weaponry while others carry the antique long-barrelled muskets.

We pass acres of young mango trees, a drug eradication crop substitution scheme, according to a sign, and as we enter Mongla I am surprised by the obvious prosperity. The downtown shopping precinct is modern, with well-stocked shops featuring plate-glass windows. I've seen nothing like this in most of Myanmar, which adds to my feeling that we have entered another country—a feeling that's accentuated when we stop at a café. Our Myanmar kyats have no currency here and are dismissed with scorn. We must pay with Chinese yuan, just as we must not speak Myanmar—only Chinese—and we must adjust to the clocks that are set to Chinese time.

It's instantly obvious that gambling is the main industry of Mongla. Casinos proliferate and, as we turn a corner, we come across a gaggle of about a hundred young people dressed in black trousers or skirts, maroon jumpers and white shirts with black bow ties. They're just one shift of croupiers on their lunch break from just one casino.

The L.T. Casino on the edge of town is a garish monstrosity of Las-Vegas-Meets-the-Orient architecture, featuring one-storey-high panels that depict glamorous gamblers in black evening garb silhouetted against a lurid lolly-pink background. The building's façade is a messy scramble of roulette wheels, dice and decks-of-cards motifs. The entrance ways are bordered by sickly bright-blue columns and arches which drip gilt, and the long sweeping driveway is bordered by profusely flowering hedges.

We pop into a lavish casino in the centre of town, the Oriental, to encounter acre after acre of cavernous rooms choking with faux marble, fake ornate pillars and gilt chandeliers. Oriental kitsch to the max.

We leave the casino and drive to the Chinese border. Mongla is confusing, but the border confuses me even more. It is a strange case of West meets East, East being Myanmar and West being China. The Chinese tourists who pour across the border are well heeled and fashionable in a Western style, arriving in gleaming new cars like downtown cosmopolitans from a fashionable Western city.

The last stand for Myanmar at the border is a drab roadside office, and Sai Zoom suggests we check with the officials in case we need to report our presence. We enter a dim interior where officials are partitioned from civilians by old ornate iron scrollwork. A sign hanging from the scrollwork is the only example of the Myanmar language I've spotted in Mongla. An English translation informs me this is a 'Saniton and Antiepedemic Station'. The officials laboriously enter information by hand in large antique ledgers, but they wave us out of the office as though we are nuisances intruding upon their Dickensian clerical duties.

The Mongla side of the border is guarded by two well-turned-out National Democratic Alliance Army soldiers standing ramrod rigid under colourful umbrellas in much the same way as guards stand at Buckingham Palace, looking straight ahead, not moving a muscle. I ask if I can take a photo and they stand mute for a few seconds, then laugh and chat. One soldier says, 'Go. Go to China, walk around the corner, there is something interesting to see.'

We walk to the end of the hundred-yard stretch of no man's land and into China. The 'something interesting' is a mini-marketplace selling brand-name belts, polo shirts and assorted souvenirs. A yellow throne sits by the side of the road with two live peacocks tethered to the throne legs by cords. Two Chinese women in extravagant yellow costumes signal me to sit on the throne, and the peacocks happily hop onto my thighs.

One of a dozen or so girls lurking nearby, all armed with new digital cameras, takes a photo. She walks to a stall on the footpath which contains a row of computers, connects her camera to a computer and within seconds a printer clacks out a laminated 2004 calendar incorporating my photo. She hands it to me, saying, 'Be happy in China. Three US dorrah for carrendar.'

I contrast this display of street-side digital wizardry with our Myanmar friends a hundred yards away, who are in another country and another time, and still in the age of handwritten ledgers. To them going digital probably means using as many fingers as possible.

I look up and spot a posing sissy or lady boy, a local trans-vestite, glaring at me, and then another. They patrol the district on their motor scooters and now they're homing in on my presence, watching me like crows checking carrion to see if it still moves. I spot them here and there, standing on one leg, with one knee on the saddle of their scooter, and they look like poster girls advertising a cheap remake of a Suzie Wong movie. When I make eye contact, they glare at me as if daring me to keep staring.

Sai Zoom says he knows some of the sissies. 'Come,' he tells me. 'We visit them at the sissy house. Sometimes they will show us their breasts, sometimes their cocks.' The sissies live in an 'international standard National Park' called Shwe Satu-gan Mya Yeik San Oo-yin, a vast acreage of verdant opulence, lawns and gardens on a lavish scale with flower-bud street lamps and posts with signage contained in elephant-head-profile metal scrollwork. Elephant statues abound and, as we stroll along a path, we come to a series of giant concrete spotted toad-stools doubling as sunshades. We come across a walk-through concrete crocodile, about the size of a small prop jet, complete with portholes, and after we walk through the crocodile we come to stinking crocodile pit. A dozen despondent saurians lie on a cement slab surrounded by a murky moat, and a strange purple dye oozes from the many lesions on their scaly bodies.

Underneath the pit some small, dank cages house two sulky, scraggly bears, and two dopey elephants saunter nearby. These are the famous soccer-playing bicycle-riding elephants, and Sai Zoom shows me a small noticeboard containing withered, weathered black and white photos depicting the famous elephants actually riding bikes and kicking soccer balls. An attendant is shovelling piles of elephant shit into one large pile, and he peremptorily says, 'Elephants is not working. Today is holiday day.'

A lurid billboard featuring the performing sissies stands on a small rise overlooking the pit, and next to the pit is a dance hall where the sissies perform. On top of the hall, jutting out toward the croc pit, is a large apartment, the living quarters for the sissies. I wonder who decided that an apartment over-looking a pit of stinking live crocodiles is an appropriate housing arrangement for an assortment of Thai and Chinese transvestites.

Transvestite detritus—sequins, spangles and small fluorescent fluffy feathers—litters the ground outside the hall, and a black spangled bra and panty set hang from the apartment window.

We return to the car and drive across town to a small, drab, asphalt car park behind the main street, the venue for the infamous wild animal market, similar to markets proliferating throughout southern China. The stallholders are just setting up and, as I look around, I spot a transvestite propped on her motor scooter, glaring at me, daring me to stare. A dwarf arrives on a pushbike with a wire crate behind the seat stuffed with live cobras. More traders arrive, setting up shop around the edges of the car park, stacking wire crates containing birds, reptiles and small furry animals. The market becomes busier and I am staggered by the sheer number and variety of critters on sale: hunched hamster-like beings about the size of bulldogs, ferociously glaring, flustered falcons, calm owls with beautiful masked faces staring curiously from wire enclosures, alert, snarling mongooses, bowls of multi-coloured, slimy toads. I spot dozens of different turtles, and plenty of pissing pangolins, which resemble pinkish-grey plasticine animal foetuses. The poor pangolins don't seem to do much except piss whenever they are moved and, when a woman holds up a tiny baby pangolin, it promptly pisses on her hand.

A man walks a two-metre-long black and yellow monitor lizard by simply holding its stiff tail and pushing it in the direction he wants to go. A woman tips the contents of a green bamboo tube onto her hands, revealing a tangle of gleaming white grubs. Several round mesh cages contain the dreaded civet cats, which obviously escaped the extermination camps just over the border in China, where they've recently been sentenced to death for allegedly disseminating SARS.

A man walks over to the dwarf, undoes the cage on the back of his bike and pulls out six feet of hissing cobra, which writhes and lunges in the air. A good cobra sells for about US$100, and the meat sells in Kyaing Tong for US$30 a kilo.

Vendors thread their way through the throng selling ice-creams, snacks and fruit. I buy mandarins and walnuts, and take photos until two officious Chinese tell me to get lost. As we leave the menagerie of sorrows, we drive past a roadside sign saying, 'Cigar can start drug abuse'.

We head toward another architectural monstrosity that stands on a hill dominating the town. The building's pink awfulness is adorned with gilt scrolls and curlicues, and it resembles an icing-sugar confection atop an Italian birthday cake. We stop at the entrance, to be confronted by a stone slab with bold brass lettering announcing we have arrived at the 'Museum in Commemoration of Opium-Free in Special Region no. 4'.

As we walk toward the museum I spot a transvestite propped on his motor scooter, glaring at me, daring me to stare. We climb the steep stairs, past a red and white umbrella shading a stall selling cheap cartons of Golden Triangle brand and Duya cigarettes, and past another sign saying 'Let us join hands in the fight against drug menace to all mankind'. We have entered the Mongla Drug Elimination Museum.

The Myanmar military love these expensive mausoleums, which they've erected throughout the Union. But the Thais have also jumped on the bandwagon and, in late 2003, they opened a US$40 million Hall of Opium near the Thai–Myanmar border. This Thai museum is also a research centre, and the history of opium in the region is represented by dioramas and displays, including reconstructions of scenes from the Opium Wars in China, a Thai opium den and the hold of a British cargo ship. The museum's Gallery of Victims represents the descent into the pit of addiction and oblivion suffered by international celebrities and addicts such as Elvis Presley, Lenny Bruce and Charlie Parker. A tragic portrait of the beautiful Chinese actress Ju Jia, who died from an overdose aged 28, fades and reappears to the strains of Louis Armstrong singing 'What A Wonderful World'.

But while the Thai museum is a commercial tourist attraction and research centre, the Myanmar Drug Elimination

Museums are mostly vehicles for the peculiar propaganda perpetrated by the junta, assailing viewers with three-dimensional weirdness and crude examples of audience inter-action, most of which aren't working when I try to interact.

The Mongla Drug Museum is smaller than the Yangon equivalent built on an old graveyard and avoided by most Myanmar, due to the alleged presence of ghosts. But both museums are alike in their presentation of artefacts, dioramas, heroic tableaux, portraiture and potted histories mainly shafting the dreaded drug-pushing colonialists.

Displays of photos show seized drug hauls with some stacks as large as small caravans. Photos of generals and overseas dignitaries are also featured, including US senators shaking hands with drug lords who were once, or still are, on the US State Department's wanted list.

Bottles containing deformed foetuses, the doomed children of junkies, are exhibited in the Yangon museum, and newspaper reports I had read claimed the Mongla museum displayed a pre-served addict's body lying in repose, similar to the mummified bodies of AIDS victims on public display at Thailand's biggest AIDS hospice in Lopburi. I can't find the body at Mongla, but I do find a display of grotesque forensic photos showing the physical ravages of drugs and/or AIDS on the human body.

I run an appreciative eye over the museum's collection of propaganda art, or prop art as I call it, and particularly admire a massive heroic diorama. It is set in a picturesque valley. In the background Myanmar soldiers with their Australian-style slouch hats denude a field of insidious poppies. Striding forth is a uniformed nurse carrying a clipboard, and in the fore-ground Chinese soldiers dismantle a clandestine jungle heroin laboratory. In the centre picture, arms behind his back, is a mysterious and slightly sinister foreign figure with a pencil-thin moustache and sunglasses, wearing a uniform without any identifying insignia. The character looks like a rendering from a 1930s *Boys' Own Annual* cover, and I take it to represent the covert US military presence.

I check the museum's guest book to see if there are any entries from the Goldwyn family, but I find no trace of them. I leave the museum and stroll toward a souvenir stand, spotting a transvestite propped on her motor scooter, glaring at me, daring me to stare. I check the shelves in the souvenir stand. There aren't any actual souvenirs of the museum, but there are shelves of liquor, cigarette cartons, and pornographic DVDs with lurid topless photos of pale, podgy, Pommy page-3 models. The women behind the counter giggle modestly and one asks, 'You want sissy photo?' She hands me a pack of cards which feature simpering, glaring, melon-breasted sissies posing in see-through string vests.

Sai Zoom's friends have been quiet all day, enthusiastically swigging cheap, clear, potent Chinese liquor from small hip-flask-sized bottles; they now lurk furtively near the display of DVD covers. Sai Zoom says, 'My friends think we should stay tonight in Mongla.' 'See naked fucking ladies,' interjects one of the friends. Sai Zoom says, 'The driver wants us to make decision now. If we will not be here for night, then we must go now because the mountain pass is not safe at night. Many bandits.'

I look at the driver. He is a family man and obviously wants to return to Kyaing Tong. 'Naked fucking ladies good, good,' interjects the drunk and hopeful friend. 'I think we should now return to Kyaing Tong,' I announce, while one of the friends lurches forward, almost knocking over the stand of dirty DVDs.

The sun is setting as we reach the car; as I get into the vehicle, I look around to spot a transvestite propped on her motor scooter, glaring at me, daring me to stare. As we drive through the outskirts we are caught up in peak hour in Rural-tania. The road is clogged with agricultural workers leaving the fields and heading home after a long day's patriotic toil. Dozens of doughty buffalo plod wearily while calves skitter across the road. Women walk by carrying loads of produce on their heads, and a group of hill-tribe women walk toward the hills carrying wicker baskets slung over their shoulders, their muscular calves encased in embroidered knee-high gaiters. Every kilometre or so we halt and permit flocks of thousands of white ducks to cross the road, tended by men in broad, round hats gently prodding their orange-beaked charges with long canes.

We come to a checkpoint. Our papers are examined and we are instructed to get out of the car and to slowly walk behind it as it crosses the barrier. On into the night again, until we come to another long stop at the Tarpin checkpoint, where paperwork is once more scrutinised. I want to get out of the car to stretch my legs, but I am instructed to remain in the vehicle.

And then we are away, into Myanmar proper, the blackness of the Golden Triangle night enveloping us as we cross the steep mountain pass. My drunken companions peacefully sleep in the back seat, probably dreaming of naked fucking ladies, as we descend into the outskirts of Kyaing Tong and the flickering of roadside cooking fires, lanterns and candles. We are back in the land of limited electricity.

Returning to the office after the Christmas break at Kyaing Tong confirmed what I'd already perceived about the international life: clichés rule. The paradigm case is that, despite cultural differences, people are essentially all the same and people the world over act the same when returning to work from leave—they do so begrudgingly.

So it was at the *Myanmar Times*. Staff reluctantly filtered into the office, turning on their computers and psyching themselves for more of the same. Another year, another story. But the office gossip carried a story everybody had missed up to now. Mick Jagger had just been and gone, after being spotted with a woman companion at some of Yangon's better restaurants, such as Le Planteur. Myanmar coverage of this event had been non-existent, but Jagger's visit didn't go unnoticed by the British press. When he returned to London, the determined and dogged anti-Myanmar movement in Britain lobbied against him, denouncing him for visiting Yangon.

Back at the office, the Myanmar staff, after establishing their presence in the office, conformed to their own stereotype by promptly removing their presence, fanning out in groups, dispersing among their favourite teashops.

I left the office and wandered down the narrow side streets, checking out the teashops, and then down along Sule Pagoda Road until I found my trainees at Madam Greedy's famous pickled tea shop. I joined them, sitting on the tiny plastic chairs that in Western countries would have been provided for toddlers; I suggested we start work by practising spoken English, indulging in yet another cliché: exchanging what-I-did-during-my-holiday stories.

Prospective business writer Maw Maw San claimed she had visited distant relatives in their native village of Chan Tar, near Mandalay, enjoying the experience of being a big-city novelty in the rustic backblocks. 'We got to a bus stop near the village,' she said, 'and we had to tell a passer-by to tell our auntie to send a bullock cart for us. It was exciting to ride in a cart on a dusty road. Actually, it was more than exciting. It was stifling because the air was full of dust.'

She said children ran after their cart to look at the city folk. 'The feeling of being the centre of attention was embarrassing but it was also enjoyable. People stared at us and whispered, "Wow, they look so nice in their clothes." Really! And when I walked around the village, almost everybody stared at me because they were not used to seeing a girl wearing sunglasses.'

When Myanmar travel within their own country, they invariably pagoda-hop, visiting as many pagodas as possible. The writer Ma (Khin Win) Thanegi recently wrote the only contemporary English-language novel about Myanmar life, a satire portraying pagoda-hopping, called *The Native Tourist—In Search of Turtle Eggs*, and Maw Maw also warmed to the theme. 'There were many pagodas,' she said. 'Chae-Yar-Daw, which had a Buddha's footprint, and Moe Nyin Than Boat Dae, which has thousands of small Buddha images. But my favourite was the famous Kan Ta Lu pagoda, built by Myanmar's most famous actress, Moet Moet Myint Aung. It is said she built the pagoda because her wish in life had been fulfilled and people go there because they also want their wishes fulfilled.'

The tourism trainee, Su Myat Hla, said she too went Christmas holiday pagoda-hopping with a group of friends at Bagan, the ancient pagoda capital of Myanmar. 'We arrived at Bagan at dawn and when I opened my eyes from my slumber I saw the image of a golden pagoda through the coach windows. This was the famous Tuyin Mountain Pagoda, said to house one of Buddha's teeth. It stands alone solemnly on a mountain and is lit by electric bulbs so, because it was still dark when I first saw it, it appeared to be floating in the air.

'In the evening we hired a horse-drawn cart, visited three pagodas and then watched the sunset from a boat on the Irrawaddy River. We experienced a rare moment as we sat in the boat, surrounded by mountain ranges on one side and ancient pagodas on the other. A beautiful white bird flying away caught our eye as the pinkish-orange sun slowly set, changing from one colour to another and spreading its colours onto the mountains directly underneath.'

The trainee sports and environmental writer, Ba Saing, said he went bush, returning to his Kayin Christian community in Pyin Oo Lwin, a former British hill station known as Maymyo. 'After a long trip I finally found myself in front of my family compound and laughed because it was a mess of green bushes and grass and I knew my job would be to clean it up,' he said. 'I walked along the dirt road of our compound shouting, "Mum, I'm home." She ran out to me and hugged and kissed me.'

Ba said he attacked his duties as No. 1 son by cleaning up the compound, and then explored his home town, taking in the changes that had occurred since he had moved to the big city for work. 'I travelled around the old town in the horse-drawn carriages we call gharries. I spoke to the gharry-walas about the town's economy and learned that the sweater-making business is enjoying high demand. The Korean television stars wear them in the popular TV series and suddenly everybody wants to buy a sweater.

'There were several music concerts during Christmas, and I saw the famous rock band, Emperor, from Yangon. There were funny scenes at that concert because some spectators climbed a tree and were shouting out loudly until a guard shot them with a catapult.'

As for most good Myanmar sons, New Year's Eve was a family affair for Ba. He said, 'I'm very much grandma's pet and she requested I spend New Year's Eve with her. We watched the Myanmar Academy Awards ceremony, which was broadcast live on MRTV at 5pm. Grandma criticised the clothes the actresses wore. Then a boy from my grandpa's house came and told me grandpa wanted to see me right away. I thought he wanted to give me the usual lecture, but I was wrong. He wanted me to pray for his health because he had low blood pressure. So I prayed to encourage him.'

The budding agricultural writer, Thein Lin, said he also spent some time with his family in Ngasutaung village praying, but mostly he built a new guest toilet for a forthcoming family wedding. 'I was late getting to my village,' he said, 'because the bus had a flat tyre. But when I finally arrived home, my mother and I talked until the sound of the midnight toll. I slept warmly and peacefully at my mother's breast like a baby. Next morning when I woke I heard the signal sound of a cock in the fen behind the house and I knew the day had started. My mother recited the Dharma of Buddha. My youngest brother and I began to build the toilet, but then my brother hit his thumb with the hammer and I worked on alone.'

Thein finished his toilet-building duties, helped his family clean the local monastery, and returned to Yangon for New Year's Eve. 'In the evening I watched the fiftieth anniversary of the Academy Awards of the Myanmar motion picture industry,' he said, 'and then went to the family home of one of my university friends. We discussed the Academy Awards and then my friend's father, who is a member of the Myanmar Women's Affairs Federation, told me he was translating the book *A World*, which contained collected extracts of speeches by the former secretary-general of the United Nations, U Thant. The book, in the English language, was copyrighted by Daw Aye Aye Thant, U Thant's eldest daughter, and my friend's father was translating it into Myanmar.

'So, instead of sitting around a campfire playing guitars and enjoying sing-alongs as I'd planned, I talked about the U Thant book until it was midnight and we all loudly shouted "Happy New Year!"'

The would-be sports writer, Saw Thiha Thway, a Christian community leader, said he'd set out to do good works during the festive season, but instead upset both his mother and his girlfriend. 'During our family Christmas dinner I was very embarrassed because of my mother's disappointed words about my long hair. I went to bed early feeling melancholy and next day I cut my hair. The New Year's Eve celebration at the Cornerstone Community Church was a thrilling time for me because I was the chairman of the New Year worship service. I conducted the programs but I was tired and at 2am, when the young people were playing games around the camp fire, I went to sleep. But it wasn't a thrilling time for my girlfriend. All the people in my church were very happy, but my girlfriend was very angry—because I had been so busy, she wasn't able to talk to me the whole night.'

The diplomatic affairs trainee, Winston Soe, a Muslim with an intellectual interest in the permutations of the many religions found on this earth, said he spent Christmas Day with his Christian friends from the Watch Tower Bible and Tract Society.

'They actually don't practise Christmas because they do not believe December 25 to be the birthday of Jesus Christ,' he explained. 'Other Christians marginalise them for their different religious beliefs and the way they represent Christendom, but I am very fond of them because of their kind attitude. Thanks to them, I had a chance to learn advanced English because they offered me many English language books.

'On the last day of the holiday period I drank beer at the Jade Garden with my friends. The price of beer had jumped about twenty per cent. Many people, even the girls, now drink beer and a beer culture has become strongly rooted in Myanmar. It is a contagious culture because many Myanmar youth try to copy the lifestyle of the West. They value material possessions too much and want to copy those who possess them. They also think that by drinking beer they will appear to be modernised.

'Later I talked to a friend, who owns an eye-glass shop, about how Myanmar people are also copying Korean and Chinese cultures, because they are so captivated by movies from those countries. We agreed that the good should be adopted and the bad filtered out, and that such cross-cultural activities contribute toward a better globalisation. My dream is to live in the global village.'

I figured that Winston had perhaps unknowingly realised his dream, because in many ways the supposedly isolated Yangon was more of a global village than the Australian cities in which I had lived. Last Saturday afternoon, for example, I'd been invited to a Yangon university graduation party at the trendy Western-style BME Dome nightclub. As I sat on the floor with my Myanmar friends watching the musicians on stage, I noticed the club was slowly filling with outrageous English-style Myanmar punks sporting spiked mohawk haircuts, contrived punk trappings and, for the men, leather jackets, despite the heat. One punk's leather jacket had the legend, 'Sex Pistils are God' painted on the back, and another boasted, 'Conflict'.

A punk band, featuring a woman singer in crotch-hugging leopard-print pants, with a black mesh top over a Union Jack singlet, burst onto the stage. They ripped into 'Anarchy in the UK' and their acolytes invaded the dance floor, throwing themselves about in a frenzy of self-conscious but supposedly abandoned aggression, clearing the dance floor, sending the soft, gentle and polite Myanmar students into exile in the shadowy recesses at the edge of the floor. At first a frisson of fear shivered through the crowd, to be replaced by seething resentment over the aggression and violence displayed by the limb-flailing punks as they dominated the dance floor.

I lost interest and left, hailing a cab that came to a sudden halt at the first crossroad about 200 yards from the club. A military parade was underway, and smartly dressed troops in tight formation marched out of a parade ground and through the crossroad. There were thousands of them in neat lines, marching with bared bayonets, garlands of flowers around their necks, their boots stamping loudly on the bitumen. The lines of soldiers were interspersed with military bands and the procession lasted for more than half an hour.

During this time I sat in the cab watching the fearful but impressive show of military might, and contrasting their precision with the anarchic madness of the punks' day out I had just witnessed. I said to myself, 'Only in Yangon'.

It's Saturday morning and I stroll though the downtown district, shopping by myself because my usual shopping companion and Unofficial Daughter No. 1, Lasheeda, has gone with her mother to the countryside. Earlier in the week I phoned Ma Ban Cherry and arranged to accidentally bump into her again later this morning at Zawgyi Café to discuss the date we discussed before Christmas.

I'd also arranged to have lunch with Joost, one of several interesting young Western entrepreneurial types who have set up shop in Yangon, trying to make a success of their business schemes. Joost is in the rattan business, designing and manufacturing fashionable rattan furniture, which he hopes to export mainly to Europe. A few weeks ago he abandoned the country residence he'd established in a village near Yangon, where he'd also rented a factory to produce his rattan ware. He'd had an idyllic image of the bucolic rural life, but this had been shattered by reality: bad phone lines, no running water, an electricity supply even more erratic than in the capital and, of course, isolation.

But it was the cobras that did him in. The gardens surrounding his rural retreat were a haven for the reptiles, and he'd ultimately been held to ransom by a large, grief-maddened male cobra mourning its dead wife. Cobras, he'd been told, often mate for life; his security guard had killed a female and thereafter its male partner circled the house angrily each evening looking to avenge its late wife, as it were. Joost was trapped in the house because he wasn't game to venture outside at night. Ultimately he packed his bags, rented a Yangon apartment, and the last time I saw him he was in the throes of opening a downtown showroom.

As I walk through the streets, I notice some vendors are selling a flower that's just come into season. I haven't seen this flower before but I have read about it. It's the legendary and revered gangaw, also known as cobra's saffron, a beautifully scented flower with large, lustrous white petals and a furry yellow button centre. Its pollen is collected by women to perfume the thanakha they wear on their faces, but the flower is also sacred. It grows on the ironwood tree, or the bodhi tree, the Buddhist tree of enlightenment, and Indian Hindus associate it with the naga, a snake-like demigod that inhabits the deep and can attain human form.

There is a brisk trade in the flower this morning because women are buying it to give as offerings at the pagodas. I buy a bunch, and this seems to amuse the locals. 'Ah, gangaw, gangaw,' people comment as I walk by. I stop at the busy Super One supermarket and several salesgirls follow me through the aisles saying, 'Ah, you have gangaw, gangaw, very beautiful.' A stylish middle-aged woman walks toward me, waving to gain my attention, and then executes a sort of pirouette, as though she is a fashion model, turning around to show me she has a gangaw flower in the bun at the back of her hair. 'Ah, very beautiful, very beautiful,' I murmur as she smiles and returns to her shopping.

I like flowers and that's another reason I love walking the streets of Yangon, because often they are alive with the most brilliant blooms. Taxi drivers buy strings or garlands of fragrant jasmine, or the even more cloyingly fragrant little butterfly or ginger lilies, to drape over the rear-vision mirrors of their vehicles as a tribute to Buddha, and women and children flit among the traffic at red lights hawking these garlands.

Soldiers march with garlands of flowers around their necks on special occasions, the warm yellow and white petals off-setting the cold glinting steel of their bayonets. Many women wear flowers entwined in the hair, or a single flower affixed by a brooch-like ornament to their hair when worn in a bun, and the heroic Aung San Suu Kyi is almost always pictured wearing flowers in her hair.

Flowers have significance in Myanmar society, often marking the changing of seasons or the onset of religious festivals. The yellow padauk flower, as we have seen, heralds the onset of the Thingyan Water Festival season. Flowers are also given to people as a mark of respect. Early every Saturday morning for the past few months, one of my former trainees, Eindra Pwint, has been paying me respect by bringing me, her sayar, bunches of flowers. She trims them in my kitchen and arranges them in vases throughout my apartment, before she rushes off to join her family.

Myanmar drips with orchids, including several rare species found in the jungles, and orchid cultivation is becoming a thriving business. A street vendor waylays me almost every week at the entrance to my apartment complex. She has dozens of multi-hued orchid flowers in a bag, living gems coated with glistening beads of moisture. She sets them out on a plastic mat on the footpath, urging me to buy this one or that one, a yellow one, a pink one, or a purplish-mauve delight. Occasionally she triumphantly produces a spectacular black and white flower with little drips of blood-red splattered over the petals. 'Ah, very beautiful,' she will coo softly as she holds it aloft.

At such times I squat on the pavement examining her offerings, and often my betel-nut-and-cigarette-selling lady will come over with her daughter and they too squat, offering suggestions as to which flowers I should buy to take home and float in bowls of water on my coffee table. Sometimes the amiable Frenchman, Kenedi, owner of the Zawgyi Café, will stroll over, smoking a cheroot, standing and smiling as he surveys the orchid transactions unfolding on the footpath.

But now I arrive at Zawgyi Café and, as I sit down, the waiter is amused because I am carrying the bunch of gangaw flowers. 'Ah, you have the gangaw flower,' he says, significantly. Ma Pan Cherry glides into the café, a brilliant smile illuminating her dusky face. She is wearing yet another of her dazzling fashion creations, an eye-catching hybrid of traditional Myanmar style and Western elegance. She looks at the bunch of gangaw flowers on the table and is obviously amused. I'm tempted to offer them to her, but I'm not sure whether we have reached the flower-giving stage yet. She orders coffee and tells me our accidental-bumping-into-each-other this morning will have to be brief because she is en route to the country to visit an array of aunts: eldest aunts, middle aunts, beloved aunts, respected aunts, and ordinary aunts.

We quickly get down to the business of the day: the date. I ask her if the date we organised before Christmas is still on her agenda and she replies affirmatively. She does the counting-on-her-fingers business again and announces that some cousins she expected to be arriving in Yangon next weekend are no longer arriving, so our date can be brought forward. We can now officially date next Saturday night.

Ma Cherry exits gracefully, rewarding me with another illuminating smile. I attack the *Bangkok Post* crossword with vigour, filling in time until my lunch appointment with Joost. Then I put the crossword aside, unable to complete the final three clues, and I am briefly joined by Aye Aye Oo, an intelligent university graduate who wants to become a journalism trainee at the *Times*, but cannot gain permission from her mother. I have met the mother, who told me she doesn't want her daughter to become a journalist because the stress might affect a medical condition she has: her blood pressure drops dramatically, causing her to collapse. But I know the real reason the mother will not grant permission is that she fears her daughter will be contaminated by association with the *Times'* foreigners.

As Aye Aye Oo sits, she looks at my bunch of gangaw flowers with amusement. 'Ah, you have the gangaw flower,' she says, significantly. We chat, and she distractedly picks up the pen I have left on the table, idly completing the crossword puzzle, effortlessly inking in the three clues that baffled me.

The day's events unfold smoothly. Aye Aye Oo leaves; Joost arrives, wearing his customary black. He's an easygoing, unflappable sort of guy with a quietly spoken demeanour, an asset here in Yangon, which allows him to operate with a modicum of success. But today he's not so easygoing. We order a bottle of Spirulina Beer and I inquire about the progress of his new showroom. 'The bloody astrologers are making my life hell,' he says, a pained, quizzical expression flitting across his face. 'The staff insist I consult the astrologers about everything. Right now I'm waiting for them to decide what day would be an auspicious opening day. I can't plan anything until I get their decision, and I don't even know when they will actually make this decision.

'My new showroom has two entrances, but the one I like and was going to use as the main entrance has been forbidden by the astrologers. Now I have to shut that entrance because my staff refuse to use it or to let it be used by others.' Joost ponders his predicament momentarily, then leans forward and says, 'But you know what's really strange? I was talking to one of my neighbouring shopkeepers, and he warned me against using this same entrance. He said it gets slippery during the monsoon and several years ago a man was badly injured when he fell and hit his head on the wall.'

Astrologers dominate day-to-day life in Myanmar, although the onset of modernity is slowly eroding the practice. Most of the military strongmen consult astrologers—Prime Minister Khin Nyunt's personal astrologer is famous and many of Ne Win's maddest decisions, such as the overnight switches to a currency divisible by nine and to driving on the right-hand side of the road instead of the left, are reputed to have been suggested by astrologers.

Astrology books flood the marketplace and sell in impressive quantities. Astrology magazines, such as *Hlyo Whet San Kyae* and *Ganbi Ya*, are popular and the astrology magazine *Nut Katta Yaung Chi* is the biggest-selling magazine in Myanmar. Incidentally, the second best selling magazine is a young woman's magazine, *Ay Pyo Sin* or *Young Virgins*.

I spend considerable time in Yangon tracking down bizarre curios, with the help of a local dealer, U Why Not, whom I hired on the basis of his name and business card, which reads: 'Attentiveness, courtesy, generosity . . . I also lie'. Recently Why Not came up trumps, delivering me one of my most prized possessions, a zata I'd been keenly seeking. A zata is the equivalent of the Western horoscope chart, and a series of complex individual horoscope symbols are artistically etched onto small bamboo sheets and bound with string. They form a little book that is compiled a few weeks after the birth of a baby, whose destiny it helps predict. The finished product is a collection of weird hieroglyphics that look as though they originated on a distant planet. Legend has it that British War Office code-breakers attempted to decodify a zata early last century, but failed.

The Myanmar astrology system is very different from ours. We rely on a solar system of twelve months, each with a corresponding sign, while Myanmar uses a lunar system. The Myanmar lunar New Year starts on 8 April and every fourth year a special month is added, much like our leap year system, which adds a day every fourth February.

In Myanmar you'll never hear the line, 'What star sign are you?' Instead the local line is, 'What day are you born?' Great emphasis is placed on this, and experts will tell you that a Sunday-born person may, for example, be incompatible with a Tuesday-born person. Each day has a sign and temperament. For example, Thursday-born is a rat and the temperament is mildness.

The first one or two letters of a person's first name can often denote what day they were born on. For example, if I have an appointment to meet Daw Khway Yo, I know I should be meeting Monday-born Mrs Dog's Bone, who may be a jealous tigress. The K in the first name, Khway, may denote Monday-born and Monday's sign is the tiger, with a temperament of jealousy.

If I were visiting someone called Ohnmar, I should be meeting a Sunday-born person with a name meaning, 'Woman so beautiful she drove men mad'. I should also suspect she is parsimonious because she is a kalon, the fabulous half-beast, half-bird guarding one of the terraces of Mount Myintmo, the centre of the universe. If I met Ma Soe, I'd be meeting Miss Naughty, a Tuesday-born lion who is therefore honest.

I myself am Wednesday-born and Wednesday is a tricky and different day, because it is the only day divided into two. I fall into the Wednesday afternoon category, which means I am born under a special constellation, yahu. Both morning and afternoon Wednesday-born are represented by elephants; morning-borns by tusked elephants and afternoon-borns by tuskless elephants. Both morning- and afternoon-borns share the characteristic of being short-tempered, but they are soon calm again, and this trait is intensified in we yahu, or afternoon-borns. Newcomers to the *Myanmar Times* office are always warned about my tendency to be short-tempered, which indeed I am.

All such details, and many more, are carefully and laboriously hand-etched onto the zata, which is given to astrologers to interpret when decisions need to be made. The zata is also hidden from people, because the information on it can enable a person of ill will to employ a wezu or wizard to cast a bad spell. But Why Not claimed that the zata he supplied to me cannot be used to ill effect because I don't know the person's identity. Plus the zata is so old that the owner has already been reincarnated and is well beyond any evil intentions I might try to conjure up with the aid of wezus.

Joost and I finish our lunch and he says he had better go and check what's happening at his showroom. Maybe the astrologers have come to a decision. I wish him good luck and when he leaves I figure I should perhaps invoke good fortune by consulting an astrologer.

I pick up the *Myanmar Times* and turn to the Western zodiac 'Extended Stars' column, where I read the entry for Taurus. It says:

> Financial gains are on the cards this week. You may find yourself on the path to a big pot of gold. But try to not take on too much work at one time. As hard as it may seem, make some time to go out for coffee. The outside air will do you good and increase your chances of meeting new and interesting people.

Bright sky-blue Myanmar fighter jets scramble and shriek overhead while I stand, together with my trainees, looking at three hobbled elephants silently and solemnly shuffling from foot to foot. They are chained to the concrete floor of a pavilion in the outer suburbs, and they are allegedly white elephants, supposedly good omens for the prosperous future of mighty Myanmar and its military rulers who acquired these pale pachyderms.

Actually the white elephants are a bit of a joke in some Myanmar circles because they're not all that white. One actually looks like a fairly ordinary elephant; the other two are a light tan, but they do appear to have some albino characteristics. Some Myanmar say they are simply undersized elephants suffering from skin disease, but such utterances are made discreetly, because they could be viewed as sedition if heard by those loyal to the military, who place great importance on these elephants.

The belief that white elephants are good omens is a legacy of the Myanmar kings, and the presence of the elephants adds credence to the belief that some of the top generals view themselves as modern-day monarchs. Senior General Than Shwe is said to deploy royal seating in his home, ensuring that he and his wife are seated at greater heights than any visitors. Than Shwe also uses a royal suffix when referring to his daughters. A Buddha image in Myanmar's holiest-of-holies, the Shwedagon Pagoda, has been given a face that's a replica of Than Shwe and this is meant to suggest that the leader has been invested with supernatural powers.

But Prime Minister Khin Nyunt also got in on the act, when

he was titled Secretary-1, claiming credit for the acquisition of the whitest of the elephants, a cute four-year-old known officially as Rita Marla. A poem published in the *New Light of Myanmar* describes Rita Marla as:

The Royal Treasure of Secretary-1
From the golden pedestal he pours water
Glorious downpour from sky to earth
The State's fate and glory.

A monk from the monastery attached to the White Elephant Park engages my trainees in conversation and explains that because the little elephant is very cheeky and destined to become the leader of the pack, staff at the park subversively call it Aung San Suu Kyi.

This visit to the White Elephant Park is one of several excursions I've embarked on during the last few days, simply to get out of the office, which has been taken over by the brat pack—the US interns—who dominate, due to their numbers. Their earnest and dogged resistance to traditional newspaper disciplines and values, such as editing, creates an atmosphere akin to a tedious, hysteria-tinged undergraduate summer camp. The quality of the newspaper suffers, and its integrity is undermined by jejune items such as a column in this week's issue written by a New York intern, describing an official visit by Major General Kyaw Win to approve (i.e. censor) an art exhibition held as a promotion by the *Times*.

Major General Kyaw Win is a mysterious, powerful and enigmatic character, a noted aesthete and artistic photographer who normally avoids the official limelight. He is the right-hand man to the number one, Senior General Than Shwe; he is also a member of the State Peace and Development Council, holding the position of Chief of Armed Forces Training. He is the liaison between the government and Aung San Suu Kyi, plus the deputy chief of Military Intelligence under Khin Nyunt.

Of his visit to check the art exhibition at the Sakura Tower building, the columnist wrote:

> My boss [Ross Dunkley] explained who exactly this General is, and I began to understand the reason for all the preparations. I was nervous as can be, but was glad that I had coincidentally worn a nice skirt that day. In the car I reapplied my foundation and lipstick . . .
>
> We heard him arrive. I jumped up, put out the cigarette, straightened my skirt, hid my juice glass, grabbed my purse and ran to greet him . . .
>
> The General walked straight up to an abstract painting with splashes of greens, blues and yellows. 'It is called hope,' said my boss. 'You don't think about what it is supposed to mean,' the General said. 'You just look and see how you feel.'
>
> Oh my goodness, I thought, the General understands abstract art . . .
>
> At one point I said, 'Are you interested in buying any (paintings)?'
>
> My boss shouted in excitement, 'He already has.'

A variety of people seemed offended by the curious piece. Women expatriates found it degrading to professional women; male expatriates found it degrading to those who consider that the *Times* should not be fawning to generals; and the *Times* freelance contributing editor, Ma Thanegi, found the piece so degrading to Myanmar and its leaders that she sent a scathing email to the columnist, accusing her of being patronising and insulting by presuming that generals are too ignorant to understand matters such as art.

Ma Thanegi's response surprised some Westerners, who

presumed that, because she'd worked as the personal assistant to Aung San Suu Kyi in 1988 and 1989 and had subsequently served three years of a ten-years-with-hard-labour prison sentence, she would be avowedly anti-government and anti-military. But Ma Thanegi is an interesting example of a modern Myanmar intellectual. Her thinking doesn't confine itself within the convenient but simplistic black and white limitations most Western writers employ to describe Myanmar politics. Intellectuals such as Ma Thanegi take exception to their leaders not being accorded respect, whether they agree with them or not, and certainly object to them being described in print as buffoons.

Ma Thanegi's view is that the outside world's solution to Myanmar's political problems borders on being a fairytale. She set out her thoughts in a controversial article called 'The Burmese Fairy Tale', published in the Lonely Planet guide book. Here she wrote that, while she loves Suu Kyi deeply, the leader hasn't made life easier for Myanmar people because of her dogged stance, which has caught the imagination of the outside world. Ma Thanegi wrote:

Unfortunately [Ma Suu's approach] has come at a real price for the rest of us.

. . . Two Westerners—one a prominent academic and the other a diplomat—onee suggested to me that if sanctions and boycotts undermined the economy, people would have less to lose and would be willing to start a revolution . . .

The naïve romanticism angers many of us here in Myanmar. You would deliberately make us poor to force us to fight a revolution? American college students play at being freedom fighters and politicians stand up and proclaim that they are striking a blow for democracy with sanctions. But it is we Burmese who pay the price for these empty heroics. Many of us now wonder: Is it for this that we went to jail?

She argues that the fairytale is now so widely accepted that pragmatism is impossible and that political correctness is so fanatical that any realistic evaluation of Suu Kyi's party or its leadership is rejected as treachery. She says, 'To simply call for realism is to be called pro-military or worse. But when realism becomes a dirty word, progress becomes impossible.'

I dated Ma Pan Cherry, triggering a romance that launched us into an intense series of further dates, meaningful meetings and accidental-bumping-intos. And then one evening it happened. We kissed.

We were at a German restaurant at the Savoy. We chatted for hours, and the staff politely left us to it until we were ready to leave, well past closing time. We walked through the dark after-hours hotel corridors looking for the exit, but halfway along a corridor we stopped, and then I kissed her.

We caught a cab but, when I dropped her off at her downtown apartment and tried to kiss her again, she squirmed out of my reach, exited the cab and vanished into the darkness.

We arranged to meet again the next morning, Sunday at 11, after I returned from a wedding reception I'd been invited to in a village on the outskirts of Yangon. It was for 7am, an unseemly hour to me, but a normal wedding hour for the Myanmar.

A couple of weeks earlier I'd been handed an ornate, pink, embossed, die-cut invitation to the wedding of Ma Wai Wai Lin to her sweetheart, Maung Kyaw Kyaw Min Soe Htwe.

Wai Wai, a staff member of the Grand Mee Ya Hta Apartment Residences, is one of my favourite Yangon people—a cutie always ready with a warm, welcoming smile—and I gladly agreed to sacrifice my Sunday sleep-in to attend her wedding.

When I was leaving my apartment at dawn to catch a cab, several of the young guys who worked in the building told me they couldn't afford to travel to the wedding and asked if they could come with me. The cab was jammed full of excited young guys and off we set through the Yangon traffic, singing along to a lilting Myanmar version of the song 'Dream Lover' oozing from the cabby's scratchy cassette player.

Yangon swept by in all its Sunday-morning busyness. Buddhist worshippers crowded around the many pagodas, and the drone of monks chanting in the pagodas competed with the honking of car horns and the shouts of street vendors.

We soon left the city behind and our progress slowed as we threaded through the many hay-carrying bullock carts cluttering the way. Road travel outside the capital is exceedingly slow—not that road travel in Yangon itself can be described as express. Major roads quickly disintegrate outside the capital. They teem with all kinds of traffic: clapped-out, clattering trucks belching smoke; crowded pick-ups; old, battered buses mostly made of wood; cyclists, motorcyclists and trishaw drivers; olive-green, ancient Chinese military trucks; and thousands of gear-gnashing, hiccupping Toyota Corollas. Nobody is in a hurry, nobody seems to care, and over time I learnt to enjoy this experience. The beauty of travelling at a snail's pace means travellers aren't cut off from the world in a speeding bubble of glass and metal. Travelling in Myanmar becomes a quaint social occasion—smiles and casual chat are exchanged with occupants of neighbouring vehicles or with locals standing or sitting by the side of the road.

Eventually the cab arrived at our destination. In a break between the paddy fields stood what looked like a shack, but it was in fact the village meeting point, the Pyone Pan Hlaing Restaurant, the wedding venue.

The brief Buddhist wedding ceremony was already underway when we arrived and the bride, Wai, decked out in an ornate, sequined traditional wedding costume, was transformed from her usual cuteness into a mature beauty. Her long, black hair was wrapped around and piled like a beehive on top of her head, with clumps of jasmine and orchids tumbling out of the centre of the arrangement.

When the ceremony finished, a PA music system blurted Myanmar wedding tunes, and a constant supply of food, mainly noodles with different sauces, passed across our table. I was the only Westerner in a group of about 200 Myanmar, most of whom could not speak English but, as usual in Myanmar, we were able to communicate in a strange way and I realised that, having attended the wedding, I was now a member of this village communal family.

I left the wedding with even more passengers piled into the taxi: the young guys I'd given a lift to were now joined by girl-friends who'd earlier made their own way to the wedding.

I arrived at the Zawgyi Café moments before the pre-arranged 11am meeting with Ma Pan Cherry. I bought the Bangkok papers from the street boys, a theoretically illegal transaction because they are banned. Newspaper shops keep Bangkok papers out of sight and produce them only on request, but the street boys openly sell them at cafés and street corners, carefully marking and displaying any news story about Myanmar or Suu Kyi as an added inducement to purchase, while keeping a wary eye open for policemen.

I read the papers and time passed; midday came and went, but no Cherry. Then, just as I was about to give up, I saw her crossing Bogyoke Aung San Road. She sat down, giving me a cursory smile. I told her she was so late I thought she wasn't coming, and she said she thought I would think that. Something was up. She opened her bag, extracted an exercise book and carefully opened it. She looked at me and said, 'I sat up until very early this morning writing you a letter. I would like you to read it now.'

She slid the open exercise book toward me and I sensed she was angry. My first thought was that I'd offended her with the kiss at the hotel and, as I looked down at the exercise book, at her neat, elegant handwriting there, the words 'cheap' and 'slut' sprung up at me. 'What do you think I am?' the letter read. 'Do you think I am a cheap girl? Do you think I am a slut?' But the letter had nothing to do with the kiss at the Savoy. It had to do with my attempted kiss in the back of the taxi. 'How dare you shame me like this, how dare you try to kiss me in front of a Myanmar man!'

I'd completely forgotten the Myanmar practice of absolute discretion in public, of not touching until married, and certainly never kissing in public. I spluttered, 'But in my country it is okay to kiss in front of the taxi driver, a quick goodbye kiss is okay.'

'Not in my country,' she said. 'It is not done and you must promise to never shame me like this again.'

I sighed, figuring I had a lot to learn about relationships in Yangon.

The journalism trainees and I head off on another excursion, to the town of Twantay, just outside Yangon, on the trail of a British colonial policeman, Eric Blair, who served in Burma between 1922 and 1927. Blair is better known to the world by his *nom de plume*, George Orwell, and his Burmese stint affected him greatly, shaping both his psyche and destiny. The book he subsequently wrote, *Burmese Days*, documenting the bizarre behaviour of British officials in Burma, was factual in its original form, but Orwell's revelations were so outrageous that his publishers instructed him to fictionalise the work and change the names of people and places to avoid litigation.

His book tells of life in Kyauktada, which in real life is the out-of-the-way northern Myanmar town of Katha. Many buildings described in Orwell's book still stand and the town has become an attraction for adventurous tourists.

But Orwell also lived in several other Myanmar towns, and Twantay was his first posting outside of the then capital, Rangoon. I'd been trying to find traces of Orwell's life in this small town, and I'd heard talk in Yangon that the house Orwell lived in during his Twantay posting was still standing. I asked the trainees to help me in the search for this house, and we ended up with the address of a Twantay man who might be able to help.

We set off on the trail of George Orwell by crossing the Yangon River in a commuter ferry, and then heading overland in a rough, rattling jeep. Half an hour later we are in Twantay and enlist trishaw drivers to take us to the house of our contact, Ko Ba Than, a local businessman. We arrive on an auspicious occasion, the opening day of his latest business venture—a food stall in the downtown market area—and his entire extended family and friends are hunkered in the courtyard, industriously preparing and then cooking food on blazing braziers.

Ba Than invites us to sit with his family while he scours Twantay to see if anybody knows anything about this foreigner, Mr Blair, also known as Mr Orwell. He disappears for almost three hours, leaving us to enjoy the shade under an ancient peepul tree. Several women stir big bowls of a gooey pink matter that will become a treat for children: flavoured icy-poles. Food and drink are brought out for us and the time drifts by in the quiet, unhurried, unworried way of the Myanmar.

Eventually Ba Than returns, announcing, 'I have not yet found the house, but I have found the oldest man in Twantay and talked to him about this foreigner's house. He is waiting to see you.'

Once again we set off by trishaw, to meet the town's oldest man. He proves to be a lovable character and, forewarned of our mission, he greets us clutching a book titled *Ten Thousand Facts and Things*. His brow wrinkles as he consults his battered tome. He sadly shakes his head, saying there is no record of this Eric Blair or of George Orwell but, he adds, there is hope. He knows of a house where a foreigner lived long ago.

Another trishaw trip takes us to this dwelling, which is now a quaint guesthouse, but nobody there can remember the name of the strange foreigner who once resided in the building. A dozen people gather in the guest-room office, and the consensus of opinion is that we might be able to find some record of this foreigner at the police station.

We abandon trishaw travel and pile into a cart drawn by a horse with flowers behind its ears. At the police station, we announce our presence and explain our intention. Any trans-action with police in Myanmar involves a long wait and this case is no exception. We sit inside the police station while a succession of officers inform us they aren't senior enough to deal with the matter and that an appropriately senior man is on his way. Soon.

Several policemen in blue singlets and longyis snooze on mats, while another officer with a grubby white singlet encasing a pot belly engages us in chit-chat. Finally the senior officer turns up, but a rowdy drunk is dragged into the police station and has to be subdued, yelled at and locked up. Then the senior officer gives us his concerned attention, listening to our request carefully and explaining that all appropriate records have been sent to Yangon many years ago. But he invites us to inspect the old prison, on the proviso that we do not take photographs. The prison is a picture-book tumble-down red brick colonial building, with weeds growing out of the timber-shingled roof. After our inspection, we are escorted off the premises by the friendly officer, who tells us that we should now pursue the matter in Yangon.

Our group strolls down the main street of town, past the Twantay post office, looking for a nice clean teashop. As we stroll, we chat about this and that, and I ask about the use of the words *ma* and *daw* to describe women. The terms are roughly equivalent to the Western Miss and Mrs, but not as clearly delineated. Almost every married woman is a daw, for example, but not every daw is married. Age also comes into it and I have been curious whether there is a precise age that ma becomes daw, but apparently there isn't. Ma can be used as a term of respect by a young woman to a woman in their company who is slightly older. The trainee Su Myat Hla, for example, is four or five years older than the other women trainees and they defer-entially refer to her as Ma Su, so I ask at what age Ma Su will become Daw Su?

Ma Su is walking a few yards ahead of the group and, as a joke, I shout, 'Daw Su'. The effect is cataclysmic. People in the street freeze and silence thuds. The woman trainee walking next to me reels across the footpath like an insect hit with a powerful spray of bug repellent. Another trainee grabs my arm and whispers, 'You cannot say this. Daw Suu is the loving term all Myanmar people use to describe Aung San Suu Kyi, but we are not permitted to say it aloud, especially in public. If the police or soldiers hear you, or if someone reports you, you will be taken to prison.'

As we cross the road towards a busy teashop, a male trainee

nudges me, pointing to an abandoned, forlorn and padlocked building: the faded markings announce that this was once the Twantay headquarters of Aung San Suu Kyi's NLD party.

We sit at the teashop ordering tea and fried bananas. I give the trainees the bad news: I am intent on returning to Yangon via the canal and river. I'd read that this was a magical journey, especially in the evening with the sun setting, but a few days earlier, when I'd asked the trainees about ferry schedules, they were vague and prevaricating. Now a trainee promptly announces, 'Not possible to return by river because we have missed the big ferry'.

I recall that a few days earlier they'd suggested there was no big ferry making regular runs on the river yet, as I look out over the Twantay canal, which is visible from the teashop, I can see lots of small ferries and boats seemingly touting for business. So I suggest we hire one of these craft. I'm promptly told, 'Not possible. These are the famous sinking ferries and many people who travel in them drown.'

I dig in, dismissing this notion and insisting that we hire a ferry. But once we start inquiring, I discover this is no simple matter because my status as foreigner is causing complications once again, given the confirmed inclination of these small craft to sink. One ferry owner says the government has banned foreigners from travelling on sinking ferries, because several years ago a Westerner drowned and it had been expensive to repatriate his body.

Another ferry owner says he'll take us, providing I hide in the hold during the journey. Eventually we find a sinking ferry owner who claims to be the chairman of a ferry owners association and says he has a special dispensation to carry foreigners.

The journey down the Yangon River is as magical as the guide book had suggested, although the trainees don't share my sentiments—every time the boat is jolted by the wake of a passing craft, they cringe nervously as if expecting to be dragged to the bottom of the earthy-brown, churning Yangon River in the coffin-like confines of a sinking ferry.

After an uneventful and non-sinking two-hour cruise, we pull up at the Strand jetty in downtown Yangon just as night sets in.

Next morning in the office, the trainees tell me they are worried they have lost face because we found no trace of George Orwell or his house. They fear they have wasted the company's time because there is no story to write.

I assure them otherwise, telling them they can write the story of our search because, while we did not find the house, we did in fact make a liminal connection with George Orwell. I reach into my desk drawer and pull out a copy of *Burmese Days*, turning the pages until I find the section where the book's main character, an Englishman named Flory—probably a fictional representation of Orwell himself—has a discussion with his friend Dr Versaswami. Flory says: 'I see them [the British] as a kind of up-to-date, hygienic, self-satisfied louse. Creeping around the world building prisons. They build a prison and call it progress . . .'

I point out the delicious irony of this passage, considering the context of our search for Orwell's traces. The only connection we were able to make with the author was our visit to the old colonial prison behind the police station—a prison that was standing in Orwell's day and a prison where, as the colonial policeman, Orwell most certainly would have set foot. Probably on some occasions there, he had to perform the odious duty he so detested, as witness to yet another execution.

We finished our picnic, visited the Buddhist nuns for late afternoon tea, entered a small wooden hut on the edge of the jungle and there, in the dim light, was a human skeleton standing erect. Ma Cherry whispered, 'This is what we Myanmar Buddhists sometimes meditate on. This is what will become of both of us when our flesh and karma are stripped away. Does it make you think?'

It made me think that the skeleton was a gruesome touch on such a warm, pleasant Sunday afternoon but, when I mentioned this to Ma Cherry, she was curious about why I felt this way. I told her that death, skeletons and dead bodies are hidden from sight in our society and not usually associated with romantic Sunday afternoon après-picnic strolls through Elysian glades. Ma Cherry said, 'That is one understanding we have of you Westerners—that you are always all so busy hiding from the reality of life.'

I nodded. She had a point and I smiled as we walked from the hut hand in hand, back down the trail that led to the lake, past a procession of children from the local orphanage, onto the rickety little jetty and into a long boat for the quick trip across the lake and then the two-hour journey by car back to another velvet evening in Yangon.

We'd arrived early in the morning of the previous day for a romantic and daring (by Myanmar standards) weekend away from Yangon, and we'd stayed in a houseboat on the lake overnight. The languid tropical night on the lake inspired lacy mosquito-netting-protected romance; the whispered murmurings of love and adoration that lapped the edges of our psyches like the soft slapping of water against the side of the old boat soon became talk of marriage.

We woke in the morning agreeing that we were officially engaged to become engaged, or perhaps our status was even unofficially engaged because, although we'd sworn eternal love to each other, we could not become officially engaged until the liaison had the sanction of her immediate family, her inter-mediate family, her extended family and her collection of sundry second aunts, beloved aunts, respected aunts and eldest aunts, not to mention the approval of beloved friends, assoc-iates, and others who exerted some form of influence over her rich, full, ultra-social life.

We had left the houseboat early in the afternoon and walked through the forest until we found a clearing and there we indulged in a Western-style picnic, complete with warm cham-pagne and a posy of scented flowers plucked along the way, while we were fanned and cooled by the collective gentle beating of the wings of a million and one brilliantly coloured butterflies. Well, there mightn't have been a million and one butterflies but there certainly were a lot, and their beating wings might not have physically cooled us but they certainly added to the splendour of the shaded afternoon in that calm forest clearing.

Afterwards we had visited nuns in their hand-built, hand-hewn timber cottage behind a forest monastery, and shared tea while Ma Cherry underwent her daily ritual of one hour of fervent prayer. It was the nuns who suggested we call in at the skeleton hut a short distance away, where the airy, free forest suddenly surrendered to gloomy, entangled jungle.

At dusk, as we settled back in the car for the return journey, I thought about the skeleton and I thought how much I had learnt during this weekend about having a relationship with a beautiful Yangon woman, and in fact how much I'd learnt since the very first date with this woman not all that long ago.

The most striking lesson I'd learnt was that the free and easy

Myanmar aren't all that free and easy when it comes to the notion of a foreigner stealing the heart of one of their eligible middle-class maidens. I should have realised, because an oft-told story in Yangon centred on Prime Minster Khin Nyunt publicly disowning his successful son for a period of time for marrying a foreigner, a Singaporean Airlines hostess. Foreigners can marry Myanmar, but the Buddhist ceremonies are not officially recognised, and no marriage certificates are issued.

We faced many nasty little incidents. One evening we attended an opening night at the National Theatre and a surly soldier glared at me, blocking Ma Cherry's path, refusing her entry and snarling something at her which she refused to repeat to me. She was only granted admission after a Myanmar man who knew her family interceded. At that moment I thought back to the descriptions I'd read of the Depayin massacre and how women were killed by having their heads bashed against the road by thugs who ranted about their being ravished by *kala*, the white man, supposedly like their heroine Aung San Suu Kyi, wife of a detested foreigner.

Smiles in the Yangon streets turned into almost sniping, baleful, sullen stares, young men whispered gutter obscenities and imprecations that obviously stung Ma Cherry, and our sunset strolls through the evening downtown streets unsettled me rather than relaxed me. But I made the mistake of telling her about my discomfort, which caused her to look hard at me, her eyes brimming with liquid sadness. She said, 'I knew that, if I was to fall in love with you, I would have to be strong. I was worried that I wouldn't be able to find such strength, but I never thought you would be the one to struggle with strength.'

Her words rekindled in me memories of my father, who was described at his funeral by an Hungarian friend who had known him during his war days as a 'lean, good-looking young army officer who had walked a long, dangerous road'. My father attained the rank of *podporucznik* in the 72nd Polish Infantry

Regiment and endured a nightmarish World War II, from which he never fully recovered and about which he rarely spoke, except to say occasionally that for him the war meant that one day bombs started to fall on Warsaw and he never saw his country or his family again. As a young man, whenever I experienced difficulty, this would be dismissed by my father with his advice that my problems were nothing in the light of the slaughter he and his comrades had faced as young men. He was right of course, but it took some time for me to understand this.

The same with the Myanmar. Their life is not easy and so they try to lessen their troubles by making their immediate life as joyous as possible for all those around them, so as to alleviate their at-times onerous lot. Consequently, whenever we foreigners complain about our situation, we are quickly reminded that we come from lands of wealth, freedom and privilege.

And so my comments about my discomfort at the blatant disapproval shown on the streets brought me no sympathy from Ma Cherry and instilled awareness in me of my spoilt Western weakness. Out of the corner of my eye, I admiringly watched her walk like a princess through the muck of public disapproval, and I resolved never to waiver or weaken again, but to hold my head up in pride, just as she did.

And I wasn't the only person in Myanmar experiencing relationship approval problems. From my observation, few couples have the fortune of having their union blessed and approved by all of those who have a say or think they have a say. Lately I've been having coffee with Win Lay, a writer I befriended and helped and who was writing a book reappraising Newton's Law of Physics according to an Asian perspective, whatever that means. He wanted advice from me about his love life, which had spiralled out of control. He'd been courting a woman I know, an intelligent country gal hailing from a village near Depayin, the scene of the recent Aung San Suu Kyi tragedy. She was now a city lawyer with a radical bent, but the problem with the relationship was that she was Buddhist and my friend was Muslim. She also came from quite an influential family. Her wealthy uncle was once a powerful military bigwig—too powerful apparently for the comfort of General Khin Nyunt, who became nervous over the uncle's control of central Myanmar districts. The uncle was shafted and quit the military, becoming a significant player in Yangon's business community.

Muslims, Christians and Buddhists co-exist relatively peacefully among the staff at the *Myanmar Times*, but tensions between Muslims and Buddhists often simmer in the wider community. One of my trainees, a level-headed guy who supported his ailing mother on his meagre salary, informed me that he avoided shopping at Muslim outlets because he didn't like the way Muslims treated Buddhists. He said if a Buddhist wanted to marry a Muslim girl, the Buddhist had to pay the parents a considerable amount of money by Myanmar standards for the privilege, about a lakh or K100 000 (approximately US$100), and he considered this an outrageous insult. This conversation took place in front of another trainee, an intelligent Muslim in his early thirties whom I had affectionately nicknamed Mullah because of his sincerity. Mullah sat with eyes downcast and did not react to this conversation, letting it flow over him.

Frictions between Muslims and Buddhists had also recently broken out in the provinces. Late the previous year several people, perhaps dozens, were killed during clashes at Kyaukse near Mandalay, and in Mandalay itself, including relatives of one of the female reporters at the *Times*. I spoke to the reporter about this, but she said she didn't want to discuss it because it made her want to cry.

But back to Win Lay's plight. The religious difference

wasn't a problem between the two lovers, but it was for the girl-friend's family. Win Lay told me two members of her family had travelled to Yangon to see him, to tell him to end the relationship. He was told his girlfriend was very close to her sick father and that knowledge of her liaison with a Muslim could result in his having a heart attack and dying. The girlfriend had no idea that a family delegation from her home town had visited her boyfriend and Win Lay declined to tell her. Instead he decided to disentangle himself from the relationship by telling her he'd been cheating with another woman and by inventing details of the other woman. Then he became remorse-ridden and mortified because his 'confession' caused her such distress, and he realised he still loved her.

When he told me all this, I launched into an explanation of how he should follow his heart and at least discuss the problems with her truthfully. Win Lay excused himself, saying that he was going at once to visit his girlfriend at the hostel where she was staying and put matters right.

But the next time I saw him he laughed nervously, shrugged and said the relationship was over. I saw his former girlfriend a few nights later in the downtown Café Aroma, surrounded by her country cousins, and she too confirmed that the relationship was over. She added that she was better off out of the mess.

Luckily, I wasn't treated with opprobrium by Ma Cherry's civilised and close-knit family, although at first our union was met with stiff, stern resistance. Eventually, the father interceded, questioning Ma Cherry, and then ruling that in his opinion the relationship made No. 1 Precious Daughter happy and that, as her happiness was paramount, the family must accept the relationship. This triggered a round of semi-official visits to her family. There were visits to her parents at their downtown apartment, where I also met her youngest brother and his girlfriend. I had been warned that, although youngest brother would probably insult me, I was not to return the insult. As it happened, youngest brother declined to insult me, although I sensed a modicum of contempt when he discovered I wasn't a fan of English football and knew nothing about Manchester United.

There were also visits to the principal aunts, uncles and cousins at the family's rural residence, about a 45-minute drive from Yangon. But the crucial visit was to the family matriarch, the paternal grandmother. Pan Cherry and I set off on the journey to No. 1 Grandmother's village late one howlingly hot Sunday afternoon. The streets were a crowded dustbowl because yet another festival was being celebrated. On the out-skirts of Yangon we passed through the Indian quarter, where a kilometre-long column of Hindu women in their finest, flashiest saris walked along the side of the road, balancing blazing candles in holders on their heads. We were delayed by a group of sadhus in the grip of a seething religious fit. They spun and swirled dervish-like in the middle of the road and pushed long, thin, shiny metal rods through their bodies, their blood glinting eerily in the dim late-afternoon light.

Eventually we reached No. 1 Grandmother's house and, according to custom, proceeded to prostrate ourselves in front of her, kowtowing three times, until she chanted the traditional go-ahead and blessing to our courtship.

Ma Cherry later informed me that we had only appeared in person before about a quarter of the family, but that was enough for an overall consensus of opinion to be arrived at, and the verdict was that we were reasonably matched, even though I was an older foreigner, and even though eldest aunty—a spinster and a former English teacher at a convent in northern Myanmar—clung to her disapproval, although not as fiercely as at first. She gently chided us that we could never be totally suited because we were night and day.

I arrive at work on the Monday after the picnic weekend, look at the calendar and my head spins, plunging me into panic, despondency, despair—my time in Myanmar is almost up, and this time there'll be no more contracts to renew because the training program has come to an end. But Myanmar is like a cancer that's taken hold of me; I can't get it out of my system, I can't achieve a clear-cut ending, I can't cut and run as I'd originally planned. I've complicated my life by falling in love and talking about marriage.

But what hope is there for a future between Ma Pan Cherry and myself? Where will we live and how will we live? I know instinctively that permanent life in the West would not suit Ma Cherry. I know if she left her family and colourful life for a future in Australia, she'd soon wilt like an exotic bloom deprived of water. On the other hand, permanent life in Myanmar for me might not be possible, and at best it would be a typical expatriate existence: precarious, due to the nation's quicksand politics. There have been glimmers of hope that the political situation will modify and become less hardline, but even now, in a climate where the moderate factions are perceived to be on the ascendancy, rumours sweep Yangon of an impending backlash by the hardliners.

Expatriates who can survive the vagaries of life in Myanmar are those who can adopt a philosophical wait-and-see-what-happens attitude and react accordingly, an attitude that's also in accord and harmony with Myanmar's overriding Buddhist ethos.

So I tell myself I must put my fears and anxieties to rest, because I have no control over any aspect of life in Myanmar.

All I can do is carry on regardless and see what happens. It's the only way to cope, and right now I have to cope with the reality that in a couple of weeks' time, I'll be Australia-bound once again—Ma Cherry or no Ma Cherry—and, from that point on, it will be a matter of *que sera sera*.

In the meantime I have a training course to finish and a final report that must be compiled for the Sasakawa Peace Foundation. Happily, life in the *Myanmar Times* office is now buoyant, with plans for expansion steaming ahead; new downtown office premises have been leased and renovations for the building are being planned. Ross Dunkley and Sonny Swe have just returned from India, where they have purchased an offset printing press that will be the biggest of its type in Myanmar.

The Myanmar staffers have started their own publishing venture, issuing a regular office newsletter that's gossipy, caustic and popular, helping boost morale in the office. The latest issue deals with the news about our leaders' trip to India to buy the press, and Sonny Swe has written a rather unusual account of the venture:

> As we went straight to the printing machine after arriving in Bombay, my stomach gave me a noisy alarm to push down some fodder. To solve the problem I decided to eat. I chose nanbya (roti) and beans with onion sauce. Ra! Chucha! Then at last we reached our Stars Hotel. After going through woes and throes, I fell to sleep from exhaustion. Noisier sounds inside my stomach woke me and Oh! Dear me! I'd a bowel motion. I had to shuttle between my room and the WC for at least a dozen times. The biggest problem was that we had no tissue paper in the closet (the hotel didn't give, how frugal are they?) Yes, they're Indians and they provided just a bowl of water to clean your ass. We're Myanmars and we know how to overcome these hitches. I had to carry a tissue roll wherever I went.

Last week my training sessions at the *Times* revolved around the all-encompassing censorship that Myanmar journalists contend with on a daily basis, and we explored the historical context. Myanmar has always been a country with high literacy rates and it was the first Asian country to experience press freedom, when the second-last monarch, King Mindon, enacted a lengthy law on 15 August 1873. King Mindon decreed:

> If I do wrong, write about me. If the queens do wrong, write about them. If my sons and daughters do wrong, write about them. If the judges and mayors do wrong, write about them. No one shall take action against the journalists for writing the truth. They shall go in and out of the palace freely.

This edict flew in the face of the Bengal Resolutions introduced by the British to regulate, or censor, the written word, and the Resolutions became known as the 'law to shut mouth'. The British moved quickly to override Mindon and restrict the press again, enacting The Vernacular Press Act in 1878.

Myanmar enjoyed several bouts of press freedom after attaining independence, the last bout being in 1988 for one month, and the country's press history is littered with the escapades of colourful journalists and editors, including the flamboyant Edward Law Yone. He was interned by the British in Delhi's Red Fort during World War II, but American OSS officers flew him to Colombo, where he was trained by the playboy-style operative S. Dillon Ripley. Many OSS officers became CIA agents after the war, and the CIA established media operations in South-East Asia, funding Daniel Berrigan's *Bangkok World* newspaper, Robert North's Far East Film Company and Jim (the 'father' of the Thai silk export industry) Thompson's operations.

The CIA bought Law Yone an old printing press and provided start-up capital so he could publish the *Nation* newsaper in Burma. But Yone bit the hand that fed him by despatching his best investigative journalist, Dr Maung Maung, to the Shan State to report on the Taiwanese-based Kuomintang's armed incursions against communist China from illegal bases in Burma. Maung Maung also exposed the extent of US participation in these covert operations. A crisis broke out between Burma and the US, with Burma raising the issue at a UN General Assembly meeting in Paris. On 22 April 1953 the UN General Assembly adopted a resolution demanding the KMT withdrawal from Burma.

I assigned the trainees to write about the censorship processes and organisations that now control the Myanmar press. One trainee interviewed the deputy director of the Censorship Board, who claimed publishing in Myanmar was being hindered not by censorship but by a shortage of censors, because the board doesn't have enough staff. The director also said that no writers are banned in Myanmar: 'The Censorship Board does not ban any writers. They can write freely . . . but if the writers are anti-government, their permission to publish will be postponed.'

The trainee wrote a news story about the Censorship Board that was accepted for publication by *Times*' editor Goddard. But this morning I pass on the news that the article about censorship has, sadly, been censored in its entirety.

Time's up. It's over. My Yangon life is finished.

I feel guilty because in the last two months I've been so

caught up in affairs of the heart that I've neglected my social life and neglected my friends. I've become a stranger to so many people and now I've tried to catch up with them all in a final whirl of farewells, but the farewells are somehow unsatisfactory. Last night I said goodbye to Unofficial Daughter No. 1 Lasheeda, but she just shrugged.

Now it's my last night in Yangon, and I'm sitting with Ma Pan Cherry at a pool-side restaurant at the Sedona Hotel. Flaming torches, fairy lights, candlelight and a sparkling, illuminated mini-pagoda in the middle of the floodlit pool create an exotic atmosphere, and Cherry looks breathtaking in a figure-hugging chartreuse cheongsam. Once again, like so many times in recent months, I feel as though I am in a glamorous oriental movie.

As a boy in the Australian bush, I read many books about tropical hearts of darkness, and I dreamt romantically of travelling to mysterious ports of call such as Rangoon, where I'd fall in love with a startlingly beautiful Asian woman in a cheongsam, with long black hair, who would whisper the ancient secrets of the orient into my ear. And here I am, half a century later, the dream come true; but, instead of long black hair, Cherry has fashionable mid-length black hair and, instead of ancient secrets being whispered into my ear, Cherry whispers teasing admonishments.

'You. I hate you,' she says, with her dazzling white-toothed wide smile. 'You ambushed my heart. You make me love you like I have never loved another man. And now, when I can't sleep at night, what do you do? You fly away from my heart, away from my life. What do I do now if I want love and you are not here, please tell me the answer to that question?'

But there is no answer.

Instead we discuss The Plan. We will part for three or four months and assess our relationship. If the flame still burns after that time, Ma Cherry will come to Australia, where we will make our unofficial engagement official and where we will try to determine how a future together can enfold.

I wake the next morning. My flight leaves late afternoon, so I phone Ma Cherry and ask her to come and say a final farewell at Zawgyi Café at lunchtime. When she arrives, I want to kiss her, but of course I can't, because we are in public. We talk, we hold hands, and again we say our goodbyes. She stands to go. She goes. I sit and watch her walk away, down Bogyoke Aung San Road, the scene of our many accidental-bumping-intos.

I can't cope. I get up and run after her, the whole street watching me. I pull up alongside her just as she is about to enter the Bogyoke Market. I look into her eyes, which are brimming with tears. I say to her, 'Dabawalone chit-me-thu.' *I will love you the whole life.* But she is angry with me. She says, 'You say this, yet you leave me?' I shrug helplessly.

We stand looking at each other. 'Goodbye, Cherry,' I say. She relents, smiles, and says, 'Goodbye, Peter.' She turns into the market and is swallowed by the crowd.

Ma Pan Cherry is gone.

I face the winter of my discontent on my return to Australia. I can't settle back into a routine, and I find life in my home town, Noosa, bland and boring. I miss Yangon and I miss Ma Pan Cherry even more. Communications between us are not as warm as I'd hoped: at first I sense she is still angry and resentful at my departure and then, as the frequency of her emails stretches from days apart to more than a week apart, I sense I am losing her.

She goes on leave from her job to celebrate the Thingyan Festival and for several weeks I hear nothing.

Then it comes: the confession. Ma Cherry writes:

I have thought about many things and now I decide to tell you something serious. Actually it is my confession to you. But before I tell you anything I want to convince you that I now know that I really love you and want to be with you as we planned.

My breaking news is that not long after you left I started going out with another guy, a Myanmar. First of all I just saw him here and there, and then after a month we started going out together as boyfriend and girlfriend.

Yes, I like him, I like his smartness and I come to know that he kind of love me. But I know I don't love him because I don't feel comfortable with him as I did with you. So finally, the day before your birthday, I tell him I don't have the desire to continue the relationship.

This is what I done and, because this is my confession, isn't it, I should be frank with you and say that this happened because I have many uncertainties and doubts about us, and my doubts were on high during the Water Festival. I asked myself if I could be brave enough to present you, an older foreigner, to my people as my man. But now I know that I miss you and that I want you. That I love you.

What are you now thinking? Please tell me exactly what is on your mind.

I read this 'confession' many times. I walk along the beach that evening, thinking, and then I sit at home at night with a bottle of wine, thinking, while the moaning winter winds whip off the sea and buffet my glass-box apartment eyrie.

PETER OLSZEWSKI

I think how much I admire Ma Cherry, as well as love her, because she needn't have sent me this confession. If she hadn't told me, I would never have known. And I think of the moral strength her actions required.

But her honest missive is also a relief to me, because I'd instinctively known all along that she had doubts and that she wondered if she would be happier with a man from her own culture, a Myanmar man.

This has been put to the test, and she has come back to me.

I write to her the next day telling her what is on my mind, exactly, that I too still want to be together with her, as planned.

And so we begin to put our plans into action, the plan being for her to come to me in Australia. Had I fallen in love with a woman from almost any other country on earth, such a plan would be simple, but I have fallen in love with a Myanmar woman. She has to acquire a passport and that, for a Myanmar woman especially, is no easy matter. It requires government permission and, for that to happen, she has to fit into one of several categories: she has to prove she wants to travel for educational purposes, for competitive sporting purposes, or for career training.

The only option available is career training and, with that in mind, I approach a local Australian media company to ask if they will grant her an internship and back this up with a formal letter of invitation. The media company agrees, and the next step is to communicate with both her family and her employer, asking them to support this initiative. The family agrees and so too does her employer, who is enthusiastic because it creates a precedent to provide international training for more of his staff. He agrees to back the application by issuing formal paperwork and, because his television script-writing company also comes under the censorship of Military Intelligence, he has to apply to MI to request them to support and guarantee the application—which they do.

Ma Cherry is now free to commence the passport application process itself, a lengthy, drawn-out bureaucratic procedure. Her background has to be checked and police reports obtained, and these then have to be notarised before being issued to the Ministry of Home Affairs for examination. The letter of invitation and supporting documents from her employer also have to be notarised and presented, and she spends several hours a week for several weeks preparing the documentation.

Finally, the application is finished and, after several more weeks, Ma Cherry is told all is in order and her passport will probably be ready for collection in the not-too-distant future. In the meantime, letters of invitation, employer statements and other documents are also prepared for the necessary Australian Embassy visa application.

The weeks roll by and in late September, Ma Cherry is told to present herself at the Yangon passport office the following week, early in October, to collect her passport. She books a flight to Australia for 26 October but, when she attends the passport office, the precious document is not ready, and their excuse is vague. She returns a few days later and the story is the same.

She emails me saying, 'I haven't had passport. Someone who sign them is going on trip and he will be back in two three days. My boss asks me again. He says we don't have much time. We are both worried.'

I am also worried about the passport. Strange stories about trouble in Myanmar are circulating in cyberspace. I receive an email report about shooting on the Thai–Myanmar border, where government troops are shutting down commodity trading businesses operated by Military Intelligence branches. Another even more foreboding email reports that troops have shut down the Phoenix Travel Company, which Military Intelligence had established at the international airport. The staff have been told to go home, computers seized, and signs have been torn down and trampled. Other companies set up by Military Intelligence have been shut down, assets confiscated and MI agents are being arrested.

Something big is up.

Then I receive an ominous email from Ma Cherry: 'Darling, I have bad news. I am frightened. Our political situation is not good at the moment. I cannot say more. A senior man here, Chan The, came and told me not to have high hopes for travel. I am so sad. If I can't come to you, what should I do?'

I phone Ma Cherry at her office. We talk about the passport, and suddenly the sound of loud, excited voices in the office can be heard over the phone. Ma Cherry breaks off the conversation and returns to say the office has just received news that the prime minister has been arrested. She says she must go.

I check the news agencies via the internet and confirm the news: not only has the prime minister been arrested under orders from Senior General Than Shwe but so too have many leading Military Intelligence officers. A purge is underway.

I email Ma Cherry's boss and he emails back: 'Yes, hmmmm, well things are unfolding and we don't have any clear details of the situation at the moment. But it will become known. As for Pan Cherry's passport, it would be difficult to make any judgement right at this point.'

I check more news services. More details emerge. The purge is far-reaching. The prime minister is under house arrest (ironically, like Aung San Suu Kyi), as is his son and his astrologer, Bodaw Teinkyar Than Hla. The prime minister's son's Bagan Cybernet internet server company has been seized by the government. About 800 Military Intelligence officers have been arrested. Brigadier General Thein Swe has been detained for questioning at the 8 Mile army barracks.

News from the *Myanmar Times* office is circumspect and cautious. The office was already in turmoil because the staff is preparing to move to their new state-of-the-art downtown premises, complete with glass washbasins in the toilets. But at this point no-one seems certain whether or not the *Times* will be allowed to continue publishing.

I receive an email from Pan Cherry, letting me know she is invoking higher powers: 'I am now praying. The beautiful concept of Buddhism is to give loving kindness to every creature. Do you remember how I pointed my forefinger to many directions after I prayed at Shwedagon Pagoda? This means I wish for every creature in every direction to have a good life. Now I pray that you and I will be allowed to have good life.'

This is followed by another email: 'I have checked with the *Myanmar Times*. Nothing happens to the paper. Don't worry. We are fine.'

Followed by: 'The email and company phone may soon stop. If something happens, I leave you this emergency number. It is one way you may be able to contact me. Chan The is teasing me. He is saying my problem is bigger than the country's.'

And finally, just despair: 'I hear nothing about passport. I phoned them this morning and I desperately wanted to cry. I needed to go into toilet to cry my eyes out. We keep going, that's all I can say now. I still have hope. I don't give up. We will meet each other again, but now I cannot say where or how.'

Emails stop coming. I try the phone and can't get through. Communication with Myanmar is down. It is over. It has all been so fast, so furious, and now it is so final.

Myanmar is purging itself and has shut out the world.

Two days pass and I hear nothing from Myanmar. I follow the news on the wire agencies, and the gist of the reports is that Myanmar has been plunged back into darkness and that Khin Nyunt has been arrested on charges of corruption.

Newspaper experts write features about the impact of the purge, and I note with much cynicism that most experts now concede that, until a few days ago, there was a moderating force within the Myanmar military, and this force was centred around Prime Minister Khin Nyunt and Military Intelligence, described by some as the 'state within the state', a network that functioned as an 'invisible government'.

I read such reports with cynicism because, until this purge, the very same media experts painted predictably bleak, black, linear and uninformed portrayals of the Myanmar military regime, either unaware or refusing to accept that there was such a thing as a moderating influence within the government.

Essentially most international coverage of Myanmar is a mish-mash of guesswork and speculation, written by foreign bureau journalists usually based in Bangkok, and comments about events inside the country are often attributed to 'un-named Western diplomats'. The journalists have no contact with Myanmar government members, and operate along club lines. Journalists who actually travel to Yangon to try to cultivate government contacts are mostly regarded with suspicious hostility by their peers and their work often dismissed as mere repetition of the government line.

During the last decade, a handful of reporters have been able to access senior Myanmar military figures and have produced the few insightful articles published about the regime, yet those same reporters have been almost universally derided as regime-sympathisers and dismissed as mere opportunists buttering up the regime for visas or whatever.

The Myanmar government is partly hoist with its own petard because it makes access for journalists so difficult but, in the past, a measure of a good journalist was the ability to work through such difficulties in an attempt to deliver the story.

It's easy to concede that it's hard for journalists to get information about Myanmar, and that reporters have their 'hearts in the right place', but the result, with the exception of one or two, such as Larry Jagan, is that coverage of Myanmar is largely based on advocacy rather than objectivity and often, sadly, the advocacy is based on ignorance.

Now suddenly reporters are writing with some insight and claim to have known all along that there are factions within the Myanmar regime and that some factions are more moderate than others. But, because they didn't report this in the past, their wisdom is now meaningless, devalued as mere hindsight. And what many expatriates living in Yangon have feared may now come to pass: life in the Delta of Sorrows may take another turn for the worse, and it may actually get as bad and as black and white in its grimness as most media reports over the past five years have suggested.

But these are just fragments of the considerations that pass through my mind while I incessantly walk along the beach at Noosa, dwelling on what I perceive as my personal tragedy, and thinking about what has been denied to myself and Ma Cherry.

I think about the comment that Pan Cherry's colleague Chan The made about her predicament, that her problems are bigger than the country's.

I think: Fuck Chan The, fuck the purge, fuck the people, fuck the international reporters, and fuck Myanmar.

I think of my early days in Yangon.

I think of the Kiss Me Softly plant I bought back at that time and how I came to understand that the plant represented an analogy of life in Yangon. Kiss softly at first because underneath the sensuous surface lurks needle-sharp danger.

I think how I have kissed the beauty of sensuous Yangon without paying due heed, and how now I am bleeding with a mouthful of painful thorns.

On 20 October the purge becomes official. I access the *New Light of Myanmar* on the internet and, in its inimitable style, the State Peace and Development Council officially informs the Myanmar people that there have been changes in their government. Under the heading, 'Permission granted for retirement', Senior General Than Shwe declares that the government has permitted Khin Nyunt to quit his post and to 'retire on health grounds with effect from today'.

Under another heading, 'Assignment of duty as prime minister', the people are informed that Lt-Gen Soe Win has been appointed prime minister 'with effect from today'.

After reading the *New Light*, and while I am online, I check my emails again, not really hoping for anything even resembling good news, but you never know. I am stunned to see an email from Pan Cherry. I open the email and read, 'Darling, I got it!!! I got the passport. I can't believe it. Say something.'

I try to phone to say something, but I can't get through. I send an email, but I hear nothing more. The next day I vet the wire services and read that there has been an easing up of conditions in Myanmar, that there's a feeling of hope that the after-effects of the purge may not be as bad as first thought. I read that the *Myanmar Times* has missed publishing an issue, but that it is now being allowed to continue publication. I read many things, but I have received nothing more from Pan Cherry since her amazing announcement that she has acquired the precious passport.

I have so many questions. What now? Has she been able to

apply for an Australian visa? Is she still coming to Australia? And if so, when?

A few days later, another email from Myanmar pops onto my computer screen. It has been sent by someone whose name I don't recognise. I open it. It reads: 'Here comes the happy message for u. Ma Pan Cherry asked me to inform u that she finds it difficult to email. She wants me to inform you about her coming and provide you with her Yangon departure date and time, her Brisbane arrival date and time and her flight no. We are happy for both of u.'

I arrive at Brisbane International airport in time to meet the Thai International flight that the email of a few days ago said Ma Pan Cherry would be on. I've heard nothing since and I try not to set my hopes too high, because I have no idea if she is actually on this flight. Maybe she was stopped from boarding when she arrived at Yangon airport, maybe not. Maybe there's been some last-minute glitch, maybe not. Who knows? The only option I have is the famous Myanmar option: wait and see what happens.

The arrivals board tells me the flight in question has landed. So I wait at the welcoming area just outside the customs bay at the airport. After a few minutes there is a flurry of people coming through the customs exit. There are several Thai International stewardesses in their sexy, distinctive uniforms, so I know that passengers from the all-important flight are now being processed.

I'm not really a nervous traveller, except the day before my flight, when I worry I will forget something crucial, and I always suffer anxiety at the end of a flight, when I am standing at the baggage collection area. I fear that my baggage will have gone astray, but eventually I always see the familiar Samsonite with its identifying stickers tumble onto the carousel and begin its circuit.

I'm feeling a similar anxiety today, only greater. I figure the best way to cope is to play a little mental game by counting the passengers as they stream through the customs exit. To make the game more interesting, I mentally bet what number passenger Ma Pan Cherry will be as she exits customs—if she does, that is. I mentally bet that she'll be passenger number 179 to pass through the exit.

I start counting. One hundred passengers have now exited. One hundred and twenty, one hundred and fifty. I'm now concentrating on the mental game, and it's helping stave off anxiety. The final countdown to my lucky number begins: passenger number 170 has exited customs, followed by passengers number 171 and 172. There's a break for a brief moment, and then passenger number 173 walks through.

Passenger number 173 is an attractive Asian woman wearing a cute pink sweater and blue jeans, and pushing a trolley with a large blue and red Polo suitcase. I look into the face of passenger number 173, into her eyes, and she looks into mine, and her face explodes into the dazzling white-toothed smile I know so well.

It's her. Ma Pan Cherry. She's made it.

Epilogue

In the wake of the October 2004 purge almost all the influential Myanmar people involved with the *Times* newspaper have been jailed.

FORMER PRIME MINISTER KHIN NYUNT was sentenced to 44 years in prison on 21 July 2005 following an excessively secret trial, even by Myanmar standards. His sons were also jailed and their businesses, including the ground-breaking Bagan Cybernet internet provider, have been taken over by the government. Khin Nyunt's personal astrologer, Bodaw Teinkyar Than Hla, was also jailed.

SONNY SWE, deputy CEO of the *Myanmar Times*, was arrested on Friday 26 November 2004, initially on charges of being a threat to national security. On 7 April 2005 Sonny was sentenced to fourteen years prison after being found guilty of bypassing the official censorship while publishing the *Myanmar Times*. The charges are a retrospective technicality: during the period Sonny ran the *Myanmar Times* he was subject to strict official censorship by the Military Intelligence office headed by his father Brigadier General Thein Swe. But after the purge Military Intelligence was declared an illegal organisation and therefore, retrospectively, Sonny Swe was guilty. He actually received two seven-year sentences, one for the *Myanmar Times* English language version, the other for the *Times* Myanmar language version. Prison sentences are not served concurrently in Myanmar.

BRIGADIER GENERAL THEIN SWE of Military Intelligence and the chief censor of the *Myanmar Times* was sentenced to 152 years prison on unspecified charges, although rumours suggested some charges hinged around treason.

It will be interesting to see whether Sonny and his father

ever make it onto the lists of political prisoners that circulate so widely among concerned libertarians in the West. Or whether the former Prince of Darkness, Khin Nyunt, does. A dissident Myanmar publication has produced a cartoon showing a sweating Khin Nyunt at gunpoint under house arrest on the phone to Amnesty International saying, 'You'll never guess who this is.'

THE OFFICE OF MILITARY INTELLIGENCE was totally disbanded after the purge and most of the 8000 operatives were fired. About 300 senior MI officers were arrested and to date more than 40 have been given lengthy prison sentences, some receiving two or three life sentences.

ROSS DUNKLEY still presides as CEO and editor-in-chief of the *Myanmar Times*, but now he is censored by the body that he so boldly announced he had sidestepped when the *Times* was launched. A further bitter pill for Dunkley is that the propagandist 'editorials' of the *New Light of Myanmar* are now being reprinted and acknowledged in his journal, including a disturbing full-page disclosure of Australian, German and US embassy staff (complete with vehicle registration numbers) who visited NLD headquarters and the dates they visited, and details of several Western tourists who also visited NLD headquarters. It also included their nationalities, occupations and Yangon hotel addresses. Colour photos of offending British, French, German, Norwegian and New Zealand tourists accompanied the text. The Orwellian tone of the denouncement served as a stark reminder to expatriates, who may have become complacent in the seemingly easy-going city, that they are constantly under surveillance and that they are indeed living in the land of a thousand eyes.

SENIOR GENERAL MAUNGAYE, Myanmar's number-two strong-man was rumoured to have been shot and killed in early January 2005, in a bizarre gun battle in the war office with Senior General Than Shwe and the new Prime Minister Lieutenant-General Soe Win. Maung Aye later appeared on television to quell the rumours, but then the fact emerged that his personal assistant, Lieutenant-Colonel Bo Win Tun was found dead in his office in a pool of blood, with a gunshot wound to his head.

AUNG LYNN HTUT, Myanmar's acting ambassador to Washington, applied for political asylum on 27 March 2005 after being ordered by the Myanmar government to return to Yangon. In a letter to US Secretary of State, Condoleezza Rice, Htut said, 'If I return to Burma, I will certainly be arrested, possibly tortured and possibly even killed.' He claimed that the Myanmar leaders had ordered the Depayin massacre of May 2003 and that ongoing contact between Aung San Suu Kyi and the former prime minister Khin Nyunt after the massacre led to his downfall.

AUNG SAN SUU KYI was informed in November 2004 that her house arrest, or detention, would be extended by a further year.

MYANMAR was spared much of the devastation wreaked on neighbouring countries by the 26 December 2004 tsunami.

This twist of fate prompted one of the many witty satires that regularly sweep through Yangon. The satire claimed that when the huge wave was about to hit the Myanmar delta, three giant fish—which represented the nation's leaders, Than Shwe, Maung Aye and hardliner General Thura Shwe Mann—rose from the waters. The nga, or fish, ordered the wave to turn back immediately and when the wave asked why, the fish answered, 'This is enough. We have already destroyed the country.'

JOSEPH MOYNIHAN, an 81-year-old US peace activist, was roughed up by police, questioned for hours and then deported to Thailand on Friday 7 January 2005 after staging a one-man protest in Yangon. During his brief protest he displayed a sign which read, BUDDHA SAYS, 'QUALITY OF SIDEWALK AND QUALITY OF GOVERNMENT IS SAME THING.'

I returned briefly to Yangon in April 2005 to note that the holes in the footpaths were bigger and more numerous than ever.

ZAWGYI CAFÉ and several of my favourite haunts were bombed in recent months. The Zawgyi Café bombing, in late 2004, was relatively inconsequential, with only one staff member injured, and the café reopened for business a few days later.

But on 7 May 2005 a series of bombs ripped through three buildings frequented by the Myanmar middle and upper classes and by foreigners. The Dagon Shopping centre and its City-mart supermarket, the Junction 8 Citymart and the Yangon Trade Centre were bombed on a busy Saturday afternoon. Thousands were crowded into the trade centre because of a Thai Trade Fair. The government claimed nineteen people were killed and 160 injured, but observers said the death toll was considerably higher.

After the bombing, there was a crackdown on civilian drivers who pretend to be army officers by placing army caps on their car dashboards to intimidate traffic police and avoid getting tickets, and to avoid paying fees at toll gates.

THE CENTRAL STATISTICAL OFFICE of Myanmar officially announced in April 2005 that the nation had the fastest-growing economy in the world, with an average rate over four years of 12.4%, outstripping the Asian tiger, China, with its annual growth of 'only' about 8%.

But Dr Sean Turnell, head of the Burma Economic Watch

of the economics department, Macquarie University, Sydney, said the reality was that Myanmar's economic growth in 2005–2006 will be zero, and that two organisations, Burma Economic Watch and the Economist Intelligence Unit, calculate that Myanmar's economy in most likelihood went *backwards* in 2003 and 2004.